Rethinking

Intelligence

Rethinking
Intelligence

confronting psychological

assumptions about

teaching and learning

Edited by
**Joe L. Kincheloe
Shirley R. Steinberg
and Leila E. Villaverde**

Routledge
New York and London

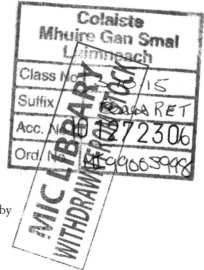

Published in 1999 by
Routledge
29 West 35th Street
New York, NY 10001

Published in Great Britain by
Routledge
11 New Fetter Lane
London EC4P 4EE

Library of Congress Cataloging-in-Publication Data

Rethinking intelligence: confronting psychological assumptions about teaching and learning / by Joe L. Kincheloe, Shirley R. Steinberg, and Leila E. Villaverde, eds.
    p. cm.
  Includes bibliographical references and index.
    ISBN 0-415-92208-9 (alk. paper).—ISBN 0-415-92209-7 (pbk. : alk. paper)
    1. Intellect—Social aspects.   2. Cognition—Social aspects.
3. Teaching—Psychological aspects.   4. Learning, Psychology of.
5. Educational psychology.   I. Kincheloe, Joe L.   II. Steinberg, Shirley R.,
1952–   .   III. Villaverde, Leila E.
BF431.R   1999   98-37301
370.15—dc21   CIP

To Elba and Jose Villaverde

Contents

Foreword

Philip Wexler

If educational discourse has remained insulated from the larger streams of cultural change and movements in social theory, how much even more so has psychology within education remained the rearguard defense of early industrial thought and practice. The intoxication of individualizing, stratifying, historically, socially, existentially and transcendentally abstracted knowledge was based not only in its abuse as an everyday drug of power, but in its idolatrous efforts at self-deification with claims of an objectivity beyond any context.

I wish I could say that this long night of factory-like, alienating type of thought and practice in education is finally over. But the educational apparatus still marches to its drummer, without any knowledge or embarrassment of the small place of this particular discourse in the historical human drama. The honest, early military use of this knowledge was forgotten by the pretentious presentation of skill sorting techniques used for organizing conscripted populations as instead a higher knowledge; trading the gods' great gift to us of human understanding for this limited substitute that was sold to educational consumers as "intelligence."

Still, the industrial education apparatus, which used and enabled this poor exchange of repackaged disciplinary practice for human understanding, now slowly responds to demands for an historically more efficient postindustrial education. And its academic partner, postmodernism, has reached the shores of education, fueling long-standing dissatisfactions with the hegemonic knowledge claims of military-industrial practice which educational academics naively represented as the core educational science of intelligence, and later, development. Not only the socioeconomic demands of a postindustrial, network society, but also its culture, in the resacralizing languages of the new age, renders the industrial educational psychology science of intelligence not merely ideological, but socially dysfunctional and culturally decadent (Castells, 1996; Wexler, 1996).

In this sociohistorical condition, there is room for an exciting constellation of alternative educational imaginations, languages, analytics,
practices, hopes and aspirations. There is intellectual space and incentive
to bring forward the suppressed dissenting theories and practices of education, to juxtapose and align them with postmodern probings, critical
theoretics, and to allow even the perspectives of existential being and
transcendental meaning. Kincheloe, Steinberg and Villaverde see this
opening and they run with it exuberantly. In this volume, we read and
feel the vibrancy of the dynamic multiplicity of this transitional time in
the network, resacralizing society

Here we begin to see what all these discursive shifts, taken together,
might imply for educational theory and practice. Kincheloe and
Steinberg earlier used the rubric of "postformal thought" to signal their
opposition to the domination of education by cognitive psychology, the
"cognitive fog" which: obscures the social context and interests working
in educational knowledge and school practice; inhibits the asking of ethical, moral and political questions as integral to education; occludes
visions of alternative social futures; and which, intellectually offends us
by dismissing from the purview of education what we know as venerable
traditions of knowledge and ways of being in the world that are different—so different from what this dressed-up, old-time-factory-school,
academicized discourse would have us believe is the true and only horizon of our human being and understanding.

Critique is not passé, when it is practiced as Kincheloe does in his
introductory essay. Self-formation in the social world, in the "planetary
society" (Melucci, 1996), increasingly requires our grounding not in the
false transcendentalism of objectivity poses, but in the truth of traditions
and counter-traditions, where knowledge, meaning, and practice are
embedded and integrated. Kincheloe replaces the hegemonic pseudo-sci-
ence of intelligence with a call to the counter authority of traditions.
From class analysis to pragmatic social psychologies, progressive education and postmodernism, existentialism and the sacred, he calls for a
rethinking of education. Instead of a narrow cognitivism, there is the
larger context of social practice and social theory, and beyond that, a
refusal to extract thought from being, and being from the historical social
world.

The contributors follow this lead, and bring Kincheloe and
Steinberg's postformal opening to illuminate a range of educational questions, going well beyond general ideology critique to classroom practice

and teacher education. Along the way, they offer critical analyses and alternatives in conceptualizing education, intelligence, development, deaf education, and schools of education. The tones range from broad scale critiques of the displacement of being by representation, "life as logos," to the comparison of teaching methods in inner city schools, derived from Kincheloe and Steinberg perspectives. Appropriately, the essays conclude with a dialogue initiated by Villaverde with William Pinar. Pinar's work on the "gendered democratization of intelligence...within" continues his "kind of social psychoanalysis," and historical analysis of the meaning of sexual politics for education. Beyond that, it fittingly ends the volume with his continuing, clear strong voice for an educational theory and practice that does not decontextualize nor disembody, but takes disciplined thought into the lived, experienced human social world in which it arises.

Rethinking Intelligence is a book of broad and open vision, of theoretical generosity, and of a keen sense of the importance of a nondualistic approach to theory and practice in education.

REFERENCES

Castells, Manuel. (1996). *The rise of the network society.* Cambridge, MA: Blackwell Publishers, Inc.

Melucci, Alberto. (1996). *The playing self: Person and meaning in the planetary society.* New York: Cambridge University Press.

Wexler, Philip. (1996). *Holy sparks: Social theory, education and religion.* New York: St. Martin's Press.

Chapter 1

The Foundations
of a Democratic
Educational Psychology

Joe L. Kincheloe

The concepts of intelligence and cognitive development often used by mainstream educational psychology are relics from another era. *Rethinking Intelligence: Confronting Psychological Assumptions About Teaching and Learning* maintains that a comprehensive theoretical overhaul of mainstream educational psychology is well overdue. Making use of dramatic changes in social theory and the development of critical pedagogies over the last twenty years, we propose to begin the task of rethinking intelligence. This reconceptualization of educational psychology is grounded on a democratic vision of inclusivity that refuses to view "others" only through the lenses of dominant (often white, Western European, male, middle- or upper-middle class) culture. This democratic vision moves psychologists to document and validate types of reasoning and intelligence that differ from those now recognized by the field and the instruments used to measure them. Such a practice democratizes intelligence by admitting new members to the exclusive community of the talented. In this reconceived context, the central criterion for aptitude no longer involves simply how closely the individual comes up to "*our* norms." Such a turn holds profound consequences for educators, who often learn from prevailing forms of educational psychology to view difference as a deficit. With such a democratic idea in mind, educators gain the capacity to learn alternative models of cognitive development from students previously dismissed as incapable.

Such a democratized view is made visible by our understanding of the culturally inscribed nature of research, psychological research in particular. Cognitive and educational psychologists look for traits of intelligence with which they are familiar. Unknown attributes of intelligence cannot be measured by psychology and are thus ignored. As a result, only a culturally specific set of indicators of aptitude is sought. In this way the intelligences of both individuals from cultures different from the psychologists' and unique thinkers or geniuses from any sociocultural background—such as an Albert Einstein—are dismissed. In a political context, those who deviate from the accepted norms of psychology fail to gain the power of psychological and educational validation so needed in any effort to gain socioeconomic mobility and status in contemporary Western societies.

The discipline of educational psychology and the educational leaders it informs have had difficulty understanding that the poor and the non-white are not stupid. Often children from working-class and lower-socioeconomic-class homes do not ascribe the same importance to the mental functions required by intelligence tests or achievement tests and academic work in the same way as do middle- and upper-middle-class students. In this context, the difference between cultural disposition and intellectual ability is lost upon the field of educational psychology. Working-class and poor students often see academic work as unreal, as a series of short-term tasks rather than something with a long-term relationship to their lives. Real work, they believe, is something you get paid for after its completion. Without such compensation or long-term justification, many times these students display little interest in school. This lack of motivation is often interpreted by mainstream educational psychologists, of course, as inability or lack of intelligence. Poor performance on standardized achievement tests scientifically confirms the "inferiority" of the poor students (Oakes, 1988; Nightingale, 1993; DeYoung, 1989; Woods, 1983).

It happens every day. Educators and psychologists mistake lower-socioeconomic-class manners, attitudes, and speech for a lack of academic and cognitive ability. Researchers report that many teachers place students in low-ability groups or recommend their assignment to vocational tracks because of their class background (DeYoung, 1989). Their rationale involves the lower-socioeconomic-class student's social discomfort around students from higher-status backgrounds—lower-socioeconomic-class students should be with their own kind. The standard practices of American schooling are too often based on a constricted view of the human capacity and an uninformed understanding of human diversity.

Intelligence in this view is defined operationally as one's performance on an IQ test, not as the unique and creative accomplishments one is capable of in a variety of venues and contexts. The social context and power relations of the culture at large and the school culture in particular are central in the attempt to understand the class and cultural dynamics of student performance (Block, 1995).

Research on the education of low-status groups in other countries provides important insight into the psychological assessment and educational performance of marginalized students in American schools. In Sweden, Finnish people are viewed as inferior—the failure rate for Finnish children in Swedish schools is very high. When Finnish children immigrate to Australia, however, they do well—as well as Swedish immigrants. Koreans do poorly in Japanese schools, where they are viewed as culturally inferior; in American schools, on the other hand, Korean immigrants are very successful (Zweigenhaft & Domhoff, 1991). The examples are numerous, but the results generally follow the same pattern: racial, ethnic, and class groups who are viewed negatively or as inferiors in a nation's dominant culture tend to perform poorly in that nation's schools. Educators, parents, and citizens must attend to the lessons of these findings in their attempt to undermine the class bias that consumes their students. Such research helps dispose of the arguments that school failure results from the cultural inferiority of the poor or the marginalized. It teaches us that power relations between groups (based on class, race, ethnicity, gender and so on) must be considered when various students' performance is studied. Without the benefits derived from such understandings, brilliant and creative young people from marginalized backgrounds will continue to be relegated to the vast army of the inferior and untalented. Such an injustice is *intolerable* in America. There is something wrong with a discipline that cannot discern the impact of the social on the psychological, that claims neutrality and objectivity but fails to appreciate its own sociocultural embeddedness, and that consistently rewards the privileged for their privilege and punishes the marginalized for their marginalization.

DEVELOPING THE VISION TO SEE THROUGH THE COGNITIVE FOG

In the spirit of Paulo Freire, the democratic vision we use to counter the elitism of educational psychology is based on an effort to rewrite the world. In this political struggle, teachers, progressive psychologists, theologians, and cultural workers create a new history, a radical commitment to a social recontextualization of those processes often represented as individualistic phenomena. Grounded on a conception of solidarity with marginalized peoples, our democratic vision seeks to connect with progressive organizations dedicated to a cultural politics of emancipatory change. In such contexts, teachers, students, and community members can become part of social movements grounded on new forms of analysis, research, and knowledge production. This is what we are attempting to do in this book: to use compelling forms of analysis, research, and knowledge production to challenge the decontextualized and antidemocratic practices of experts hiding behind the mantle of objective science. Such a critique emerges as a product of democratic cooperation, a manifestation of what happens when cognition is questioned in the light of historical consciousness intercepting personal experience. Drawing upon William Pinar's conception of *currere,* postformalists begin this ambitious task (Pinar, 1994).

In this informed context, democratic teachers can begin to expose hidden forms of subordination in "validated knowledges." Such oppressive dynamics, progressive students of educational psychology understand, create inequities among racial, class, and gendered groups. Exposé, however, is merely this first step of this democratic process. As progressive educational psychologists and teachers open a new conversation about such concepts, this book seeks to facilitate their ability to imagine more just and cognitively challenging perspectives. Learning from untapped forms of intelligence and ways of seeing, all of us come to view the world and our relationship to it in unprecedented and multidimensional ways. This process of psychological reconceptualization initiates the long process of making possible new ways of being human that are more humane, more connected, wiser, and more reflective. Grounded by our democratic vision we carefully begin to understand the limits of Cartesian-Newtonian formal thinking.

Mainstream educational psychology operating in the tradition of the modernist scientific revolution fails to recognize the kind of beings that we are: culturally embedded entities wracked by the unpredictable dynamics of rationality and irrationality, struggling to make our way and understand our actions in the complex interactions of everyday life. Without an appreciation of such realities, widely accepted psychological explanations of human behavior in general and of learning in particular are misleading. Indeed, the types of educational practices that are spun off from such explanations can be harmful on a variety of levels. In this context, the cognitivism that has dominated the field of educational psychology over the last few decades, brilliant though it has been at times, is marred by its disconnection from a more complex view of *being*, its own historicity as a socially constructed way of seeing, and a democratic vision to guide the questions it asks.

At the basis of this cognitivism, of course, is the work of Jean Piaget, who theorized formal thinking as the highest order of human thought. Such thinking implies an acceptance of a Cartesian-Newtonian mechanistic worldview that is caught in a cause-effect, hypothetical-deductive system of reasoning. Unconcerned with questions of power relations and the way they structure our consciousness, formal operational thinkers accept an objectified, unpoliticized way of knowing that breaks an economic or educational system down into its basic parts in order to understand how it works. Emphasizing certainty and prediction, formal thinking organizes verified facts into a theory. The facts that do not fit into the theory are eliminated, and the theory developed is the one best suited to limit contradictions in knowledge. Thus, formal thought operates on the assumption that resolution must be found for all contradictions. Schools and the makers of standardized tests, assuming that formal operational thought represents the highest level of human cognition, focus their psychometric efforts on its cultivation and measurement. Little thought is given to either the cultural dynamics at work in the construction of these cognitive theories or the political dynamics shaping who is punished and rewarded by these assumptions.

MAKING NEW FORMS OF HUMAN BEING POSSIBLE

It is in this critique of cognitivism's formal intelligence that Shirley Steinberg's and my theory of postformalism emerges. In the name of democratizing intelligence, we ask what type of thinking might surface as individuals operate outside the boundaries of formalism. Utilizing recent advances in social and educational theory, we have attempted to construct a sociopolitical cognitive theory that understands the way our consciousness, our subjectivity, is shaped by the world around us. Such a perspective grants us a new conception of what "being smart" might entail. This postformal view of higher-order thinking induces psychologists and educators to recognize the politicization of cognition in a manner that allows them to desocialize themselves and others from mainstream psychology's and school-based pronouncements of who is intelligent and who is not. Postformalism, as the various authors of this book use it, is concerned with questions of justice, democracy, meaning, self-awareness, and the nature and function of the social context. Such concerns move postformal thinkers to a meta-awareness of formalist concerns with "proper" scientific procedure and the certainty it must produce. In this manner, postformalism grapples with purpose, devoting attention to issues of human dignity, freedom, power, authority, domination, and social responsibility.

The point being made here involves the recognition that the postformal vision is not only about revealing the humanly constructed nature of all talk about cognition (postformal talk included), but also about creating new forms of human being and imagining better ways of life. Democratizing intelligence involves the political struggle to reshape educational psychology in the service of progressive values. As it lurks in the shadows of pseudo-objectivity, educational psychology denies its political complicity. In contrast, postformalism embraces its own politics and imagines what the world could become. As Gaile Cannella puts it in her chapter, human possibility is enhanced when the tyranny of dominant ideology, formalist reason, and Cartesian-Newtonian science is removed. Moving into the conversation from another philosophical locale, Aostre Johnson contends in her chapter that cognitive formalism undermines the expression of human multidimensionality by excluding spiritual dimensions of being. Cognitivism, she maintains, subverts our vision of human possibility by proclaiming the individual rational mind as the central organizing dynamic in cognition and action.

The new forms of democratic living that postformalism attempts to make possible are indelibly linked to an alternative rationality. Contrary to the claims of some of our critics in mainstream educational psychology, postformalism does not seek to embrace irrationalism or to reject the entire enterprise of empirical research. We borrow the phrase "alternative rationality" from Stanley Aronowitz (1988), whose critique of mainstream science helps shape our vision of postformalism. In this schemata, new rationalities employ forms of analysis sensitive to signs and symbols, the power of context in relation to thinking, the role of emotion and feeling in cognitive activity, and the value of the psychoanalytical process as it taps into the recesses of (un)consciousness. The effort to democratize intelligence extends Aronowitz's powerful alternatives by asking ethical questions of cognition and action. Such inquiries induce educational and cognitive psychologists to study issues of purpose, meaning, and ultimately worth. Do certain forms of thinking undermine the quest for justice? Do certain forms of research cause observers to view problematic ways of seeing as if they involved no issues of power and privilege (Shotter, 1993; Usher & Edwards, 1994; Cannella, 1997; Schleifer, Con Davis, & Mergler, 1992)?

Educational psychology has simply never encouraged a serious conversation about the reasons humans engage in certain behavior, about the purposes of so-called higher-order thinking, or about the social role of schooling in a democratic society. For the most part, the discipline has never considered the implications that Paulo Freire's notion of *conscientization* holds for the work of practitioners. What happens in the realm of cognition when individuals begin to gain a new consciousness via the process of (1) transforming themselves through changing their reality, (2) grasping an awareness of the mechanisms of oppression, and (3) reclaiming their historical memory in order to gain an awareness of their social construction, their social identity (Freire, 1970)? Understanding the implications of this process, Phillip Wexler (1997) describes an alternative rationality that involves the effort to move beyond the limitations imposed by the discipline of psychology. In recent scholarship on the ethnography of being, alternative rationalities emerge as analysts study altered states of consciousness. In such moments of transcendence, individuals gain insight into the constructed nature of what is labeled normal Western consciousness—an insight that allows for a reframing of experience in exciting new ways. Postformalism has much to learn from Wexler's work, as it brings together questions of knowledge (epistemology) with questions of being (ontology). Such a synthesis moves scholars to consider critical analyses of power's role in shaping consciousness vis-à-vis the effort to live more fully—Wexler calls it the process of enlivenment. In the synergistic fusion of these compelling considerations, postformalism opens new paths to human development and insight.

DEMOCRATIC EMPOWERMENT VIA THE EXPANSION OF THE BOUNDARIES OF INTELLIGENCE: GETTING SMARTER

One of the key ways to rethink intelligence is to expand the boundaries of what can be called sophisticated thinking. When such boundaries are expanded, those who had been excluded from the community of the intelligent seem to cluster around categories based on race (the nonwhite), class (the poor), and gender (the feminine). Mainstream educational psychology tends to construct intelligence as fixed and innate—a mysterious quality found only in the privileged few. Such a view has stressed biological fixities that can be altered only by surgical means. Such an authoritarian view is a psychology of hopelessness that locks people into rigid categories that follow them throughout their lives (Bozik, 1987; Lawler, 1975; Maher & Rathbone, 1986). When we begin to challenge these perspectives in the process of democratizing intelligence, dramatic changes occur in our perceptions of who is capable of learning. Such a challenge moves educators to take a giant first step in the effort to make schooling a democratic enterprise.

Such a democratic move is furthered by embracing the simple psychological notion that not only is intelligence expressed in diverse ways, but it is learnable. In many ways it is amazing that such an argument would need to be made at the end of the second millennium. Individuals of various ages, backgrounds, and even IQ scores can learn conceptual systems that help them make meaning, that facilitate their understanding of and ability to negotiate the world around them. They can gain the ability to focus their passions and cultivate their dispositions to direct energy toward certain tasks. They can seek out talented individuals who possess well-developed abilities and sophisticated understandings in order to listen and watch and eventually reflect upon their interactions with them. Such assertions are in many ways nothing but common sense, but they run contrary to the logic of much that passes for mainstream educational psychology. Postformalism does not accept cognitive hopelessness and is grounded on the idea that intelligence is learnable and can be taught in schools, in the workplace, in civic organizations, and any other place where people interact. As a psychology of empowerment, postformalism promotes the highest levels of understanding possible.

Before we proceed with our specification of the process of rethinking intelligence, a brief description of the theoretical traditions that have shaped postformalism is in order. Most of these traditions have played a minor role in shaping modern educational psychology.

DRAWING UPON A VARIETY OF THEORETICAL POSITIONS TO RETHINK INTELLIGENCE

In this context of delineating theoretical traditions, I am not going to present a history of educational psychology. I will not trace the behaviorist and cognitivist perspectives that have shaped the field in the twentieth century. While I hold great respect for the Piagetian tradition, I will view it here (at least the part of it co-opted by Anglo-American mainstream educational psychology) as part of the existing tradition of educational psychology and will focus on the critique of it.

Vygotskian Psychology

Lev Vygotsky theorized in the 1930s that individuals do not develop in isolation but in a series of interconnected social matrices. This understanding is central to the postformal effort to rethink intelligence and reformulate education in a transformative manner. Since mental activity, he maintained, takes place in a social and cultural context, thought will operate differently in diverse historical situations. Cognition thus is shaped by the interactions among social actors, the contexts in which they act, and the form their activities assume. Such a perspective motivated Vygotsky to move prevailing brain-centered psychological conceptions of mind to a more holistic notion that viewed mind as existing outside of the brain and even the skin. Cognition was no longer viewed by Vygotsky as an exclusively individual dynamic but was seen more as an intermental or social function. In a sociopsychological theoretical context, therefore, Vygotsky's work creates a space where integration between macro social forces and micro psychological forces occurs. Analysis of this integrated space becomes a central activity for a democratic postformal educational psychology concerned with the way identity is formed by large social forces and mediated by individuals operating in specific environments. Such understandings allow us to imagine pedagogies that move individuals to greater understandings of themselves and their relation to the world, to higher orders of thinking previously unimagined (Vygotsky, 1978; Marsh, 1993; Driscoll, 1994; Wertsch & Tulviste, 1992; Weisner, 1987).

Bringing psychological and anthropological concerns together, Vygotsky was interested in how we come to be certain types of individuals. As he studied this production of self, Vygotsky criticized Piaget for his lack of attention to questions of culture and language and their role in the construction of consciousness. Without a Vygotskian-type social understanding, Piagetian cognitivist educational psychology can explain poor academic performance only in terms of low individual ability. Such a viewpoint offers little hope for the effort to democratize intelligence through an understanding of the cultural dynamics that shape both learners and the discourse of educational psychology. If one's social environment plays an important role in shaping one's cognitive orientation, as

Vygotsky argues, then a postformal educational psychology maintains that cognition can be reformulated for differing purposes. Those who are deemed incapable by individualistic educational psychology—often those who are unfamiliar with the cultural practices and values necessary for school success—can be taught how to maintain their own abilities *and* do well in schools as presently constructed. Indeed, they can also learn to rethink schooling in light of diverse cultural ways of making meaning and being intelligent.

Postformalists interested in the democratization of intelligence have much to learn from Vygotsky. Understanding the social dynamics of the learning process and the goal of fostering cognitive self-direction, we realize the need to reconceptualize educational psychology, learning theory, and the organization of the instructional process. Postformal educational psychologists and teachers have much to think about in their efforts to rearrange their professional practice in a way that accounts for the social aspects of what mainstream psychology has seen as individual processes. Obviously, there are numerous ways to interpret Vygotsky's implications for a democratic psychology, but postformalists agree that the benefits justify the effort. Written in the 1920s and 1930s, Vygotsky's work reflects the *Zeitgeist* (the spirit of the times) in its Eurocentrism— European cultural tools and cognitive orientations were thought to be superior to others, the culmination of a modernist notion of humanity's evolutionary process. Obviously, the postformal engagement with Vygotsky will reveal the need to update the social theory he employed seventy-five years ago and to correct the tendency of his followers to focus on a limited, face-to-face usage of the meaning of social context. The advances in social theory achieved over the past thirty years will move Vygotskian understandings to a new level and allow his insights to better inform theorists and practitioners. Vygotskian psychology is an open system that lends itself to interaction and combination with other social, political, psychological, and pedagogical traditions. Such an integration is a major feature of the postformal attempt to democratize intelligence and develop a transformative educational psychology and education (Moll, 1991; Vygotsky, 1978; Wertsch & Tulviste, 1992; Wertsch, Del Rio, & Alvarez, 1995; Weisner, 1993; Nicolopoulou, 1993).

Neo-Vygotskian Situated Cognition

Situated cognition explores the contextually situated character of human learning, understanding, and communication. The cognitive theory is much indebted to Vygotsky and is sometimes referred to as neo-Vygotskianism. Students of situated cognition are interested in the social engagements where learning takes place. Much of their research has asked which forms of social engagement provide the best context for learning. Their answer to this question involves the context where learners engage in the skills needed to perform particular tasks. Here learners study the ways experts perform their tasks, noting in particular the ways they interact with their environment and make use of tools. The evolution and development of the field of study known as situated cognition is grounded on the study of environmental interaction and usage of cultural tools—what Vygotsky called mediational means or mediated action. Learners gain access to the world only through a filter created by the sociocultural context in which they operate. Postformalists appreciate the significance of this understanding in their effort to democratize intelligence. Given the nature of students' mediational means, postformal educational psychologists understand that such individuals' position in the world, their power or powerlessness, is profoundly affected. Informed by the work of situated cognitivists, postformalists gain a more sophisticated picture of the sociocultural and political dynamics of how humans learn. Such insights allow educational psychologists to appreciate that much of what has traditionally been labeled an individual mental process is far more affected by physical settings and social tools than previously believed.

The research of situated cognitivists challenges the traditional definitions of learning by asserting that the verbal meaning learners acquire is shaped by their interpretive activities, not by some unmediated memorization of the content of a lesson. These interpretive activities, students of situated cognition assert, are constructed in relation to some form of action—not within self-contained mental structures. Thus, the knowledge and abilities a student brings to instruction become essential knowledge for a teacher attempting to design a curriculum that connects to a learner's relationship with his or her mediational means. Such educational insights dramatically change mainstream educational psychological assumptions about developmental processes and skills hierarchies. An understanding of the contextual dynamics of mediational means tells psychologists and educators that the cognitive process, not to mention the relationship between the cognitive process and instruction, is much more complex than previously assumed. Postformalists argue that in light of such knowledge, teachers must be better equipped to study and make sense of the social context in which their students are situated. They must become researchers of their students, understanding the ways learners' backgrounds mesh and conflict with the culture of schools. In this context, teachers come to understand themselves, their own mediational means, and their relationship to the contexts of those they teach (Wertsch, Del Rio, & Alvarez, 1995; Damarin, 1993; Hanks, 1991; Raizen, 1989).

Deweyan Progressivism

John Dewey's progressive pedagogy plays an important role in our critique of educational psychology. Dewey was always mindful of the connection between learning and the objects and acts of everyday experience. Much of the learning that takes place in school, he contended, is useless because of the break school induces with the child's previous experiences. This decontextualization, Dewey wrote in *How We Think,* undermines cognitive growth because higher thinking always references some lived context. Only in relation to this lived context can individuals aspire to Dewey's sociopolitical cognitive goals: the reorganization and reconstruction of experience and the progressive transformation of one's actions for democratic participation. Dewey was harsh in his criticism of the educational psychology of his day, maintaining that it was antithetical to preparation for life in a democratic society. He was especially critical of those psychologists and educators who argued that many students—especially those from lower-socioeconomic-class backgrounds—were incapable of working with their minds. The "hand-minded," many psychologists and educators contended in the first decades of the twentieth century, should be tracked into nonacademic courses and encouraged to seek less demanding, low-status, low-wage jobs. Dewey vehemently fought this line of thinking, repeatedly pointing out its undemocratic impact.

As a philosopher of democracy and democratic education, Dewey provided insights that are indispensable in the postformal effort to democratize intelligence. Dedicated to the struggle against education as a method of adapting individuals to the status quo, Dewey called for the cultivation of cognitive inventiveness rather than imitation. Inventiveness, as Dewey employed it in this political context, involved a radical modification of an individual's foundational understandings and purposes. Speculating in the domain of cognition, Dewey referred to these dynamics as aspects of a larger notion of "social intelligence." Individuals with sophisticated social intelligence would ask questions concerning whose interests were being served by specific political and educational actions. A central feature of a progressive pedagogy would involve helping all students gain access to the skills associated with this social intelligence. Such an ability is a basic skill in Dewey's progressive educational vision—an educational philosophy that is founded on the objective of preparing students for present and future participation in the democratic life of the community (Farber, 1989; Simon, Dippo, & Schenke, 1991; Block, 1995; Dewey, 1933; Wirth, 1983; Lakes, 1985).

Social intelligence, as Dewey conceptualized it, involves developing a cultural perspective. Such a way of seeing is centered around the construction of a broad social meaning that facilitates the contextual understandings necessary for transformative democratic action. Thus, as we consider democratizing the definition of intelligence, Dewey helps us concurrently consider the nature of democratic cognition or, as he put it, social intelligence. Postformalists learn from Dewey that there are two separate but complementary aspects to democratizing intelligence: (1) expanding the boundaries of intelligence to include the cognitive activities of different cultures, and (2) learning to think and act democratically in ways that foster egalitarian and just practices. Dewey did not advocate the study of history merely for the purpose of helping students recite a litany of important events in America's past. Historical understanding, he trusted, would provide the context in which students could detect patterns of injustice. Such an awareness would generate both the knowledge and the disposition to engage in transformative acts of citizenship. Dewey's goal was to make these qualities of mind available to all citizens—an objective shared, of course, by postformalism.

Critical Pedagogy

Critical pedagogy raises one of the central issues in postformalism's critique of mainstream educational psychology and the effort to democratize intelligence: Whose interests are served by particular psychological and educational perspectives? Such a question, of course, drags mainstream psychology kicking and screaming into the political arena, the sphere of society that involves the struggle for the organization and distribution of power. Students of critical pedagogy are always concerned with the way this political dynamic operates, the way various institutions and interests deploy power in the effort to survive, shape behavior, gain dominance over others, or, in a more emancipatory vein, improve the human condition. Realizing that power is not simply one important force in the psychosocial process, proponents of critical pedagogy understand that humans are the historical products of power. Men and women do not arise outside of the process of history; our identities are fundamentally shaped by our entanglements in the webs that power weaves (Samuels, 1993; Thiele, 1986; McLaren, 1994).

An educational psychology informed by critical pedagogy is concerned with the specific nature of these entanglements, the way power shapes subjectivity in general and classroom practices in particular. Viewing these processes of power as having naturalized themselves to the point of invisibility, a critically informed educational psychology wants to expose them for all to see. In this context the postformal critique pays special attention to the critical pedagogical analysis of the relationship among knowledge, authority, and power (Giroux, 1994). Traditional educational philosophies viewed pedagogy as a body of techniques and skills used to teach a designated core of subject matter. Because of such a definition, pedagogy has been viewed with condescension within the academy. Postformalists maintain that the critical rearticulation of pedagogy propels it to a central position in higher education, social theory, the humanities, and psychology. Thus, pedagogy in this critical context becomes not only a school practice but a cultural practice that exists wherever power produces knowledge, shapes values, and constructs consciousness. These pedagogical and power-related features are inseparable from both an understanding of educational psychological processes and the postformal quest to democratize intelligence.

Paulo Freire (1970), operating in this critical tradition, spoke frequently about "reading the world." In this context Freire was referring to these power dynamics, as he moved his students to make connections between social and educational knowledge and the political forces that shaped it. An understanding of power's complicity in the production of society's validated knowledge, its educational knowledge in particular, is essential information for racially, ethnically, and economically marginalized students who are trying to figure out why they are deemed slow and incompetent in the schools they attend. With an understanding of the role of power in education and the knowledge of school, they begin to make sense of what happens when intelligence is not democratized. A dramatic and hopeful transformation occurs when marginalized students grasp this power-related dynamic, a change of consciousness that allows them a critical X-ray vision to see through psychological evaluations of their *lack of* ability (Macedo, 1994; Martin-Baro, 1994).

The Postmodern Paradigm Shift

The word *paradigm* comes from the Greek word for "pattern." A paradigm, as most academics know by now, is a pattern, a schema for understanding the nature of the world. Although Thomas Kuhn (1962) was not thinking about psychological science when he popularized the term, individuals now employ the word in medical, political, educational, and psychological contexts. Modernist educational psychology hangs on as a bastion of resistance to paradigmatic conversation. In the physical sciences, researchers who hoped to solve the questions emerging from Newton's pattern of the universe were frustrated, as data from Einstein's, Niels Bohr's, Werner Heisenberg's, and David Bohm's research in physics refused to fit the pattern. As the Cartesian-Newtonian paradigm was strained, new patterns began to emerge and new questions arose. The linear, cause-effect Cartesian-Newtonian paradigm began to crumble. In much the same way, the work of Vygotskians, neo-Vygotskians, critical theorists, and postmodern students of psychology has undermined the foundations of modernist mainstream psychology.

The postmodern notion of a paradigm and paradigm shift is more than merely a conceptual framework of an academic discipline. In this framework, a paradigm becomes a cultural dynamic, a sociopolitical schema of concepts, values, assumptions, epistemologies, ontologies, and practices that shape both academic practice and everyday life. The postmodern paradigmatic critique maintains that the modernist paradigm has given meaning to life in Western societies. Science and its companion, technology, have become sources of ultimate truth that provide this-worldly rewards of efficiency and economic prosperity to those who will accept their authority. As critical theoretical scholars recognized decades ago, the sci-tech paradigm—especially in a psychology context—becomes a mechanism of social control and regulation. As Aimee Howley, Linda Spatig, and Craig Howley argue in their chapter, the postmodern critique reveals modernist psychological science as a technology of power that colonizes the processes of self-formation. Such a practice, postmodernists contend, adjusts individuals to the existing society in a manner that avoids questioning the ethical and moral nature of the process (Shotter, 1993; Capra, Steindl-Rast, & Matus, 1992; Aronowitz, 1993; Martin-Baro, 1994).

Snared in a discursive world of its own making, modernist educational psychology is unable to appreciate the constructed vantage point from which it views psychology and learning. The postmodern shift induces educational psychologists to study both their subject and themselves, especially the nature and impact of their value assumptions, cultural context, and research methods. When such reflective analysis is undertaken, postmodernists argue, psychologists begin to understand that they assume the existence of a given, transcendent self. As a preformed entity, the self requires no sociocultural analysis. Psychological features that are produced by specific historical processes are deemed natural manifestations of universal human experience. Intelligence thus becomes an innate quality that individuals possess regardless of the context in which they operate. Embedded in modernist paradigmatic psychology is a mechanism that erases the social experiences that shape us as humans. Sociopolitical influences are reduced to personality quirks; thus, the discipline recognizes few differences between, for example, former U.S. secretary of education William Bennett and one of Paulo Freire's peasant students in northeastern Brazil. In such a context the political struggle to democratize intelligence is irrelevant—individuals would still possess the same "amounts" of intelligence regardless of how ability was constructed by psychologists.

While our critically grounded, postmodern, postformal educational psychology seeks to democratize intelligence by expanding what counts as intelligence and helping individuals to draw upon their own sociocultural abilities to become more intelligent, modernist educational psychology has held very different goals. From the vantage point of a new paradigm, we can more easily comprehend that one of the most central concerns of mainstream educational psychology has been the identification of a central processing mechanism (Shweder, 1995) in the human brain that can be represented mathematically. This phantom power train of the mind, like any other mechanical device, can be measured in terms of its efficiency, its torque, and its actual and kinetic energy. The power train has been constructed by a discipline grounded on a natural-science model that sees itself in search of scientific laws about human activity. How powerful is the phantom power train in particular groups? Relative to different groups? Within particular individuals (Usher & Edwards, 1994; Cushman, 1995; Shweder, 1995)?

Postformalists, as postmodern psychological researchers, move into our observations with different attitudes and objectives than our modernist counterparts in the discipline. We are not as concerned with producing universal truths as we are with exploring activities, contexts, and critical uses to which our tentative insights can be put. We are much more aware of the cultural situatedness of the beliefs about knowledge production and the discipline of educational psychology we bring with us and the way they tacitly shape what we see. Such concerns are of great practical importance, for they change the very purpose of what we do in the name of educational psychology. They are central features of the effort to rethink and democratize intelligence.

Cultural Studies

Cultural studies is an interdisciplinary, transdisciplinary, and sometimes counterdisciplinary field that functions within the dynamics of competing definitions of culture. Unlike traditional humanistic studies, cultural studies questions the equation of culture with high culture; instead, cultural studies asserts that myriad expressions of cultural production should be analyzed in relation to other cultural dynamics and social and historical structures. Such a position commits cultural studies to a potpourri of artistic, religious, political, economic, and communicative activities. In this context, it is important to note that while cultural studies is associated with the study of popular culture, it is not primarily about popular culture. Cultural studies interests are much broader and tend to involve the production and nature of the rules of inclusivity and exclusivity that guide academic evaluation—in particular, the way these rules shape and are shaped by relations of power.

The rules that guide academic evaluation are inseparable from the rules of knowledge production. Thus cultural studies provides a disciplinary critique that holds many implications for educational psychology— we have already analyzed many of these dynamics, however, within the boundaries of critical pedagogy and the postmodern critique. The boundaries between cultural studies, critical pedagogy, and the postmodern critique have become increasingly blurred in recent years, an understanding that needs to be kept in mind in our effort to delineate the traditions upon which postformalism draws in its rethinking of educational psychology. Thus, in this examination of the role of cultural studies in the postformal project, we focus our attention on the domain's concern with contemporary popular culture and its impact on the production of identity.

Cultural studies advocates argue that the development of the mass media has changed the old rules of how culture operates. Media have become sufficiently powerful to produce both new ways of seeing the world and new meanings for lives and work. Media produce and validate data described as knowledge. Thus media shape identities and self-images. It is safe to say that our lifetimes have witnessed a major transformation in how knowledge is produced. If this is true, cultural studies proponents argue, then we should expand the types of issues we study in school in general and teacher education in particular. For example, while we should, of course, continue to study books and print as academic artifacts, we should also begin to study the values that aural and visual media produce, market, and distribute in TV, film, CDs, computer networks, advertising images, and so on. A major transformation has taken place in cultural epistemologies, and educational psychology and other academic disciplines have been as yet unequipped to account for such change. Cultural studies has positioned itself as a social force determined to confront these systemic changes and their implications for the purposes of academic institutions.

In the jargon of cultural studies, such cultural changes are described as creating a new era, the postmodern condition of hyperreality. In this new cultural domain new forms of social domination are produced as the distinction between the real and the simulated is blurred. This blurring effect of hyperreality (Baudrillard, 1983) constructs a social vertigo characterized by a loss of touch with traditional notions of time, community, self, and history. New structures of cultural space and time generated by a bombardment of electronic images from local, national, and international venues shake our personal sense of place (Aronowitz & Giroux, 1991; Gergen, 1991; Kincheloe, 1995). This proliferation of signs and images characteristic of information-soaked hyperreality functions as a mechanism of control in contemporary Western societies. The key to a successful counterhegemonic cultural studies pedagogy hinges on (1) its ability to link the production of the representations, images, and signs of hyperreality to power blocs in the political economy, and (2) its capacity, once this linkage is exposed and described, to delineate the highly complex and ambiguous effects of the reception of these images and signs on individuals located at various race, class, and gender coordinates in the web of reality. No easy task, this effort—but to avoid it is to turn our backs on the democratic experiment and the possibility of social justice. This is why the effort to trace the effects of power in the ways the power bloc represents reality is so important.

Cultural studies maintains that a discipline such as educational psychology, especially in its democratic articulation, must transcend disciplinary confines and move into interdisciplinary waters. Thus an encounter with cultural studies may help educational psychology transform itself into a transdisciplinary notion of "educational psychological studies." Such a transformation would consciously politicize the discipline—presently it is tacitly politicized—in the sense that educational psychology would consider both the political consequences of its own work and the ways in which the formation of identity is a political process in contemporary hyperreality. A politicized educational psychology would study the ever-present political dynamics of learning and contemplate the ways the educational process is always politically and historically situated. In this context it would study the ways learners can respond to these dynamics in a manner that heightens their capacity for self-determination.

Depth Psychology and Poststructuralist Psychoanalysis

Drawing upon depth psychology and poststructuralist psychoanalysis, postformalists are empowered to dig deeper into the complexity of the fundamental and primordial aspects of the human psyche. Psychoanalysis has traditionally been concerned with the forces of irrationality and the ways they shape both consciousness and behavior. Any force that shapes agency in a manner that is contradictory to the ways in which we ourselves think of an experience is important—even if the notion of self is not as stable and knowable as early psychoanalysts assumed. Indeed, it is psychoanalysis that allows us to view the formation of identity from unique vantage points not attainable via other methodologies. In such a procedure, analysts often discern the unconscious processes that create resistance to progressive change and induce self-destructive behavior. Psychoanalysis offers hope to postformalists concerned with social justice and the related attempt to democratize intelligence as it explores the possibilities of human potential. When psychoanalysis takes into account the Deweyan, the Vygotskian, and more recently the postmodernist rejection of Freud's separation of the psychic from the social realm, it becomes a powerful tool in cognitive and educational psychology (Alford, 1993; Henriques et al., 1984; Russell, 1993).

In this context the contributions of the field of depth psychology, an admittedly old-fashioned term associated with psychoanalysis, are important to the political concerns of postformalism. I choose depth psychology as a tradition worthy of contribution in the attempt to democratize intelligence because of the specificity of its concerns and their direct relevance to a reconceptualized educational psychology. Depth psychology is focused on the analysis of irrationality, the emotions, the complexity of "personality," creativity, artistic endeavor, and morality. No educational psychology worthy of its important task can ignore these issues and their relationship to learning, motivation, school performance, and the nature of the teaching process. In addition, a depth psychology aware of the insights of the postmodern turn in social theory can motivate interest in the way an individual subjectively experiences social, cultural, political, and educational structures. In this context public issues can be viewed at the private level, modernist boundaries between the political (external) and personal (internal) can be erased, and the separation between subjectivity and intelligence can be reconceptualized. Postmodern social theory's concerns with identity, difference, and power can be directed to the broad notion of psychological studies by way of the interests of depth psychology (Samuels, 1993).

Thus in the name of emancipation and a critical democracy, postformal educators and psychologists call for an analysis of such issues in relation to educational practice. As we begin to grasp the importance of a socially situated unconsciousness in the production of identity and in the learning process connected to it, practitioners gain vital insight into the ways education might be reconfigured. In this context postformalists are quick to note that their appreciations of psychoanalysis and depth psychology are cautious and very selective. Following the lead of many feminist psychoanalysts, postformal psychologists and educators employ only those aspects of the tradition that are conscious of the problematic nature of defining psychic health as conformity to dominant cultural norms. Taking their cue from feminist theory, such psychologists and educators understand the patriarchal inscriptions of traditional psychoanalysis and struggle to avoid the hegemonic landmines hidden in the field. To the postformalist, psychoanalysis and depth psychology possess progressive features that in conjunction with a critical postmodernist awareness can be used to create a more just and better-educated world, a resacralized society where human beings are studied and appreciated in terms of their unique abilities and hard-to-quantify talents (Ventura, 1994; Elliot, 1994; Henriques et al., 1984).

Thus, the postformalist vision of psychoanalysis is a poststructuralist psychoanalysis—poststructuralist in the sense that it reveals the problems embedded in the sciences emerging from modernity and the "universal structures" it constructs (Slattery, 1995; Block, 1995). As poststructuralist psychoanalysis makes use of the subversive aspects of the psychoanalytical tradition, it presents a view of humans quite different than the modernist psychological portrait. In the process it challenges the modernist erasure of feeling, valuing, and caring in contemporary Western societies and attempts to rethink such features in light of power and its construction of consciousness. In this context the poststructuralist impulse challenges Freud's positioning of the pleasure principle in opposition to the reality principle. In many ways, poststructuralist psychoanalysts argue, such an oppositional construction places Freudianism squarely within the boundaries of Western logocentrism, with its structures of rationality over irrationality, masculinity over femininity, civilization over primitivism, and logic over emotion.

From the poststructuralist perspective, therefore, the psychoanalytic tradition is complicit in the regulatory objectives of modernist science. In its effort to produce a healthy (read conformist) population, traditional psychoanalysis has in the same manner as its modernist brother, educational psychology, set out to repress desire. Poststructuralist psychoanalysis has often embraced unconscious desire as a positive feature with the social revolutionary potential to unfasten the hegemonic straitjacket of modernist psychology. Poststructuralism admonishes the discipline of psychology to accept the undesirability of what it is trying to accomplish (Henriques et al., 1984; Elliot, 1994). Psychology must also understand that its rationalistic views of *being* and its faith in an unexamined rationality are ill-suited for an everyday life riddled and destabilized by affective intensities and powerful forces of libidinal desire. Humbled by the poststructuralist critique, traditional psychoanalysis timidly looks into the mirror of self-reflection and begins to discern the relationship between suppressed desire and political power, the affiliation between the fear of passion and cultural reproduction. These understandings hold profound consequences for students of cognition and learning.

Gardner's Multiple Intelligences

The appearance of Howard Gardner's *Frames of Mind: The Theory of Multiple Intelligences* in 1983 marked an important advance in both cognitive and educational psychology. Grounded on the argument that Western societies and Western sciences have thought of intelligence very narrowly, Gardner's theory proposed a new theoretical framework for thinking about the topic. Gardner was convinced that intelligence, despite psychometric pronouncements, was not a monolithic hereditary dynamic that could be accurately measured by a short "objective" test. He understood that the same mind-set that viewed intelligence in this reductionistic psychometric manner tended to produce educational strategies based on memorization and drudgery. In opposition to Piagetian theory, Gardner rejected universalistic notions of stages, accepting a more Vygotskian notion that individuals in different cultural contexts possess diverse relationships to socially constructed stages. Unimpressed with

Piaget's culturally inscribed emphasis on verbal ability, his theory's remoteness from everyday activities, and its neglect of creativity and originality, Gardner sought to move beyond the tenets of Piagetianism.

In this context Gardner offers his theory of multiple intelligences to help make sense of evidence that seems to be at odds with traditional cognitive theories. Understanding multiple intelligences, he maintains, will facilitate the effort to explore, appreciate, and expand the complex notion of intelligence. In Gardner's expansion of the concept of intelligence, we find his relevance not only to postformal democratic effort but also to the attempt to educate intelligence. If we know better what intelligence involves and the variety of forms it takes, we have a much better chance of cultivating it. Thus Gardner believes that an informed education can make us smarter and better able to deal with the world that surrounds us. As we become more acquainted with the ways the various intelligences are used in various social settings, psychologists and educators gain a clearer picture of human potential. With this assertion Gardner makes a radical move within the conservative confines of cognitive theory, contending that "nearly every normal individual can attain impressive competence in an intellectual or symbolic domain" (Gardner, 1983, p. 316). Such a pronouncement induced conservative psychometricians Richard Herrnstein and Charles Murray (1994) to label Gardner a "radical."

At times Gardner seems paradigmatically aware that all theories of intelligence are social constructions reflecting the values of individuals from particular cultural locations at specific times in history. At other times he views intelligence as a universal, transcultural truth that seeks some form of final scientific validation to prove its reality. Sometimes, as for example in his critique of Piaget, Gardner understands the cultural specificity of all cognitive theory: Piaget, he argues, delineated a picture of cognitive development that is inseparable from abilities valued most highly by the European scientific and philosophical traditions. Yet he later betrays this cultural insight by writing of the possibility of a general theory of motivation, as if such an animal is possible given the vast cultural differences that separate human endeavors.

One suspects that Gardner is caught between paradigms. This observation is made with no implication that one must pursue some form of paradigmatic purity; indeed, understandings gleaned from various paradigms are important. But in Gardner's case he seems unable to sense the epistemological and methodological contradictions that emerge from his speculations and mixed feelings. Also, his work suffers from a lack of critical understanding of what psychological theory and the education it supports can do to harm students. Without this appreciation, Gardner tends to see the purpose of his cognitive work as helping elite students reach a higher level of achievement. The role of schooling as a cruel and unfair sorting machine around cognitive categories does not seem to concern Gardner in the same way as it does postformalists. In this context Gardner is unable to anticipate the postformal critique of his work or fathom the purposes of a postformal turn in cognitive and educational psychology. Such a reality remains paradoxical in light of the implication of Gardner's work for the political goals of postformalism.

With these theoretical foundations delineated, the etymologies of the authors' contributions in this work take on more clarity. To some degree all of the traditions referenced help us understand cognition and intelligence in a more contextualized and complex manner. Each position is concerned with broadening the understanding of self and the production of self. In these ways they help us confront the naturalization of the psychological assumptions that shape teaching and learning. All of the following chapters extend these concerns as they rethink the nature of intelligence.

REFERENCES

Alford, C. (1993). "Introduction to the special issue on political psychology and political theory." *Political Psychology, 14* (2), 199–208.

Aronowitz, S. (1988). *Science as power: Discourse and ideology in modern society.* Minneapolis: University of Minnesota Press.

Aronowitz, S. (1993). *Roll over Beethoven: The return of cultural strife.* Hanover, NH: Wesleyan University Press.

Aronowitz, S., & Giroux, H. (1991). *Post-modern education: Politics, culture, and social criticism.* Minneapolis: University of Minnesota Press.

Baudrillard, J. (1983). *Simulations.* New York: SemioText(e).

Block, A. (1995). *Occupied reading: Critical foundations for an ecological theory.* New York: Garland.

Bozik, M. (1987). *Critical thinking through creative thinking.* Paper presented to the Speech Communication Association, Boston.

Cannella, G. (1997). *Deconstructing early childhood education: Social justice and revolution.* New York: Peter Lang.

Capra, F., Steindl-Rast, D., & Matus, T. (1992). *Belonging to the universe: New thinking about God and nature.* New York: Penguin.

Cushman, P. (1995). "Ideology obscured: Political uses of the self in Daniel Stern's infant." In N. Goldberger & J. Veroff (Eds.), *The culture and psychology reader.* New York: New York University Press.

Damarin, S. (1993). "Schooling and situated knowledge: Travel or tourism?" *Educational Technology,* 27–32.

Dewey, J. (1933). *How we think.* Lexington, MA: Heath.

DeYoung, A. (1989). *Economics and American education.* New York: Longman.

Driscoll, M. (1994). *Psychology of learning for instruction.* Boston: Allyn and Bacon.

Elliot, A. (1994). *Psychoanalytic theory: An introduction.* Cambridge, MA: Blackwell.

Farber, K. (1989). *The use of psychological foundations to inform teaching for critical reflectivity.* Paper presented to the American Educational Research Association, Chicago.

Freire, P. (1970). *Pedagogy of the oppressed.* New York: Herder and Herder.

Gardner, H. (1983). *Frames of mind: The theory of multiple intelligences.* New York: Basic Books.

Gergen, K. (1991). *The saturated self: Dilemmas of identity in contemporary life.* New York: Basic Books.

Giroux, H. (1994). *Disturbing pleasures: Learning popular culture.* New York: Routledge.

Hanks, W. (1991). "Introduction." In J. Lave & E. Wenger (Eds.), *Situated learning: Legitimate peripheral participation.* New York: Cambridge University Press.

Henriques, J., et al. (1984). *Changing the subject.* New York: Methuen.

Herrnstein, R., & Murray, C. (1994). *The bell curve: Intelligence and class structure in American life.* New York: Free Press.

Kincheloe, J. (1995). *Toil and trouble: Good work, smart workers, and the integration of academic and vocational education.* New York: Peter Lang.

Kuhn, T. (1962). *The structure of scientific revolutions.* Chicago: University of Chicago Press.

Lakes, R. (1985). "John Dewey's theory of occupations: Vocational education envisioned." *Journal of Vocational and Technical Education, 2* (1), 41–47.

Lawler, J. (1975). "Dialectical philosophy and developmental psychology: Hegel and Piaget on contradiction." *Human Development, 18,* 1–17.

Macedo, D. (1994). *Literacies of power: What Americans are not allowed to know.* Boulder, CO: Westview.

Maher, F., & Rathbone, C. (1986). "Teacher education and feminist theory: Some implications for practice." *American Journal of Education, 94* (2), 214–235.

Marsh, D. (1993). "Freire, Vygotsky, and special education, and me." *British Columbia Journal of Special Education, 17* (2), 119–234.

Martin-Baro, I. (1994). *Writings for a liberation psychology.* Ed. A. Aron and S. Corne. Cambridge, MA: Harvard University Press.

McLaren, P. (1994). *Life in schools: An introduction to critical pedagogy in the foundations of education.* White Plains, NY: Longman.

Moll, I. (1991). *The material and the social in Vygotsky's theory of cognitive development.* Paper presented at the biennial meeting of the Society for Research in Child Development, Seattle, Washington.

Nicolopoulou, A. (1993). "Play, cognitive development, and the social world: Piaget, Vygotsky, and beyond." *Human Development, 36,* 1–23.

Nightingale, C. (1993). *On the edge: A history of poor black children and their American dreams.* New York: Basic Books.

Oakes, J. (1988). "Tracking in mathematics and science education: A structural contribution to unequal schooling." In L. Weis (Ed.), *Class, race and gender in American education.* Albany: State University of New York Press.

Pinar, W. (1994). *Autobiography, politics, and sexuality: Essays in curriculum theory.* New York: Peter Lang.

Raizen, S. (1989). *Reforming education for work: A cognitive science perspective.* Berkeley, CA: NCRVE.

Russell, D. (1993). "Vygotsky, Dewey, and externalism: Beyond the student/discipline dichotomy." *Journal of Advanced Composition, 13* (1), 173–97.

Samuels, A. (1993). *The political psyche.* New York: Routledge.

Schleifer, R., Con Davis, R., & Mergler, N. (1992). *Culture and cognition: The boundaries of literacy and scientific inquiry.* Ithaca, NY: Cornell University Press.

Shotter, J. (1993). *Cultural politics of everyday life.* Toronto: University of Toronto Press.

Shweder, R. (1995). "Cultural psychology: What is it?" In N. Goldberger & J. Veroff (Eds.), *The culture and psychology reader.* New York: New Yok University Press.

Simon, R., Dippo, D., & Schenke, A. (1991). *Learning work: A critical pedagogy of work education.* Westport, CT: Bergin & Garvey.

Slattery, P. (1995). *Curriculum development in the postmodern era.* New York: Garland.

Thiele, L. (1986). "Foucault's triple murder and the modern development of power." *Canadian Journal of Political Science, 19* (2), 243–260.

Usher, R., & Edwards, R. (1994). *Postmodernism and education.* New York: Routledge.

Ventura, M. (July/August, 1994). "The age of endarkenment." *Utne Reader, 64,* 63–66.

Vygotsky, L. (1978). *Mind in society: The development of higher psychological processes.* Ed. M. Cole et al. Cambridge, MA: Harvard University Press.

Weisner, T. (1987). "Review of J. Wertsch, Vygotsky and the social formation of mind." *American Anthropologist, 89,* 479–80.

Wertsch, J., Del Rio, P., & Alvarez, A. (1995). "Sociocultural studies: History, action, and mediation." In J. Wertsch, P. Del Rio, and A. Alvarez (Eds.), *Sociocultural studies of the mind.* New York: Cambridge University Press.

Wertsch, J., & Tulviste, P. (1992). "L. S. Vygotsky and contemporary developmental psychology." *Development Psychology, 28* (4) 548–57.

Wexler, P. (1997). *Social research in education: Ethnography of being.* Paper presented at the International Conference on the Culture of Schooling, Halle, Germany.

Wirth, A. (1983). *Productive work—in industry and schools.* Lanham, MD: University Press of America.

Woods, P. (1983). *Sociology and the school: An interactionist viewpoint.* London: Routledge and Kegan Paul.

Zweigenhaft, R., & Domhoff, G. (1991). *Blacks in the white establishment.* New Haven: Yale University Press.

Chapter 2

Developmentalism
Deconstructed

Aimee Howley, Linda Spatig, and Craig Howley

Not only are American *children* shaped and marked by the larger political forces of political maneuverings, practical economics, and implicit ideological commitments, *child psychology* is itself a peculiar cultural invention that moves with the tidal sweeps of the larger culture in ways that we understand at best dimly and often ignore. (Kessen, 1979, p. 815)

Following Kessen (1979), this essay evaluates developmentalism as an ideology. In order to avoid grandstanding—that is, simply presenting an ideological refutation of developmentalism from an equally totalizing but opposing vantage—we present a series of critiques from distinct and often mutually exclusive frames of reference. This approach enables us to argue that developmentalism is something other than the set of neutral theories it purports to be. As a theoretical frame of reference, developmentalism would be amenable to debate, criticism, and emendation. As an ideology, it functions as a series of tacit assumptions within various academic and practical discourses. For example, within the discourse of early childhood education, developmentalism serves as the rationale for certain forms of "child-centered" instructional practice (Lubeck, 1996). At the same time, it functions as the basis for discrediting other instructional practices that, under other sets of assumptions, would also reveal themselves as centrally concerned with children's development.

We start from the premise that there can be no first principle that accounts for life, growth, or improvement. Another way to say this is that concepts as apparently indisputable as "alive" or "young" really embed a host of socially constructed meanings (see also Katz, 1995). Apart from these meanings, the concepts have no fixed referents. By saying these things, we do not intend to argue that bodies do not exist or that birth and death are essentially arbitrary. These points are arguable in some contexts. Here it is sufficient to confront the conventional positivist wisdom at the moment when it converts what we experience as the course of our lives into a necessary and predictable sequence of developmental events.

Confrontation takes various shapes in this essay because our purpose is hermeneutic. What we are doing is primarily critique—arguing against—rather than positive assertion. And our goal is to use more than one discourse as the basis of critique. If this suggests a kind of ganging up on developmentalism, we confess to taking this approach. We want to examine how wrong-headed developmentalism might be; others' quarrels with this ideological constellation are pointedly relevant. Furthermore, we suspect that there may be a sort of strength in numbers. If developmentalism looks wrong to neoconservatives, for example, then the supposed errors of its ways may simply instantiate the incommensurabilities of discourse. We might say, in this circumstance, that developmentalists and neoconservatives are unable to talk across their different assumptions. If, however, developmentalism looks wrong to neo-Marxists and to feminists too, then we might conclude, at the very least, that its claims to objectivity are premature and arrogant. Putting forth little effort to address competing interpretations, "developmentalist" theory begins to look self-serving and defensive (see also Morss, 1992).

Acknowledging that our approach is somewhat arbitrary, we present in the subsequent sections of this essay five critiques of developmentalism, each grounded in a different ideological position. Within some of these positions, there are several bases for critique, not all of which are addressed in the essay. Moreover, several of the ideological positions sometimes seem to support the same critique. Our purpose, however, is to illustrate the nature of various critiques rather than to present an exhaustive review of all critiques of developmentalism.

THE CONSERVATIVE CRITIQUE: THE PAMPERED CHILD

The generation raised after September 1945, when Benjamin Spock's *Baby and Child Care* was published, was to be the generation raised right, according to modern (that is, liberal), scientifically guided principles. Dr. Spock's child care manual rivaled the Bible in sales. Indeed, following successful battles against great discouragement (the Great Depression) and against evil incarnate (Hitler's dominion), parents must finally have found the world comfortable and safe enough to accommodate the proper raising of children. The obstacles had been cleared away, progress in all fields was manifest, and normalcy could at last be realized and duly cherished.

When the generation that was supposedly raised right came of age in the 1960s, however, it earned a reputation for deviance, self-indulgence, and negativity (Bell, 1973). Many asked where the enterprise of child rearing had gone wrong.

One answer, from a neoconservative perspective, has entailed a critique of a kind of misguided child rearing and schooling that infused the postwar ethos most particularly, but which persists today. On this view, the reported longing of young adults to get back to normal life following the early- and mid-twentieth-century European and American catastrophes was by no means a simple "return." It was instead a return to something new, a progressive return, so to speak. Psychology had for some time suggested that the best upbringing conformed to the progression of child development and that errors of timing produced unnatural distortions of normal development. Normalcy and proper development determined one another; they were mutually dependent and axiomatic for adequate adjustment to life.

Adopting this modern view, the new, postwar theories of child rearing displaced the Victorian ethos of obedience, propriety, and self-denial (Kessen, 1979), which in the enlightened midcentury was condemned as unnatural and therefore harmful (e.g., Spock, 1976). Informed by progressive science, the new child rearing was more in tune with the nature of childhood and its "stages." Hence in the 1950s and 1960s when a child appeared unruly, the middle classes spoke of "going through a stage," meaning, in popular parlance, a passing and inconsequential period of misbehavior for which little if any correction was really necessary.

Forceful correction of any sort, in fact, was unnecessary under the modern ethos: Children were good by nature, and parents and teachers could rely on children's innate virtue—so long as the natural course of development was not tampered with. This viewpoint, which reinscribes original sin as original virtue, is a legacy of the Enlightenment, as Stone (1996) suggests.

In this interpretation, children are not simply innately good but appear in, and to, nature as *originally virtuous*. To call children originally (naturally) virtuous rather than originally or naturally sinful, however, has a serious drawback, which may outweigh the presumed benefits of the seemingly enlightened position. The drawback is that original virtue is a kind of pinnacle virtue, from which a fall (from grace) is inevitable. Upbringing can only abet the fall, and the very best, under ideal circumstances, that might be done on children's behalf is to do no harm.

From the conservative (and even the liberal) perspective, the idea that virtue is a natural state of existence seems misguided and dangerous. If original sin is problematic, certainly original virtue is as well. An alternative, however, is to acknowledge children as originally harmless but with a natural *tendency* toward either virtue or sin. The question of tendency is where liberals and conservatives do diverge, for a tendency to evil clearly requires a regimen of schooling that differs from that required to address a tendency to virtue. The question becomes whether one bends the child contrary to (sinful) nature or in conformity with (virtuous) nature. The former view prevailed under the sway of a strong church; to espouse it is historically and culturally—and not just politically—conservative. The latter view might be said to represent "the latest findings of research" (see Kessen, 1979).

Note that the key grounding rests on a reading of biblical text, but that a literal reading of the fall from grace does not necessarily represent the sort of ignorance often attributed by liberals and radicals to Christian conservatives. The conservative reading does not construct all nature as evil; in fact, among believers the natural world is more often taken as literal evidence of God's benevolence. Whereas nature may harbor the devil, the devil does not characterize nature. Rather, the devil has special access to the human heart, and that access constitutes human frailty, the need for redemption (and humility), and the child's tendency to evil. All humans share this tendency equally and redeem themselves from it only through a relationship with Christ.

Religious doctrine notwithstanding, traditional parenting practices die hard (as do traditional teaching practices), and few parents then or now undertake the experiment, or folly, of raising children in conformity with the latest findings. When overwrought parents come to the conclusion that their children are bad, most frequently they shoulder the blame personally (rather than blaming bad science, rotten natures, or God's scheme of predestination). And, it must be observed, a fetishism of "latest findings" is likely to produce a pastiche of revised and inconsistent nostrums, making it difficult for even the most savvy children to predict parental expectations. Only the most insecure, most leisured, and most shortsighted of parents could indulge such a fetish.[1] That is, the position is tenable mostly among the simultaneously neurotic and comparatively affluent.

The assumption that children are innately good is contrary to a pan-Christian assumption that humans are born (in)to sin. Sinful human beings *do* require corrections, and children, who are unformed and without indoctrination, can by no means be left to the devices of their own natures. Few sects believe that the flesh of children needs continually to be humiliated to cultivate virtue, but some do. The more common belief is that children need to be closely watched for evidence of the influence of the devil or, less literally, marks of sinfulness. The first education law in the British colonies promoted education on this basis (Cremin, 1979). Sin means error, and in this case error is interpreted variously as deviance from any of a diverse set dogmas, each of which insists on its overarching truth. Error must be corrected, not just to ensure gracious day-to-day conduct, though certainly for that, but most particularly to secure the kingdom of heaven. When the evil to which humans, on this view, are naturally subject unequivocally manifests itself, not only the individual but the community, the church, and the afterlife are placed in jeopardy.

The conservative critique of the pampered child, whether religiously informed or not, requires the same thing that conservative forms of schooling require—*rigor*. Rigor is the corrective for sin, and because pampered children never experience the corrective, their evil is compounded. They are doubly damned—on sacred terms *and* on secular terms.

The resultant evil for the nation is clear. According to this critique, as children mature they will fail to recognize their obligations; they will seek to minimize the pain that naturally accompanies the human condition and with which they must cope; and, ultimately, they will be incapacitated in terms of the struggle to improve themselves, their communities, and most importantly the national economy.

As adults, many previously pampered children will expect, according to this argument, to be provided for, rather than to produce. Thus, in addition to developing soldiering workers, schooling on the developmentalist model also helps ensure the continuing existence of the liberal welfare state. In cultural terms, pampering reduces the child's odds of success in the war of all against all. In the conservative estimation, education should stand as a defense against human nature, rather than fall mistakenly into step with it.

THE USEFUL ADULT: THE NEO-MARXIST CRITIQUE

In the conservative critique of developmentalism, rigor is valued as a tonic for children's wills. Struggle characterizes the adult world, and therefore children must be educated to, by, and for it. Neo-Marxists, who attribute less significance to individual will and character and more significance to concerted political action and the structure of social institutions (that is, they view *socialized* will and character as more significant for the needed transformation of the "social relations of production"), interpret differently the issue of rigor.[2]

For neo-Marxists, schools are not at all what they seem or claim to be, nor are the mainstream professional ideologies used to legitimate schooling forthcoming about the reality that schools support. Schools do not exist to educate, ennoble, or improve; they do not exist to cultivate creativity or thoughtfulness very widely; and they do not exist to create democratic-minded citizens. Among structural neo-Marxists, in particular, the durability of teaching practices constitutes strong evidence that schooling serves to reproduce, and indeed actually to *enforce*, the class relationships of capitalist society.

For this reason schools are not really subject to legitimate reform efforts, according to neo-Marxists. Reform is needed only to make schools *conform* more faithfully to the requirements of capital. Dominant reformation (or conformation) proposals since the Reagan ascendency have nearly always accorded particular solicitude to business interests. "What business requires of schools" is of key interest to contemporary school reformers, and the emphasis is on big business, not on small-scale entrepreneurship. The liberal-conservative ideology of schooling and its kit of theory and practice are, to neo-Marxists, durable lies—complex lies, but nonetheless more or less total, purposive misconstructions of reality.

Neo-Marxists believe, predictably enough, that schools do exist as an extension of *labor discipline*—a form of socially imposed rigor that attempts to make capitalism seem natural to workers (e.g., Bowles & Gintis, 1976). Rigor, on this view, is an ideological device to obscure workers' class interests, making it seem to them that a minimum wage might not be an affront to human dignity, that part-time jobs instead of full-time employment is an agreeable bargain, that society really cannot afford to construe health care as a right (and especially not for impoverished families), that fabulous wealth is the happy fortune of the virtuous, and that significant income and wealth redistribution are incompatible with the principles of (liberal) democracy.

Where the conservative critique sees failure in the enterprise of schooling, neo-Marxists see success (e.g., Bowles & Gintis, 1976). Capitalism functions smoothly to exploit workers, and, in line with this logic, schools prepare students to accept their inevitable exploitation in a liberal-democratic political economy. The chastisement of schools by (liberal-democratic) conservatives is merely the form that labor discipline takes for those who work in and around them, that is, students, teachers, administrators, and educational researchers (Apple, 1988). The strategy is successful: *Accountability* is a word on the lips of every politician, State Education Agency (SEA) official, and school administrator. Teachers, structurally somewhat closer to the interests of labor (Wright, 1979), seek to dab it off their chins, but it is continually thrown back in their faces. Schools *will* do what business requires. Teachers—the real laborers in schools—have been effectively disciplined, according to the neo-Marxist view.

In general, neo-Marxists, like most people, have little difficulty believing that children exhibit a predictable sequence of accomplishments associated with their maturation. But given their perception that schooling is a bastion of labor discipline, neo-Marxists are not inclined to argue that school practices ought to be "developmentally appropriate." We suspect they would be more likely to agree with Stone's (1996) assessment of the extreme difficulty of making inferences about both a child's developmental status and the appropriate educational treatment responsive to that status.

Whereas neo-Marxists would consider it a good thing to make schooling more humane, they must interpret the interminable and inconclusive professional disputes over "developmental appropriateness" as an ornate game, little concerned to affect the real conditions of lives in impoverished and working-class families. On this view, the professional disputes of educationists serve the same purpose in the construction of the capitalist world as religion—class-based distractions keeping the working classes from directing the class struggle (i.e., ensuring that it is the bourgeoisie that directs the class struggle, as it must in a capitalist regime).

Neo-Marxists are also likely to find the *substantive* purposes of developmentally appropriate instruction suspect in a capitalist regime of schooling. In approximating developmentally appropriate instruction (whatever it may be), schools aim to produce productive and well-adjusted citizens, sorting children into academic groupings that ready them for different and unequally rewarded job categories (Spring, 1989). The few students who nonetheless become pessimistic about the workings of capitalism, who exhibit socialistic tendencies, or who develop a critical bent of any sort are very likely to be regarded as maladjusted troublemakers. Ethnographers have amply shown how apparently commonplace this perspective is in classrooms (see, e.g., Willis, 1977).

On the neo-Marxist view, what society at large considers proper development has its proper end in useful adults ready, willing, and able to serve the interests of capital and little interested in engaging the class struggle. Some will serve in the (post-) industrial reserve army; some (e.g., teachers) will bolster the institutions of bourgeois culture; and some (e.g., the Bill Gateses) will direct core enterprises. Few will perceive that they have been miseducated, and the most fortunate among them will surely have enjoyed a developmentally appropriate education.

This view is easily extended to the various developmentalisms devised for adult education; the cultivation of leadership or creativity; and, in particular, regional, rural, national, and international economic development. Once a *natural* sequence is discovered among children, one can be inferred almost anywhere to good bourgeois purpose. Adults are thereby "discovered" to have a predictable sequence of (supra-) maturation, leaders a predictable sequence in the exercise of power, and rural areas and third-world nations a natural progression in aspiring to achieve the developmental pinnacle of the metropolis, on one hand, or of first-world nations, on the other (Williams, 1988).

What is important to neo-Marxists in all of the developmentalisms—micro and macro—is the rush to confirm a developmental sequence that validates the naturalness of capitalism. In education, the dominant theorists of development are nearly all apologists or functionaries, both witting and unwitting, of capital. As with liberals and conservatives—who seem so different but are so similar, according to North American neo-Marxists—the structurally preapproved end for all kinds of developmentalists is the same: the cultivation of dispositions, habits, and skills that are useful to the capitalist system. The scientific claim that all these developments proceed from a natural essence makes capitalism seem, if not actually just, then most certainly inevitable.

THE ONE BEST CHILD: THE CRITIQUE
FROM CULTURAL PLURALISM

One of anthropology's major contributions to contemporary thought is the observation that there are few (perhaps no) cultural universals. Cultural practices vary among contexts, different cultural groups attribute different meanings to similar activities, and the life cycle unfolds within cultures according to socially negotiated assumptions about desirable ways of being in the world. These observations—based in an ecological understanding of the connection between children and their environments—support a dynamic and pluralist view of development (Harkness, 1996). Furthermore, as Lillian Katz (1994) suggests, such an interpretation gains support not only from portraits of development in cultures other than our own. Developmental variation *within* our culture also warrants the dynamic and pluralist view.

This view, which accounts for the cultural basis of development and admits broad interpretations of what is normal, tends to confound efforts to identify predictable sequences of development, normative milestones of developmental accomplishment, and reliable indices of the achievement of adult status (Harkness, 1980; LeVine, 1980). Furthermore, it challenges mainstream psychological assumptions about what constitutes meaningful differences within and between individuals (Nunes, 1995).

Despite admonitions to take a broader view of development, many psychologists and practitioners who work with children expect children's performance to match norms derived from observations of white, middle-class children only (Artiles, 1996; Kessen, 1979). These expectations contribute to the practice of judging children from some groups to be less able than mainstream children and then treating them as inferior and potentially dangerous (New, 1997; Rist, 1970). Furthermore, the engineered failure, indeed "abnormality," of certain groups of children contributes to racist and classist recommendations for social policies, which in a self-serving and tautological fashion support prevailing inequities in the distribution of power and resources (e.g., Herrnstein & Murray, 1994).

The mechanisms of such failure are documented in anthropological accounts of schooling, such as Rosenfeld's (1976, p. 228) dramatic portrait of "Harlem School":

> Harlem School was not solely an agency of cultural transmission in an educational sense, but an agency of personality restriction. It did not serve to connect the child and the larger cultural world so that the child would eventually be passed into the world in confidence; it served more to tell the child that he was unacceptable as he was, and that he would have to be substantially changed in order to fit the images others had of him.

In schools like this, children diminish their hopes and confirm teachers' fears by learning "not to learn" (Rosenfeld, 1976). Similarly, in the culture at large, members of disenfranchised groups acquire the reputation for "not growing up," a reputation that serves to legitimate the practice of treating them like children. Whether it is by offering paternalistic salves to the less fortunate or by locking up the deviant, social programs speak to the putative deficiency of unassimilated individuals and groups.

Multicultural education, which purports to value diversity rather than to encourage assimilation, also fails in many cases to confront the ideologies that denigrate persons and cultures differing from the mainstream. Some versions of multicultural education, in particular, exemplify the way that a culturally sensitive stance can devolve into an approach that trivializes and marginalizes those who are different. This abasement occurs when writers and educators treat cultural differences superficially, rendering as harmless the power relations that shape the contest between dominant and subordinate groups. Silent on the practices of colonization, disenfranchisement, and economic oppression, this treatment fosters a myth of cultural difference. Central to the myth is the construction of culture as entertaining, sometimes quaint or stylish, and politically inert.

The developmentalist rendition of the myth accounts for differences, particularly in the cognitive development, of children from different racial and ethnic groups by positing variations in learning style. Accepting the conventional view that children from some groups are developmentally delayed with respect to their cognitive performance, this approach seeks to attribute the seeming delays to differences in field dependent or independent, visual or auditory, synthetic or analytic preferences (see, e.g., Browne, 1990; Rhodes, 1988; White, 1992). Educators who subscribe to this approach construct a type of "culturally sensitive" teaching that tries to address the supposed differences in children's styles of learning (Kleinfeld & Nelson, 1988). The effect, though, may be to disconnect processes of learning and modes of thinking from the cultural contexts in which they typically take place. This disconnection misconstrues situated sense-making as learning technique. Moreover, it assumes rather naively that the "one best system" of school practice will somehow become flexible in deference to a precise specification of individual need (cf. Tyack, 1974). Culturally sensitive teaching replaces the hegemonic construction of the "one best child" with a trivializing image of childhood as a more or less common experience that varies only in terms of its picturesque details.

In addition to these critiques, a viewpoint based in cultural pluralism offers a more fundamental way to see through developmentalism's illusion of objectivity. Rooting developmentalism in a Western tradition that constructs selves as discrete individuals, this critique uses examples from less individualistic cultures to challenge the positivist assumption that development inheres in the individual (Kessen, 1979). In the positivist version, "the child—like the Pilgrim, the cowboy, and the detective on television—is invariably seen as a free-standing isolable being who moves through development as a self-contained and complete individual" (Kessen, 1979, p. 819).

Using examples from African, Hispanic, American Indian, and Asian cultures, pluralists show that the self may be defined in collective and interdependent—rather than individualistic—ways (e.g., Greenfield & Cocking, 1993; Markus & Kitayama, 1991; Mudimbe, 1988; Simonelli, 1993; Staples, 1978). In many of these cultures, social or narrative practices replace individual performances as valid markers of self (Miller & Goodnow, 1995). The notion that self might be manifested in the idiosyncrasies of personal behavior makes little sense when normation is viewed as a socially negotiated process rather than a scientifically ascribed one.

THE UNDERDEVELOPED MAN: THE FEMINIST CRITIQUE

There is no one feminism, so to speak of "a" feminist critique essentializes feminist thought in a way that belies the spirit of this essay. We base our discussion, therefore, on one construct of feminist theorizing, Benhabib's (1987), which assumes (1) that the gendered organization of social systems is a fundamental rather than a contingent construction of social reality and (2) that the gendered social systems that have emerged thus far in history have contributed to the oppression and exploitation of women. On this view, the tasks of feminist critique are to expose the oppressive features and consequences of social practices (in this case, developmentalist psychology) and to create alternative, even utopian, visions of how to organize society on different terms.

Just as in social science generally, mainstream developmental psychology has been dominated by privileged white male heterosexuals who control the production and legitimation of knowledge. Feminists within psychology have criticized traditional theories of human development, and feminists both within and outside psychology have criticized mainstream social science more broadly. The feminist critiques have in common a concern for women and the extent to which they are ill-served by mainstream social science.

Feminist challenges within psychology address every aspect of the discipline, from grand theoretical issues to specific researchers and their methodologies. According to Naomi Weisstein (cited in Walsh, 1992, p. 293): "Psychology has nothing to say about what women are really like, what they need and what they want, essentially, because psychology does not know." Weisstein's comments suggest that, in the construction of influential theories of human behavior, personality, and development, psychology has virtually ignored women and their experiences. As a consequence, women continue to be judged as deviant or deficient in relation to theories of human development—based almost entirely on the study of males.

Perhaps no single theorist has come under greater attack from feminists than Sigmund Freud. In the early years of the second wave of feminism, there seemed to be a consensus that Freud's psychoanalytic theory was a destructive ideology, useful only for demeaning and controlling women. For example, Kate Millett (1970) described psychoanalytic theory as the major (and scientific) source of ideological support for a "patriarchal social order." More recently, Hannah Lerman (1986) argued that women cannot benefit from any attempt to refine psychoanalysis. Because it ignores women and the uniqueness of their life experiences, psychoanalysis, in Lerman's view, is fundamentally flawed.

Beginning in the 1970s, however, some feminists attempted to make connections between psychoanalysis and feminism, arguing that Freud's theories provided powerful descriptions of human development *in the context of* patriarchal societies (e.g., Mitchell, 1974). Perhaps the most widely read work of feminist psychoanalysis is Nancy Chodorow's (1978) study of mothering in which she argues that, rather than deriving from processes determined biologically or cultivated intentionally, mothering is reproduced through psychological processes that are induced and sustained by the social structure.

Keller (1985) also used a "reformulated" psychoanalytic approach to address the failure of Freudian theory to incorporate the experiences of women. She noted in particular that Freudian accounts of the development of self-other relations (i.e., object relations) focus on the development of individual autonomy and ignore the development of the relational capabilities and understandings that undergird individual's connection with others. Keller also argued more generally that modern science is characterized by the stance of objectivity—in her view, the cognitive counterpart of psychological autonomy. Taking what she called a "feminist perspective on science," Keller described both gender and science as "socially constructed categories" (p. 4).

Building on Chodorow's work, Carol Gilligan (1982) exposed masculine biases in the work of psychologists concerned with psychosocial and moral development, focusing particular attention on the work of Erikson, Piaget, and Kohlberg. Gilligan, for example, critiqued Kohlberg's theory of moral development, a theory based on the study of eighty-four males over a twenty-four-year period.

> Although Kohlberg claims universality for his stage sequence, those groups not included in his original sample rarely reach his higher stages.... Prominent among those who thus appear to be deficient in moral development when measured by Kohlberg's scale are women, whose judgments seem to exemplify the third stage of his six-stage sequence. At this stage morality is conceived in interpersonal terms and goodness is equated with helping and pleasing others. (Gilligan, 1982, p. 18)

Like Gilligan and her colleagues, Belenky, Clinchy, Goldberger, and Tarule (1986) deplored psychology's inattention to women, citing in particular the lack of knowledge about the development of interdependence, intimacy, caring, and nurturance. They faulted traditional scholarship on intellectual development for "studying the intellectual capacities most often cultivated by men rather than . . . identifying aspects of intelligence and modes of thought that might be more common and highly developed in women" (p. 7). *In Women's Ways of Knowing,* Belenky and associates discussed the developmental insights they gleaned from extensive interviews with women. In particular, they described five different positions women adopt in approaching knowledge. These positions reflect women's development of "connected knowing," which is "contextual and emphasizes understanding another person's view, learning through actual experience, and relating ideas and theories to personal events" (p. 112).

Feminist psychologists—including the "insiders" discussed above—have played a vital role in furthering the feminist cause generally. Just as feminists exposed and challenged sexism in other arenas of society, feminist psychologists "accused social science of distortion, bias, myopia, ethnocentrism, heterosexism, and androcentrism," showing how "both science and society used knowledge as a form of violence to silence women and make them invisible" (Reinharz, 1992, p. 424). Whereas these feminists offered important antidotes to traditional developmentalist theorizing, in doing so they may have created or reinforced false dichotomies between the so-called nature of men and women (Enns, 1991). By speaking, for example, of *"women's* ways of knowing," these feminists may have essentialized femaleness without paying adequate attention to the differing experiences of women in different social contexts (e.g., Thompson, 1996).

For the most part, insider critiques of mainstream developmental theories accept without question the tenets of positivist science, its stance of methodological objectivity, and its reliance on correspondence theories of perception (Spender, 1992). Failing to challenge the prevailing norms of scientific practice, these critiques represent what Harding (1986) calls "feminist empiricism" (see also Reinharz, 1992). Along the same lines, Alcoff sees the work of developmental theorists such as Gilligan and Chodorow as an attempt to improve social scientific theories by bringing them into alignment with feminist principles, and "in effect purifying social science of its non-objective elements" (Alcoff, 1989, p. 88).

Discrediting the search for a "value-neutral" science, many recent feminist scholars take a different stance. No longer concerned to amend the findings of mainstream research or to expand theory to account for the experiences of women, these critics challenge the methodology of science itself. From this vantage, feminists undertake the "revolutionary" project of transforming the "foundations both of science and of the cultures that accord it value" (Harding, 1986, p. 9).

According to Harding (1986, p. 19), many feminist critics "have been so preoccupied with responding to the sins of contemporary science in the same terms our culture uses to justify these sins that we have not yet given adequate attention to envisioning truly emancipatory knowledge-seeking." While recognizing the contributions of "feminist empiricism," Harding urges feminists to go beyond such "reform"-oriented work, encouraging them to consider the ways that patriarchal relations of power constrain inquiry and, ultimately, human understanding (Harding, 1986). Claiming that value neutrality does not improve objectivity, Harding calls for science to be guided overtly by values, in particular participatory and emancipatory—antiracist, anticlassist, antisexist—values. By emphasizing the moral and political underpinnings of inquiry, scholars such as Harding construe science as one way of knowing among many. From this vantage, science is less central to the construction of truth than it is under an Enlightenment worldview.

With regard to development, this more inclusive approach to inquiry suggests that the life cycle ought to be examined from a variety of perspectives, rather than from a scientific perspective only. Moreover, it implies that the scientific account of development is no more "true" than accounts derived from other ways of knowing—introspection and mothering, for example (cf. Griffith, 1995). Many postmodern theorists, feminist or not, make similar claims. They are concerned to expand the definition of knowledge to accommodate multiple voices, often those of people who were previously marginalized or disqualified from participating in the production of knowledge.

THE SELF-PERFECTING OBJECT: THE POSTMODERN CRITIQUE

Following Foucault primarily, we base our postmodern critique on several assumptions: (1) science is a rhetorical construct, (2) knowledge (in this case, the scientific knowledge of development) is deployed as a technology of power, (3) technologies of power provide an apparatus by which the state can intrude upon—colonizing, regulating, and appropriating—processes of the formation of the self, and (4) intentional processes of formation of the self can defeat state efforts at domination and provide a basis for emancipatory praxis that links personal and political freedoms (see e.g., Foucault, 1977, 1980, 1982; Saul, 1992).

From a Foucauldian perspective, developmentalism can be included among the technologies of power that function to make persons into *individuals,* ensuring at one and the same time their well-being and their utility to the state. Among these technologies, Foucault directs particular attention to physicians' interrogations of bodies (Foucault, 1973), psychiatrists' illumination of individuals' particular madnesses (Foucault, 1971), teachers' classifications of students' talents and ineptitudes (Foucault, 1977), and pastors' inquiry into the truth of each person's soul (Foucault, 1982, 1988).

Each of these technologies provides a kind of knowledge about individuals that invests the state with power over them. And this same knowledge, which the state uses to colonize individuals, also contributes to the formation of their identities (Carlson, 1997). The way that power infuses this process of formation of the self reduces the need for the state to maintain centralized mechanisms for actively constraining personal and group behavior.

Founded in techniques of surveillance, the technologies associated with the human sciences specify with precision the nature and utility of each individual's attributes (Carlson, 1997; Foucault, 1988; Gandy, 1993). Moreover, human technicians (e.g., teachers, psychologists, doctors) exhort individuals to scrutinize themselves for signs of dysfunction and aberration. Self-monitoring and self-governance replace the arm of the state as the most prevalent methods for exerting control over individuals' actions and destinies.

Like any of these technologies, knowledge about development offers sets of standards and repertoires of practices for examining and normalizing so-called individuals—in this case children primarily. According to Lubeck (1996, p. 156), "Child development theory orients us to an abstracted schema that becomes the 'mismeasure' of the child who displays a different developmental trajectory." Whereas this "mismeasure" may provide a rationale for marginalizing (even ostracizing) a minority of children, its more ubiquitous service is in cultivating the majority of them. By identifying (or manufacturing) children's distinct capacities, developmental practices assist in the process of sorting, training, and, among the elite, manicuring them for adult roles (Carlson, 1997; Spring, 1976; Howley, 1986). These processes enable and constrain children, often at the same time. They establish the conditions of each child's uniqueness, and, when the technology works optimally, these practices shape children's perfect utility for serving the interests of the state (Foucault, 1988; Gandy, 1993).

According to Foucault, selves are created through such processes of normalization. These processes involve relational production and are neither unidimensional nor always totalizing (Carlson, 1997). Relational production undermines hegemonic determinism by enabling the subject to resist the normalized identity that the state attempts to impose strategically through the local application of technologies of power. The subject seeks freedom by enacting a counterstrategy, care of the self, which may involve refusal to accept professionals' characterization of his or her attributes, involvement in experiences that test the limits of the normal, and revolt against oppressive practices (Foucault, 1978).

While providing opportunities for personal resistance, relational production also enables the technologies of power to respond flexibly to changing conditions. As mechanisms of surveillance and social control, these technologies exploit occasions of resistance—co-opting, neutralizing, and reinscribing them as trivial or merely stylish (Hebdige, 1979). These processes take place simultaneously at the local level, in schools and other social service agencies, and at the mass level, through the popular media. At the local level, for example, teachers co-opt the language of students' rebellion (e.g., rap), reconstituting it as an innocuous classroom tool for improving the relevance of instruction (e.g., Anderson, 1993; Jeremiah, 1992). At the mass level, popularizers extract the symbols of rebellion and market them to as wide an audience as possible (cf. Hebdige, 1979). By turning the symbols of resistance into fads and "product lines," the state is able to strip them of ideological force as well as to control their impact and trajectory.

Like other technologies of power, developmental theories and practices seem to respond to forms of resistance in contradictory ways. For example, while some developmentalists celebrate the resilience of street-smart children from the inner city (e.g., Wang & Gordon, 1994), others recommend that such children be sent to juvenile facilities for "shock incarceration" (e.g., MacKenzie, 1993). The apparent contradictions in the theoretical and practical approaches taken by developmentalists signal the potential strength and flexibility of the technology, not its fragility.

Implicit in Foucault's analysis and explicit in the analyses of other postmodernists is the idea that the "other" is necessary for the constitution of the self. This claim has important ontological ramifications, but its relevance to the critique of developmentalism primarily involves its political import. In a political context, "others" serve as points of reference for subjects as they identify and expand the boundaries of self-definition. Thus, "others" can function in contradistinction to "self" as the representations of what the self is not; "othering" from this perspective involves exclusion (Karskens, 1991). "Otherness" is also a property of selves who struggle to extend the boundaries that normalization imposes on their identity. From this perspective, "other" is an alternate reading of self—in a transcendental sense, a reading of self under conditions of freedom. Recognizing the "other" as potential within the self invites openness to difference.

Attending primarily to individuals and their differences in propensity and attainment, developmentalism advances an exclusionary interpretation of "other." This interpretation supports a politics of identity that emphasizes the special character of groups of individuals who share some common feature of their identity. It also encourages a proliferation of special developmentalisms attuned to the distinct qualities of special groups (Lubeck, 1996). Thus in the education literature we encounter, among other separate bodies of literature, a literature on "African-American development," "lesbian and gay development," "gifted development," "girls' development," and so on. These developmentalisms have the effect of essentializing difference by providing technical assistance to the more widespread social project of defining and defending the borders between groups.

Approaches that encourage border crossing, by contrast, promote a critical multiculturalism that invites dialogue about difference and across differences. These approaches comprehend the possibilities for personal liberation implicit in exchanges with the "other" and with the "other" within one's self. Because such exchanges have no specified aim, however, they cannot properly be understood as necessary steps toward some type of development—even toward the development of self-determination. Rather, they embed possibility, which is necessarily indeterminate. Indeterminacy, however, encourages understandings of self that are playful, rich, and flexible (Doll, 1993).

FORMATION OF THE SELF UNDER CONDITIONS OF FREEDOM

As the five critiques suggest, though in different and sometimes incompatible ways, developmentalism is a form of restraint. For neoconservatives, developmentalism interferes with parents' and schools' freedom to bend children's character away from evil and toward a productive and virtuous life. Neo-Marxists, by contrast, see developmentalism as the ideological support for a type of labor discipline that obscures and constrains workers' emancipatory praxis. Focusing on cultural diversity, pluralists demonstrate how developmentalism narrows definitions of human potential by imposing artificial hierarchies of competence and value on the full array of cultural patterns and performances. And feminists note that, in particular, developmentalism demeans women and diminishes their opportunities for self-determination. Construing developmentalism as a technology of power, a postmodern critique examines the mechanisms by which developmental discourse and practice control and colonize processes of formation of the self.

However we look at it, developmentalism seems to be a limiting force. But what it obstructs differs within each critique. Similarly, the freedom that developmentalism impedes is, in each case, imagined differently. Recognizing this, we affirm the social construction of both developmentalism and the possibilities for development that it conceals. Moreover, we expose a discourse about freedom that at once connects it to the idea of how the self is formed and to the imagined worlds that selves—formed in whatever ways—might inhabit and continually reshape.

NOTES

1. Note, however, that the perpetual cycles of school reform depend on and, indeed, sanctify just such a fetish.
2. Marxism can, itself, be construed as a type of developmentalism. Marx's formulation of a necessary historical succession of stages in the organization of production has a distinctly developmentalist flavor. That Marx's analysis of the mechanisms of capitalism underestimated both its adaptability (which suggests another kind of development) and its tenacity (which suggests a kind of static essentialism) lends credence to a *neo*-Marxist interpretation that links resilient school practices to processes of social reproduction.

REFERENCES

Alcoff, L. (1989). "Justifying feminist social science." In N. Tauna (Ed.), *Feminism in science* (pp. 85–103). Bloomington: Indiana University Press.

Anderson, E. (1993). "Rap music in the classroom?" *Teaching English in the Two-Year College, 20* (3), 214–221.

Apple, M. W. (1988). "What reform talk does: Creating new inequalities in education." *Educational Administration Quarterly, 24* (3), 257–271.

Artiles, A. J. (1996). "Teacher thinking in urban schools: The need for a contextualized research agenda." In F. A. Rios (Ed.), *Teacher thinking in cultural contexts* (pp. 23–52). Albany: State University of New York Press.

Belenky, M. R., Clinchy, B. M., Goldberger, N. R., & Tarule, J.M. (1986). *Women's ways of knowing: The development of self, voice, and mind.* New York: Basic Books.

Bell, D. (1973). *The coming of postindustrial society: A venture in social forecasting.* New York: Basic Books.

Benhabib, S. (1987). "The generalized and the concrete other: The Kohlberg-Gilligan controversy and feminist theory." In S. Benhabib & D. Cornell (Eds.), *Feminism as critique: On the politics of gender* (pp. 77–95). Minneapolis: Univesity of Minnesota Press.

Bowles, S., & Gintis, H. (1976). *Schooling in capitalist America.* New York: Basic Books.

Browne, D. B. (1990). "Learning styles and Native Americans." *Canadian Journal of Native Education, 17* (1), 23–35.

Carlson, D. (1997). *Making progress: Education and culture in new times.* New York: Teachers College Press.

Chodorow, N. (1978). *The reproduction of mothering: Psychoanalysis and the sociology of gender.* Berkeley: University of California Press.

Cremin, L. (1979). *American education: The colonial experience.* New York: Harper & Row.

Doll, W. E., Jr. (1993). "Curriculum possibilities in a 'post'-future." *Journal of Curriculum and Supervision, 8* (4), 277–292.

Enns, C. Z. (1991). "The 'new' relationship models of women's identity: A review and critique for counselors." *Journal of Counseling and Development, 69,* 209–217.

Foucault, M. (1971). *Madness and civilization: A history of insanity in the Age of Reason.* Trans. R. Howard. New York: New American Library.

Foucault, M. (1973). *The birth of the clinic: An archaeology of medical perception.* Trans. A. M. S. Smith. New York: Pantheon.

Foucault, M. (1977). *Discipline and punish: The birth of the prison.* Trans. A. Sheridan. New York: Pantheon.

Foucault, M. (1978). *The history of sexuality.* Trans. R. Hurley. New York: Pantheon.

Foucault, M. (1980). "Two lectures." In *Power/knowledge: Selected interviews and other writings, 1972–1977* (pp. 78-108). Edited by C. Gordon. New York: Pantheon.

Foucault, M. (1982). "The subject and power." In H. Dreyfus & P. Rabinow (Eds.), *Michel Foucault: Beyond structuralism and hermeneutics* (pp. 208–226). Brighton, Sussex, England: Harvester.

Foucault, M. (1988). "The art of telling the truth." In *Michel Foucault: Politics, philosophy, culture: Interviews and other writings, 1977–1984* (pp. 86–95). New York: Routledge.

Foucault, M. (1988). *Politics philosophy culture: Interviews and other writings, 1977–1984.* New York: Routledge.

Gandy, O. H. (1993). *The panoptic sort: A policial economy of personal information.* Boulder, CO: Westview.

Gilligan, C. (1982). *In a different voice: Psychological theory and women's development.* Cambridge, MA: Harvard University Press.

Greenfield, P. M., & Cocking, R. R. (Eds.). (1993). *Cross-cultural roots of minority child development.* Hillsdale, NJ: Lawrence Erlbaum Associates.

Griffith, A. I. (1995). "Coordinating family and school: Mothering for schooling." *Educational Policy Analysis Archives, 3* (1). (On-line), http://olam.ed.asu.edu/epaa/v3n1.html

Harding, S. (1986). *The science question in feminism.* Ithaca, NY: Cornell University Press.

Harkness, S. (1980). "The cultural context of child development." In C. M. Super, & S. Harkness, (Eds.), *Anthropological perspectives on child development* (pp. 7–13). San Francisco: Jossey-Bass..

Harkness, S. (1996). "Anthropological images of childhood." In C. P. Hwang, M. E. Lamb, & I. E. Sigel (Eds.), *Images of childhood* (pp. 36–46). Mahwah, NJ: Lawrence Erlbaum Associates.

Hebdige, D. (1979). *Subculture, the meaning of style.* London: Methuen.

Herrnstein, R. J., & Murray, C. (1994). *The bell curve: Intelligence and class structure in American life.* New York: Free Press.

Howley, A. (1986). "Gifted education and the spectre of elitism." *Journal of Education, 168* (1), 117–125.

Jeremiah, M. A. (1992). "Rap lyrics: Instruments for language arts instruction." *Western Journal of Black Studies, 16* (2), 98–102.

Karskens, M. (1991). "Alterity as defect: On the logic of the mechanics of exclusion." In R. Corbey & J. Leerssen (Eds.), *Alterity, identity, image: Selves and others in society and scholarship* (pp. 75–90). Atlanta: Rodopi.

Katz, L. G. (1994, April). *Child development knowledge and teacher preparation: Confronting assumptions.* Paper presented at the annual conference of the Midwest Association for the Education of Young Children, Peoria, IL. (ERIC Document Reproduction Service No. ED 385 374).

Katz, S. (1995). "Imagining the life-span: From premodern miracles to postmodern fantasies." In M. Featherston & A. Wernick (Eds.), *Images of aging: Cultural representations of later life* (pp. 61–75). London: Routledge.

Keller, E. F. (1985). *Reflections on gender and science.* New Haven: Yale University Press.

Kessen, W. (1979). "The American child and other cultural inventions." *American Psychologist, 34* (10), 815–820.

Kleinfeld, J., & Nelson, P. (1988). *Adapting instruction to Native Americans' "learning styles": An iconoclastic view.* (ERIC Document Reproduction Service No. ED 321 952).

Lerman, H. (1986). *A mote in Freud's eye: From psychoanalysis to the psychology of women.* New York: Springer.

LeVine, R. A. (1980). "Anthropology and child development." In C. M. Super & S. Harkness S. (Eds.), *Anthropological perspectives on child development* (pp. 71–86). San Francisco: Jossey-Bass.

Lubeck, S. (1996). "Deconstructing 'child development knowledge' and 'teacher preparation.'" *Early Childhood Research Quarterly, 11* (2), 147–167.

MacKenzie, D. L. (1993). "Boot camp prisons in 1993." *National Institute of Justice Journal,* (227), 21–28.

Markus, H. R., & Kitayama, S. (1991). "Culture and the self: Implications for cognition, emotion, and motivation." *Psychological Review, 98* (2), 224–253.

Miller, P. J., & Goodnow, J. J. (1995). "Cultural practices: Toward an integration of culture and development." In J. Goodnow, P. Miller, & F. Kessel (Eds.), *Cultural practices as contexts for development* (pp. 5–16). San Francisco: Jossey-Bass.

Millett, K. (1970). *Sexual politics.* New York: Doubleday.

Mitchell, J. (1974). *Psychoanalysis and feminism.* New York: Random House.

Morss, J. (1992). "Making waves: Deconstruction and developmental psychology." *Theory & Psychology, 2* (4), 445–465.

Mudimbe, V. Y. (1988). *Liberty in African and Western thought.* Washington, DC: Institute for Independent Education. (ERIC Document Reproduction Service No. ED 302 612).

New, C. A. (1997). "Perception of African-American male achievement." In F. A. Rios (Ed.), *Teacher thinking in cultural contexts* (pp. 85–103). Albany: State University of New York Press.

Nunes, T. (1995). "Cultural practices and the conception of individual differences: Theoretical and empirical considerations." In J. Goodnow, P. Miller, & F. Kessel (Eds.), *Cultural practices as contexts for development* (pp. 91–104). San Francisco: Jossey-Bass.

Reinharz, S. (1992). "The principles of feminist research: A matter of debate." In C. Kramarae & D. Spender (Eds.), *The knowledge explosion: Generations of feminist scholarship* (pp. 423–437). New York: Teachers College Press.

Rhodes, R. (1988). "Holistic teaching/learning for Native American students." *Journal of American Indian Education, 27* (2), 21–29.

Rist, R. (1970). "Student social class and teacher expectations: The self-fulfilling prophecy in ghetto education." *Harvard Educational Review, 46* (3), 411–451.

Rosenfeld, G. (1976). "Shut those thick lips! Can't you behave like a human being?" In J. I. Roberts & S. K. Akinsanya (Eds.), *Schooling in the cultural context: Anthropological studies of education* (pp. 226–238). New York: David McKay.

Saul, J. R. (1992). *Voltaire's bastards: The dictatorship of reason in the West.* New York: Free Press.

Simonelli, R. (1993). "Seeds of diversity: A training program based on Native American principles and values." *Winds of Change, 8* (1), 28–36.

Spender, D. (1992). "The entry of women to the education of men." In C. Kramarae & D. Spender (Eds.), *The knowledge explosion: Generations of feminist scholarship* (pp. 235–253). New York: Teachers College Press.

Spock, B. (1976). *Baby and child care* (rev. ed.). New York: Pocket Books.

Spring, J. H. (1976). *The sorting machine: National educational policy since 1945.* New York: Longman.

Spring, J. H. (1989). *The sorting machine revisited: National educational policy since 1945.* New York: Longman.

Staples, R. (1978). *The black family: Essays and studies* (2nd ed.). Belmont, CA: Wadsworth.

Stone, J. (1996). "Developmentalism: An obscure but pervasive restriction on educational improvement." *Education Policy Analysis Archives, 4* (8). (Online), http://olam.ed.asu.edu/epaa/v4n8.htm.

Thompson, A. (1996). "Critique of Between voice and silence: Women and girls, race and relationship." *Educational Studies, 27* (3), 253–261.

Tyack, D. (1974). *The one best system: A history of American urban education.* Cambridge, MA: Harvard University Press.

Walsh, M. R. (1992). "Psychology and feminism." In C. Kramarae & D. Spender (Eds.), *The knowledge explosion: Generations of feminist scholarship* (pp. 291–302). New York: Teachers College Press.

Wang, M., & Gordon, E. W. (Eds.). (1994). *Educational resilience in inner-city America: Challenges and prospects.* Hillsdale, NJ: Lawrence Erlbaum Associates.

White, S. E. (1992). *Factors that contribute to learning difference among African American and caucasian students.* (ERIC Document Reproduction Service No. ED374 177).

Willis, P. (1977). *Learning to labor: How working class kids get working class jobs.* New York: Columbia University Press.

Wright, E. O. (1979). *Class, crisis, and the state.* London: Verso.

Chapter 3

The Personality Vacuum: Abstracting the Social from the Psychological

Pepi Leistyna

> Psychology with its notion of the isolated, developing individual allows for the interpretation that all societal problems can be ultimately located at the door of the individual actor. This allows for an interpretation of society as an aggregate of individuals rather than a totality that is much greater than its individual parts. (Sullivan, 1990, p. xii)

Mainstream educational psychology, in its various forms, has generally focused on what is perceived as a unitary and self-contained individual. From this perspective, it is as if the cognitive and psychological makeup of each person were somehow formulated outside of history and politics and thus unaffected by ideology, power relations, and such socially constructed categories as capitalism, race, class, gender, and sexual orientation. In fact, this myopic point of analysis systematically ignores the reality that the personal world is, in large part, an intersubjective cultural form.[1]

Unfortunately, formal pedagogy and curricula are largely the products of mainstream psychology's structuralist and positivist stranglehold on conceptions of the mind. In this essay I would like to illustrate, using a specific example of my own experience in a clinical research course at the Harvard Graduate School of Education, ways in which the sociopolitical nature of identity is virtually abstracted from all analysis and understanding of the individual—creating what I refer to as the "personality vacuum."[2] It will be my conclusion that filtering out the political nature of identity and difference plays an extremely important role in the organization and maintenance of dominant institutions and practices in our society.

CLINICAL RESEARCH AND TEACHER EDUCATION

In a radically depoliticized environment such as the Harvard Graduate School of Education, professors, for the most part, turn a blind eye to the inherently ideological nature of their assumptions, perspectives, and courses.[3] In other words, they fail to name and engage in the classroom the values and beliefs that inform their locations, hiding behind the modernist notion that knowledge and research are universal and objective.

The clinical research course that I was required to take as a doctoral candidate was taught by a person whose work is grounded in Piagetian theories around the nature and development of intelligence. The class was designed as an attempt to recognize the multiple perspectives of our students and to develop ways of understanding them as individuals. The professor introduced the course with the following statement:

> Textbooks, standardized tests, many teacher education programs, and many curriculum programs feed into the belief that there is one best way of understanding. And this is linked with another pervasive, pernicious belief—that students who do not understand it in our way are not smart enough to understand it at all. This course explores the diverse ways that people come to their understanding. What kind of experiences affect a learner's construction of knowledge, and what, then, can be a teacher's role? (Harvard University Graduate School of Education Course Catalogue, 1993–94, p. 118)

As I was looking for additional insight into the complexities of multicultural education, this particular class, at least in description, promised a great deal of insight—it implied a rupturing of positivism and the modernist conceptions of the individual.[4] I was especially intrigued to know how a person who embraced Piaget's structuralist approach to cognitive development would deal with the implications of social interactionism (Au & Jordan, 1981; Bakhtin, 1981; Gee, 1996; Heath, 1983; Kincheloe & Steinberg, 1996; Michaels, 1981; Moll, 1990; Moll, Diaz, & Lopes, 1991; Voloshinov, 1986; Vygotsky, 1978; Wertsch, 1991). That is, how would she address the postmodern realities of diversity, contingency, and difference?

In the name of "understanding individual differences and alternative perspectives," the course was centered around having the whole class observe the moon for the entire semester. As such, each and every day was dedicated to a discussion of what different people saw in the night skies. Another typical classroom exercise consisted of attaching a string to our nose, with the opposite end fixed to a mirror on the ceiling—so that we could see each other from various angles. There were also show-and-tell sessions in which some students presented their own personal crayon drawings to the entire class.

As these inane exercises continued week after week, I couldn't understand how this type of pedagogy would help develop self-reflective, multilensed, and critical researchers and practitioners. In addition, I couldn't help but wonder what any of this had to do with the fact that back in the cultural patterns that constitute social reality, schools and the streets are virtual war zones where drug abuse, teenage pregnancy, school dropouts, illiteracy, and a long list of oppressive practices and social injustices that directly affect the educational process are running rampant. How would the methodology of this particular graduate course help teachers to understand the dialectical relationship between intergroup strife and struggle and individual psychology?

At one point during the semester, the class participated in observing two young black girls engage in a cognitive exercise of solving puzzles. In light of the current debates and conflicts concerning poverty, racism, sexism, and other forms of discrimination, especially the media blitz around the release of Richard Herrnstein and Charles Murray's *The Bell Curve* (1994), a book that makes claims to the genetic inferiority of blacks and other groups, I was extremely uncomfortable with a roomful of privileged white people (there was only one black in the class) hanging over two black girls for the sake of clinical observation.[5] This was especially difficult for me in the sense that we as a group did not problematize the realities that have led to these two girls' choice to attend an African-American private school. The fact that they self-segregated themselves into an environment that nurtures and respects them in order to maintain their own cultural capital and avoid total domination was ignored by the roomful of budding researchers.[6]

Finding this radical omission disconcerting, to say the least, I openly expressed to the class the importance of context in understanding the multiple and contingent social identities of people and how such social identities, within unequal relations of power, invoke particular kinds of behavior and interaction. When I asked why, as a group, we had neglected to make the connections among the current national debates, the sociopolitical realities of these low-SES black girls, what Harvard represents as an "elite"institution that is predominantly white, and the contingent nature of cognition, the professor responded: "This is one important and complex set of questions to look at. I think that one can also look at other things." With one swift and empty statement, these "important and complex issues" were simply dismissed. The professor further defended her refusal to analyze group experience by insisting that "there are the risks of stereotyping." In the name of observing "the individual," she simply psychologized experience so as to depoliticize the social reality that these girls live in on a daily basis, that is, the realities of the multiple and interconnecting relationships of race, capitalism, class, gender, and so on that speak to a more dialectical understanding of the politics of identity and difference, as well as to the social influences on cognition, psychology, performance, and what is called intelligence.[7]

This statement about "the risks of stereotyping" epitomizes the resistance prevalent in many graduate schools of education to a theoretical engagement of the social. In fact, theory itself is often completely ignored. Even those "liberal" classrooms that in their treatment of educational psychology and human development break with traditional methodological restraints and pedagogical absolutes—like the one that I experienced at Harvard—are usually mutated into feel-good therapy sessions in which theory is stifled at the level of description.[8] In other words, students and teachers share life stories as if they haphazardly fell out of the sky, but they are rarely encouraged to engage, so as to understand, the historical and sociopolitical realities that in fact have shaped such experiences.

Theory constitutes the ways in which we make sense of the world around us, that is, how we interpret, critique, and draw generalizations (hooks, 1994; McLaughlin, 1987). Generalizations that are not constantly problematized do risk stereotyping and objectifying, and therefore theories should always be flexible heuristics prone to change. As critical educators, we need to keep a healthy tension in our understanding of the dialectical relationship between the individual and society, so as to never essentialize and objectify the individual (e.g., to assume that all Puerto Ricans are the same), but also to not disregard group experience—what it means to be marked by race, class, nation, and so on. The reality of walking the fine line between analytic distinctions and stereotypes should never inhibit educators from attempting to develop a critical understanding of what we observe. The point of using analytic categories such as "race" is by no means meant to essentialize—to imply that racial groups are fixed and exclusive, to assume that all racially subordinated groups and individuals think about is their oppression, or to argue that behavior manifests itself in deterministic or monolithic ways. Contemporary African-American culture, for example, "is radically complex and diverse, marked by an intriguing variety of intellectual reflections, artistic creations, and social practices" (Dyson, 1993, p. xiii). However, "race"—implying racism and racialization (along with a long list of other significant points of analysis)—is a significant shaper of culture and identity. A more sociocognitive approach to clinical research and practice would require the exploration of the ideological construction of such categories, and their implications and possibilities. There is a great deal of critical literature and research, none of which was presented to the class at Harvard, that explores the effects of racism and racialization, sexism, classism, and other forms of exclusion on students' reactions to schooling. In fact, terminology such as "internalized oppression," "learned helplessness," and "resistance" is frequently used in the literature to refer to the relationship between the social and the psychological.

If fear of stereotyping and objectifying the research participants in the clinical research course at Harvard was really the issue at hand, then why hadn't the class discussed the realities of representational politics, the malleability of theory, and the ideological foundation of each person's particular point of view as a researcher? Why hadn't we discussed the sociohistorically and ideologically constructed (and relational) conceptions of "blackness" and "whiteness," capitalism, gender, or class in this country, and how they work to shape our perspectives? None of these categories that define a politics of identity and difference showed up in any of the readings. The index of the professor's own well-received book, which was used as the course's main text, did not have a single mention of these crucial points of analysis.

In addition, if understanding alternative perspectives were really the goal of such a methodology, then why hadn't we discussed in depth (that is, beyond the rhetoric of the course description) the social construction of cognition and literacy, and how schools reinforce only certain kinds of language use, values, beliefs, bodies of knowledge, and learning styles—white, affluent, heterosexual, male ways of knowing? These issues were clearly avoided. The end result was that the professor simply imported black students from the ghetto for clinical observation, only to send them back.

Legitimating this vampire style of pedagogy, and contradicting her reluctance to engage the social via issues such as race, gender, and class, the professor stated, "It is good for these children to be around Harvard; it builds their self-confidence." When I asked, "What has led to a lack of self-confidence, and how have such affective dispositions impacted educational attitudes and cognitive performance?" I was completely ignored. It comes as no surprise that the professor, who discouraged critical reflexivity among her students, never questioned her own assumption that the children lacked self-confidence. In fact, such a disposition was never voiced by the girls themselves, nor was it apparent in their performance during the exercise.

I was getting the feeling that, in the eyes of the group, my questions were being perceived as disruptive rather than as potentially edifying. What often happens in these "learning" environments is that a deceitful form of democracy is used in order to make the teacher's interactions with students' ideas appear just. For example, a critical question is avoided by a response such as "Okay, but because of the limited time, let's hear from someone else" (a common response to my questions during the semester). The apparent emphasis on equal opportunity to participate disrupts any possibility for profound theoretical engagement and analysis among classroom participants. Such limiting practices are strategically used in public institutions as mechanisms of ideological control that work to privilege and exclude particular perspectives, voices, authorities, and representations.[9]

A major role of critical research and interpretation should be to expose and transform inequities of power. However, educational psychology and its concomitant pedagogical practices for the most part completely sidestep such an ethical dimension. As Joe Kincheloe and Shirley Steinberg (1996) observe, "This is the great paradox of contemporary schooling and teacher education: educators speak of empowerment as a central goal, but often ignore the way power operates to subvert the empowerment of teachers and students" (p. 191).

For the next assignment, we were asked to do fieldwork that entailed having random people read and interpret Audre Lorde's poem "Progress Report." When I asked in class if we should get any background information about our participants, the professor responded, "No! We cannot draw conclusions about a particular group from one person's response." Again, any effort to get inside ideological formations that shape the structures of meaning, forms of life, and norms and social practices, in order to make sense of them through and beyond the individual, were thrown out the window. From this perspective, Audre Lorde's subject position as a black woman who is also a lesbian (among other defining characteristics) would have to be considered irrelevant to understanding her expressive work as well. Any theoretical inquest was reduced and dismissed by the professor as "We can never really know the person." This particular stance, which categorically precludes the social, serves to reinforce the myth of individualism in this country. It also minimizes the interpretive role and ideological lens of the researcher, to say nothing of contradicting the ostensible purpose of the course itself.

Psychological development and the production of knowledge are sociocognitive processes, and socialization thus plays a significant role in shaping the individual. This shaping process was evident in watching the professor's own ideology about individualism grow in the minds of her students. For example, on one occasion a white woman was asked to participate in a math experiment in front of the class. She told the group, in no uncertain terms, that she had been treated poorly by her male math teachers and that she had ultimately done poorly in this subject area. Approaching the task, the participant was clearly nervous and sweating in anticipation. These important social-psychological manifestations and insights went untouched, even after I raised some concerns about sexism and cognitive performance. Not a sound was heard from the forty other students who, following the professor's logic, made no connection from the personal to the social, let alone to the political.

Instead, I heard students describe the personality of the woman as introverted or extroverted, inhibited or uninhibited, field-dependent or field-independent. Not once did I hear people interrogate the history of the participant, or the immediate context of the classroom and the task, in order to address why it is that a learner may sometimes be motivated, extroverted, and confident and at other times unmotivated, introverted, and anxious. Nor was there a discussion of why in one set of circumstances there may be greater social distance and antagonisms (whether we are conscious of them or not) between a specific group of learners, and less in others.

Educational psychology is certainly concerned with issues of affect—which include the learner's motivation, self-confidence, and level of anxiety. But, as illustrated in this clinical research class, all of these variables are far too often relegated to the confines of the individual and abstracted from the social context. It is absolutely ridiculous to assume that stress in working on particular assignments is simply the result of intrapsychic factors. As Bonny Norton Pierce (1995) argues, "We need a theory of social identity that integrates the learner and the learning context, and how relations of power in the social world affect social interaction between learners and teachers and among peers" (p. 7).

On a similar occasion, a black male student was asked by his peers in the class, who were in the process of celebrating their personal stories, to share his experiences growing up. He replied, "How can you ask me to speak when, for so many years of my life, my voice, my people's voice, has been taken away?" Regardless of the blatantly obvious overtones of this powerful statement, the conceptual understanding of racism in this classroom was reduced to the individual's world of experience. In other words, caught in the paradigm of individualism, acts of racism were not interpreted by the white students as social and institutional. Racism was psychologized into individual and pathological behavior. As such, any oppression along racial lines was disarticulated from white supremacy. Consequently, the black student was met with sympathy for having to face such harsh treatment from "those people" but was never rewarded with the anticipated self-critical and social reflection that he was looking for from his immediate white colleagues—with the recognition that it is whites' responsibility to transform such institutionalized sociocultural inequities. He never again contributed to the class discussions.[10]

"Whiteness" has been a sociopolitically and institutionally sanctioned marker of status in the United States. Racialized cultural patterns are embedded in the practices and institutions of white America. As John Ogbu points out, "Feelings of aversion, revulsion, and disgust they [negative images of other racial groups] evoke come to be incorporated into the culture of the dominant group and children learn them 'naturally' as they learn other aspects of their culture" (1987, p. 260).

Educational institutions continue to perpetuate cultural racism through their curriculum (e.g., which [and whose] values, beliefs, voices, and representations of history, identity, and difference are included), teacher assumptions and teaching styles, and de facto segregation of racially subordinated students via tracking. But few whites recognize the impact that such racism has had on shaping our own values, beliefs, personal and social interests, and actions. With the help of the professor, the students did not see themselves as white, privileged, and perpetuators, whether consciously or not, of racism and other forms of discrimination. They were never encouraged to explore the history of the racialization of identities, which clearly reveals how white supremacy has historically been an important mechanism of cultural production and reproduction in the United States, that is, how hundreds of years of Anglo domination have been a fundamental part (as opposed to an external or separate feature) of most institutional and everyday cultural practices in this society. The classroom participants did not understand how the psychological makeup of individuals—the vehicle through which researchers and practitioners see and interpret the world—is, among other things, racially driven.[11]

It has been my experience that the type of pedagogy based on psychological models of the unified individual leads to future teachers who actually believe that they can be bias-free in their classrooms. By not recognizing whiteness as a racial identity, most whites see themselves as race-free and less ethnic than "others," and consequently take for granted the privileges they secure by such an ideologically charged racial marker (Alba, 1990; Allen, 1994; Dyer, 1997; Frankenburg, 1993, 1994, 1997; Franklin, 1995; Fusco, 1988; Hill, 1997; hooks, 1992; Macintosh, 1990; McCarthy & Crinchlow, 1993; McIntyre, 1997; McLaren, 1994; Roediger, 1994). It is thus essential that educators and citizens interrogate the unspoken centrality of white, male, middle-class, heterosexual identity. As Peter McLaren (1994) insists,

> Unless we give white students a sense of their own identity as an emergent ethnicity—we naturalize whiteness as a cultural marker against which Otherness is defined.... White groups need to examine their own ethnic histories so that they are less likely to judge their own cultural norms as neutral and universal. (p. 59)

In the graduate courses that I teach that deal with issues of whiteness and other forms of oppression, there are always teachers who argue against drawing attention to racial and other cultural differences. "I see my kids as individuals, I don't see color" is a common response. However, as well-intentioned as they may be, this lack of acknowledging and engaging such ideological markers has negative consequences. As Sonia Nieto (1992) asserts,

> To see differences, in this line of reasoning, is to see defects and inferiority. Thus, to be color-blind may result in *refusing to accept difference* and therefore accepting the dominant culture as the norm. It may result in denying the very identity of our students. (p. 109)

By no means is Nieto implying that skin color predisposes behavior; rather, she is emphasizing that in this society the sociohistorical and ideological construction of race and the concomitant realities of racialization

and racism dramatically impact cultural practices and personal experience. It is thus theoretically insufficient and dangerous to simply psy-
chologize experience via the notion of "individuality," abstracting it from
the realities of social and institutional practices. Articulating the psychological effects of racialization, Howard Winant states, "Despite exhorta-
tions both sincere and hypocritical, it is not possible to be 'color-blind,'
for race is a basic element of our identity" (1995, p. 31).

An elementary school teacher in one of my graduate courses at the
University of Massachusetts recounts the following story. She observed a
group of thirteen children between the ages of three and five years old,
who were asked to describe themselves. The children, looking at pictures
of themselves, responded, "happy," "angry," "sad," "bored," and so on.
They then began describing their clothing. The final angle of inquiry per-
tained to skin color. When it was the African-American girl's turn to
describe herself,

> she became suddenly and unusually troubled and very apprehensive. At first
> she hesitated, then without conviction, described herself as "white." A Euro-
> American child shouted at the top of his lungs, "Black, black, you are
> black!" With lots of embarrassment she brought herself to say "brown."[12]

The young girl from India also identified herself as being white, even
though her skin tone was darker than that of the African-American girl.
The Mexican child "simply said *'blanco'* and then withdrew from the
group." The teacher later commented,

> It's important to note that none of the students, although very young, have
> problems distinguishing between the seven basic colors. The difficulties
> started when the children were to describe their own skin color. When it
> was my turn to describe myself, the students volunteered to identify my
> skin color. Out of the entire group, only two Euro-American children
> labeled me, hesitatingly at that, as brown. It was not until I described
> myself as brown that the Mexican child consented to rejoin the group with
> a big smile. In subsequent descriptions, I noticed a propensity for all non-
> white children to describe themselves as brown.

It is clear from this anecdote that the process of racialization, regardless of whether or not we choose to recognize and address it, begins at an
early age. The children reveal not only an internalized stigma about color,
but also how whiteness has come to signify the norm, as well as serve as

a marker of intelligence and beauty. It seemed apparent to the students that the Dominican woman could only be "a teacher" if she were white. When the positive attributes of intelligence and power were then identified as belonging to a brown person, the kids suddenly found comfort, solidarity, and motivation in their racial identities. The Mexican child's rejoining of the group is symbolic of the necessary process of rupturing internalized oppression and cross-cultural ambivalence.

The clinical research course that I have been describing at Harvard does absolutely nothing to prepare educators for this type of predicament. It does not help them develop the interpretive tools to understand and use this incident as a pedagogical moment to engage the realities of racism and whiteness—or any form of exclusion, for that matter. Such graduate courses provide no opportunity for students to develop the presence of mind (i.e., critical awareness) necessary to understand what constitutes difference and how the dominant referent shapes "otherness." In most cases, deskilled teachers simply sweep such forms of discrimination under the rug with the false hope that they will simply go away.

Within the uncritical and abstract environment of this research course, students came to believe that the minds of individual "other'" minds were simply different, and that diversity of this sort was okay. The central problem, as I saw it, was that the participants in this class could clearly articulate their own perspectives, but they had no idea where these thoughts were generated from, nor were they encouraged to explore such avenues. As such, the referent that they were using to define "difference"—what the professor loosely described as "our ways of understanding"—went uncontested. Who is the "our," and how has it become the norm at the exclusion of "others"? Why are some cultural portraits deemed more valuable than others, and how have the antagonistic relations that have emerged over the struggle for a place in these exclusionary practices and institutions led to certain attitudes toward different worldviews, literacies, education, and learning styles? If educational psychology is really "a scientific discipline that is concerned with producing general knowledge about how the educational process affects students" (Royer & Feldman, 1984, p. 6), then one is compelled to address such crucial questions; certainly we must do so if we are ever to really engage what the professor described as "the diverse ways that people come to their understanding" and how different kinds "of experiences affect a learner's construction of knowledge." Unfortunately, this type of inquiry was discouraged in this graduate classroom.

Within any relativistic paradigm of similarities and differences, the dominant group in society is perceived as the norm, and its plethora of inherent inequalities and injustices are uncontested. As such, even if educators were able to successfully teach other people's children (assuming that they are willing to do so) in terms of recognizing and building on what they bring to the classroom, this does not mean that as soon as those children leave the safety of the classroom they will not face socially and institutionally sanctioned forms of exclusion and abuse.

A classroom discussion about the politics of identity and difference would surely raise dangerous questions about the relationship among power, capitalism, language, race, gender, class, sexual orientation, identity, and exclusion. However, such critical questions in this country are for the most part, with the help of mainstream discourses of psychology, avoided at all costs. As a diversionary tactic, mainstream pedagogy simply abstracts the learner's identity from the institutions and socially sanctioned practices that produce inequality, injustice, and cultural resistance—institutions and practices that ultimately remain intact.

The unwillingness to engage the complex interrelationships that constitute identity and social reality serves only to fragment and disarticulate experience from its sociohistorical construction. In fact, fragmentation of knowledge is largely the norm at the Harvard Graduate School of Education. A prevailing rebuttal among faculty to critical and interdisciplinary comments is "That's not our particular field of study, that's politics." As Noam Chomsky states in response to the question "How can you talk about moral development and violence without talking about the larger social, cultural, and economic environments in which people live and develop?":

> You can't! On the other hand, if you simply talk about the world in the accepted ways, that would not be called politics, that would be being reasonable. It becomes "ideological" or extremist when it deviates from the accepted patterns. (Chomsky, Leistyna, & Sherblom, 1996, p. 125)

This disarticulation of knowledge, via the fragmentation of disciplines, serves to obscure political awareness; clarity can be achieved only through an interdisciplinary view of the world, what C. Wright Mills (1959) refers to throughout his work as "the sociological imagination."

The disarticulation of the social and the psychological is not surprising in a school of education that houses its courses in literacy and language acquisition in the Department of Human Development and Psychology, with very little connection to the Department of Learning and Teaching—as if the reason that millions of people in this country are illiterate has predominantly to do with cognitive, internal processes rather than the sociopolitical climate of the classroom and the greater society. As Jim Gee (1990, p. 6) argues when discussing the so-called failure problem of students, "We need to question several 'commonsense' assumptions inherited from the discipline of psychology":

1. Thinking and speaking are functions of individual minds.
2. Literacy is an individual mental skill involving the ability to read and write.
3. Intelligence, knowledge, and aptitude are states of individual minds.

Within these closed-world presuppositions that Gee contests, the responsibility for success, or lack thereof, resides within the individual. Accordingly, problems are individualized away from the social conditions within which the learning process is taking place. At best, this leads to a mean-spirited, victim-blaming meritocracy that demands that everyone pull themselves up by their bootstraps. At worst, it supports the idea that the reason that certain groups are disproportionately not "succeeding" in schools and the workplace is that, as argued in *The Bell Curve,* these people are categorically and biologically inferior to the white mainstream.

Discarding these two fundamentally racist and oppressive conclusions, educators need to understand that thinking, speaking, knowing, and literacy are functions of social groups, and that "intelligence and aptitude, as measured by tests, are artificially constructed measures of aspects of social practices taken out of context and attributed to individuals" (Gee, 1990, p. 7). Critical educators need to stress the social nature of the mind, the ideological nature of perception, and the fact that the way in which we learn to think and feel is the product of the groups we belong to and value. If any course of study truly hopes to "explore the diverse ways that people come to their understanding" and "the kinds of experiences that affect a learner's construction of knowledge," as the Harvard professor claimed, then we need to move immediately away from the personality vacuum. For, within this abstract space, the psychological realities of such oppressive institutions as white supremacy go unseen and thus untouched.

NOTES

1. I do not mean to imply that the internal biological predispositions, such as gender, sexuality, language faculties, or other cognitive capacities, are not connected to the social. In fact, the relationship is inextricable. It would be more productive for critical educators to move beyond the false binarisms of structuralism versus poststructuralism, modernism versus postmodernism, formalism versus postformalism, et cetera, and instead begin to understand the complex matrix of relationships among these concepts so as to be able to critically appropriate and reinvent the theoretical tenets therein, and use them to inform our transformative practices. For example, in my mind there are important and complementary insights in both structuralism and post-structuralism. Human beings are biologically predisposed with certain cognitive structures, such as the language acquisition device—which endows humans with the ability to grow systems of communication (Chomsky, 1965). However, this device by no means shapes sociocultural identities, the ideological nature of surface languages, or the politics of exclusion in such onslaughts as the English-only movement. Nor does the LAD determine whether or not kids in the ghetto are going to learn dominant languages.

2. I was a master's and doctoral student at the Harvard Graduate School of Education from 1990 to 1998.

3. For an analysis of its conservative practices and ideological impositions, see Leistyna, 1998a.

4. It is important to note that a course in clinical research was required for doctoral students; however, there was no formal encouragement to take a course in antiracist multicultural education.

5. For an extensive discussion of the issues raised in *The Bell Curve,* see Kincheloe, Steinberg, & Gresson, 1996.

6. While I by no means embrace imposed or de facto segregation, this short-term solution for dealing with oppressive conditions of dominant institutions can be effective. The backlash from such efforts at group solidarity is often centered around the accusation that it represents a form of "separatism" or "balkanization." By blaming the victim instead of addressing the unjust conditions within which a great many people live, conservatives of the likes of Arthur Schlesinger, E. D. Hirsch, William Bennett, and Diane Ravitch, among others, claim that these people will be responsible for the "disuniting of America"—as if it has ever been united.

7. Capitalism is a major force in shaping racism and other oppressive cultural manifestations. While racism can't solely be reduced to capitalist social relations, understanding the links is imperative (Du Bois, 1935).

8. *Liberal* is a word that carries very little meaning in that its semantic reality has shifted dramatically over time. Its present reification is also experiencing change. I use the term in an ambiguous way to refer to an ideological

middle ground where one speaks of democracy but hides behind existing relations of power. For an interesting discussion of the transformations of the term *liberal,* see Green, 1987.

9. However, cultural reproduction via the socialization process is by no means deterministic: Culture is ever shifting and forming, and there is always room for teacher and student resistance and agency.
10. The additional information about the young black girls, the white woman who participated in the math exercise, and the black man was taken from conversations that I had with them after class.
11. For an extensive discussion of the history and effects of whiteness and racism on identity and perceptions, see Leistyna, 1998b.
12. This quote was taken from the observing teacher. The identification with whiteness recalls the research conducted by Kenneth Clark (1955), a professor of psychology at City College of New York, in which the black children involved in the study chose to identify with the white dolls over the black dolls. This incident also recalls the central theme of Toni Morrison's *The Bluest Eye* (1970).

REFERENCES

Alba, R. D. (1990). *Ethnic identity: The transformation of white America.* New Haven: Yale University Press.

Allen, T. (1994). *The invention of the white race.* London: Verso.

Au, K. H., & Jordan, C. (1981). "Teaching reading to Hawaiian children: Finding a culturally appropriate solution." In H. T. Trueba, G. P. Guthrie, & K. H. Au (Eds.), *Culture and the bilingual classroom.* Rowley, MA: Newbury House.

Bakhtin, M. M. (1981). *The dialogic imagination.* Austin: University of Texas Press.

Chomsky, N. (1965). *Aspects of the theory of syntax.* Cambridge, MA: MIT Press.

Chomsky, N., Leistyna, P., & Sherblom, S. (1996). "A dialogue with Noam Chomsky." In P. Leistyna, A. Woodrum & S. Sherblom (Eds.), *Breaking free: The transformative power of critical pedagogy.* Cambridge, MA: Harvard Educational Review.

Clark, K. (1955). *Prejudice and your child.* Boston: Beacon.

Du Bois, W.E.B. (1935). *Black Reconstruction in America, 1860–1880.* New York: Atheneum.

Dyer, R. (1997). *White.* New York: Routledge.

Frankenburg, R. (1993). *The social construction of whiteness: White women, race matters.* Minneapolis: University of Minnesota Press.

Frankenburg, R. (1994). "Whiteness and Americanness: Examining Constructions of race, culture, and nation in white women's narratives." In S.

Gregory & R. Sanjek (Eds.), *Race*. New Brunswick, NJ: Rutgers University Press.

Frankenburg, R. (1997). *Displacing whiteness: Essays in social and cultural criticism.* Durham, NC: Duke University Press.

Franklin, J. H. (1995). "Ethnicity in American life: The historical perspective." In A. Aguire & D. Baker (Eds.), *Sources: Notable selections in race and ethnicity.* Guilford, CT: Dushkin.

Fusco, C. (1988, December). "Fantasies of oppositionality." *Afterimage.*

Gee, J. P. (1990). "Discourses, socio-culturally situated educational theory, and the failure problem." Paper presented at the University of Delaware.

Gee, J. P. (1996). *Social linguistics and literacies: Ideology in discourses.* London: Taylor & Francis.

Green, D. (1987). *The language of politics in america: Shaping political consciousness from McKinley to Reagan.* London: Cornell University Press.

Heath, S. B. (1983). *Ways with words: Language, life, and work in communities and classrooms.* Cambridge: Cambridge University Press.

Herrnstein, R., and Murray, C. (1994). *The bell curve: Intelligence and class structure in American life.* New York: Free Press.

Hill, M. (1997). *Whiteness: A critical reader.* New York: New York University Press.

hooks, b. (1992). *Black looks: Race and representation.* Boston: South End Press.

hooks, b. (1994). *Teaching to transgress: Education as the practice of freedom.* New York: Routledge.

Kincheloe, J., & Steinberg, S. (1996). "A tentative description of post-formal thinking: The critical confrontation with cognitive theory." In P. Leistyna, A. Woodrum, & S. Sherblom (Eds.), *Breaking free: The transformative power of critical pedagogy.* Cambridge, MA: Harvard Educational Review Press.

Kincheloe, J., Steinberg, S. and Gresson, A. (Eds.). (1996, 1997) *Measured lies: The bell curve examined.* New York: St. Martin's Press.

Leistyna, P. (1998). "Veritas: The fortunes of my miseducation at Harvard." *Presence of mind: Education and the politics of deception.* Boulder, CO: Westview.

Leistyna, P. (1998b). "Racenicity: The whitewashing of ethnicity." In *Presence of mind: Education and the politics of deception.* Boulder, CO: Westview.

Macintosh, P. (1990, winter). "White privilege: Unpacking the invisible knapsack." *Independent School.*

McCarthy, C., & Crinchlow, W. (1993). *Race, identity, and representation in education.* New York: Routledge.

McIntyre, A. (1997). *Making meaning of whiteness: Exploring racial identity with white teachers.* Albany: State University of New York Press.

McLaren, P. (1994). "White terror and oppositional agency." In D. Goldberg (Ed.), *Multiculturalism: A critical reader.* Cambridge: Blackwell.

McLaughlin, B. (1987). *Theories of second-language learning.* London: Edward Arnold.

Michaels, S. (1981). "Sharing time: Children's narrative styles and differential access to literacy." *Language in Society, 10,* 423–442.

Mills, C. Wright. (1959). *The sociological imagination.* London: Oxford University Press.

Moll, L. (1990). *Vygotsky and education: Instructional implications and applications of sociohistorical psychology.* New York: Cambridge University Press.

Moll, L., Diaz, S., & Lopes, L. M. (1991). "Making contexts: The social construction of lessons in two languages." In S. Arivzu & M. Saravia-Shore (Eds.), *Cross-cultural and communicative competencies.* New York: Horizon.

Morrison, T. (1970). *The bluest eye.* New York: Washington Square.

Nieto, S. (1992). *Affirming diversity: The sociopolitical context of multicultural education.* New York: Longman.

Ogbu, J. (1987). "Variability in minority responses to schooling: Nonimmigrants vs. immigrants." In G. Spindler & L. Spindler (Eds.), *Interpretive ethnography of education.* Hillsdale, NJ: Lawrence Erlbaum Associates.

Pierce, B. N. (1995, Spring). "Social identity, investment, and language learning." *TESOL Quarterly, 29 (1).*

Roediger, D. (1994). *Towards the abolition of whiteness.* New York: Verso.

Royer, J., & Feldman, R. (1984). *Educational psychology: Applications and theory.* New York: Knopf.

Sullivan, E. (1990). *Critical psychology and pedagogy: Interpretation of the personal world.* New York: Bergin & Garvey.

Voloshinov, V. N. (1986). *Marxism and the philosophy of language.* Cambridge, MA: Harvard University Press.

Vygotsky, L. S. (1978). *Mind in society: The development of higher psychological processes.* Cambridge, MA: Harvard University Press.

Wertsch, J. (1991). *Voices of the mind: A sociocultural approach to mediated action.* Cambridge, MA: Harvard University Press.

Winant, H. (1995). "Dictatorship, democracy, and difference: The historical construction of racial identity." In M. P. Smith & J. R. Feagin (Eds.), *The bubbling cauldron: Race, ethnicity, and the urban crisis.* Minneapolis: University of Minnesota Press.

Chapter 4

An Exchange

of Gazes

Suzanne Gallagher

We are never independent of the social and historical forces that surround us—we are all caught at a particular point in the web of that reality.... [Our] project is to understand what that point on the web is, how it constructs our vantage point, and the ways it insidiously restricts our vision. (Kincheloe & Steinberg, 1993, p. 302)

Before I had a sense of the real challenge the above quote could convey to educational psychologists, I had a glimpse of understanding that its meaning was important for me personally. Kincheloe and Steinberg (1993) were introducing me to the possibility of a postformal educational psychology. They were encouraging me in the work of becoming aware of my own "ideological inheritance" and its relationship to the "beliefs and value structures, interests, and questions" (p. 302) connected to the professional life of an educational psychologist. This is important work, for we have not only the right but the responsibility to read, understand, and transform (Freire & Macedo, 1987; Giroux, 1987) our experience of being a learner-teacher of the discipline. We need to recognize how our taken-for-granted way of thinking from within the discipline's meaning-making system impacts the educational process in perhaps unintended ways. The work is critical because, beyond the question of theory, the discipline impacts the lives and, even more directly, the bodies of children who have become entangled in its structure (Foucault, 1995; Freire & Faundez, 1992). Yet the discipline "works" and makes sense through generally unexamined assumptions. We can become conscious and critical of these assumptions as we "step back from the world as we are accustomed to perceiving it" (Kincheloe, 1993, p. 109) and learn to see and to "read" the discipline differently.

My aim in this chapter is to focus on the discipline's discourse as a way of entering the conversation regarding the prospect of constructing a postformal educational psychology that supports a critical pedagogy. I wish to make problematic the modernist and commonly accepted view of the discipline of educational psychology as a "neutral" body of knowledge that has as its goal facilitating more effective teaching and learning. Animated by a Foucauldian skepticism regarding the human sciences, I focus on how the discourse of this modern discipline is connected to the way modern societies manage and regulate their citizens (Foucault, 1995). One of the ways this government is actualized is through technologies of power that authorize those embedded in its meaning-making web to name and define persons, especially as "normal" and "abnormal." In this way the discipline casts its "normalizing gaze" (Foucault, 1995). I return the discipline's normalizing gaze with a critical one by viewing the discipline's discourse in its contextual complexity.

Much of this work is driven by the question of who benefits (Star, 1991). It is a question of power and a question of whom the discourse serves (Foucault, 1980c). By reading the discourse differently and by questioning its unexamined assumptions, it becomes possible to critique the ideological inheritance of the discipline. It is also possible to participate in the construction of a more critical postformal educational psychology, one committed to social justice.

THE IMPORTANCE OF READING INTERTEXTUALLY

A major concern in educational endeavors is literacy. This is no less a concern for educational psychologists and students of the discipline. Yet there are differences in how educationalists take up notions of literacy, especially reading.

Reading is often understood in the mechanical sense of decoding words and their meanings. The consumption metaphor (Scholes, 1985) is frequently used, as readers are often assigned the role of "consumers" of texts encouraged to "bite into" and "chew" the information found there. Readers often seek to "digest" the meaning of the text in the hope of internalizing it so that it can become a resource that can be used at some future time. Literacy, from this perspective, is a matter of acquiring the technical skills to be able to access the information that the author wishes to convey. Teachers often take a position of assisting students in the interpretation of texts "so that the truth [of the text] may stand revealed" (Scholes, 1985, p. 13).

Following this connotation of reading, teachers and students alike assume an almost reverential stance (Scholes, 1985) regarding textbooks, as they are considered authoritative sources of the discipline's discourse, or "virtual cornucopias of knowledge bases" (Houtz & Lewis, 1994, p. 5). Meaning is understood to be *in the text*. The text contains an authoritative site of "truth." Textbooks, for example, are considered to gather the knowledge that the discipline wishes to transmit to future generations; as Kuhn says, they are "pedagogic vehicles" (1970, p. 137). This mode of "reading" fits the "transmission model" or "banking" notion of education (Freire, 1970).

Critical educators take up another sense of reading. From a critical perspective, the mainstream texts of a discourse community are understood as social artifacts (Apple, 1991; Aronowitz & Giroux, 1991). Thus texts are seen as the social constructions of members of a particular scientific community embedded in a particular meaning-making system, that is, as ideological inheritance. Texts are positioned in a web of other texts; in other words, they have political, historical, and social contexts. As Scholes (1985) explicates, all texts exist "intertextually." If the ideological, political, economic, and social contexts of any text are ignored, then a form of illiteracy results. Sandra Harding (1996) makes a similar point for participants in the natural sciences, insisting that if scientists refuse to acknowledge, examine, and critique the ideological, political, and cultural positions of their discourse, then those scientists are illiterate.

Educational psychologists need to consider the texts of their own discursive community in their intertextuality, their web of constructed meaning. The focus needs to shift from a passive reading and consumption of texts accepted as authoritative sources of a neutral, scientifically generated knowledge and practice to a reading of the discipline's discourse with an active and critical analysis of the contexts that made the text possible. Critical educational psychologists assume that a discourse always represents a particular worldview and serves the interests of a particular group. Any discourse (including this one) incites multiple countertexts that offer a critique. This opens the possibility of a critical literacy.

Educational psychology's discourse is embedded within a particular meaning-making system, a modernist worldview that employs a technical rationality to solve the problems of education. This modernist world-view is the issue to which I turn next. I present a countertext by troubling this modernist worldview in an attempt to make its ideological inheritance, particularly technical rationality, more perceptible.

EDUCATIONAL PSYCHOLOGY
AND A MODERN WORLDVIEW

The ideological inheritance of educational psychology comes from its being embedded in a modernist worldview. Scientific reasoning is understood as the basis of development of knowledge and progress in society. The modernist program is aimed at discovering and delivering the "truth" about the objective world so as to be able to predict and control it. Mainstream educational psychologists persevere in the belief that the discourse of their discipline is developed and regulated through rigorous scientific activity (Cherryholmes, 1988) yielding a neutral body of systematic knowledge. Applications of this knowledge base to the practice of teaching (i.e., the discursive practices of the discipline) are thought to yield effects that are "enlightening and empowering and which thus enable effective action" (Usher & Edwards, 1994, p. 48).

The influence of this modern discipline of educational psychology is ubiquitous, and its authority is evident in the frequency with which its research, constructs, and practices inform classroom life, teacher education programs, and public conversation around educational reform. A significant group of members within the discipline are optimistic regarding the potential of the discipline to improve the educational experience. For example, the authors of the *Handbook of Educational Psychology* (Berliner & Calfee, 1996) declare:

> It is clear that our field has been and continues to be highly productive and remarkably influential. Its findings, concepts, methods, and points of view are widely adopted by scholars in other disciplines and cross a wide range of research and evaluation activities.... The field is alive and growing. (p. 1020)

The scientific reasoning—that is, technical rationality—that provides the foundation and grounding of the discipline often remains unquestioned. Technical rationality is the meaning-making system that reflects "the basic aims, interests and values of the group" (van Dijk,

1993a, p. 258)—specifically, the prediction and control of objective reality through neutral, scientific methods. Questions that arise in the educational setting can be constructed only as technical questions. Often this means that phenomena must be reduced to trivial variables so that they can be manipulated by scientific methods (Kincheloe, 1993). However, it also means that political, social, and cultural questions are recast as technical questions. The result is a reverencing of technique.

Authors of textbooks in educational psychology articulate the assurance that their texts will help preservice teachers "accomplish the tasks of teaching" (Gage & Berliner, 1991, p. 47), and they are written so that students of the discipline "will have the foundation for becoming an expert [teacher]" (Woolfolk, 1995, p. 18). This implied "promissory note" (Soyland, 1994) is particularly appealing to students of educational psychology, who are often preservice teachers eager to learn a discipline that promises to aid their future practice. Preservice teachers are encouraged to consume the discourse of this modernist discipline, which assures them that expertise is theirs if they are willing to put forth the effort to learn the discipline's "truths."

TROUBLING THE MODERNIST VIEW

However, enthusiasm for the progressive character of the discipline does not pervade the field of education. A growing number of members of the educational psychology community present alternative perspectives and speak with voices that are positioned both within and against the discipline (Lenzo, 1995). Some educational psychologists recognize that there are additional dynamics at work in the discipline that are not progressive. They question whether preservice teachers are learning how to be critical intellectual workers (Giroux, 1988) or are actually learning to think narrowly from within the discipline's implicit rationality. Critical educational psychologists are troubled by what is really going on as newcomers are initiated into the discipline, as "novices become members of practitioner communities" (Doyle & Carter, 1996, p. 27). Is what preservice teachers are learning actually a form of deskilling by way of enculturation into the discipline's discourse (Kincheloe, 1993)? It is possible that preservice teachers are enthusiastically, albeit unwittingly, colluding in their own deskilling. Educational psychologists may find queries from literary theory instructive. Scholes (1985), for example, observes that a student in a particular area of study may seem to be learning the subject, but what he is truly learning is to give the teacher what he wants. He seems to be learning about the real solid world in a perfectly transparent language, but actually he is learning how to produce a specific kind of discourse, controlled by a particular scientific paradigm. (p. 132)

While the meaning-making system of the discourse may be considered a resource, a "grounding," from a traditional modernist standpoint, it also presents problematics when read critically. I am using the term problematics to mean the process of grasping an assumption, that is, a taken-for-granted way of thinking, and turning it into a question (Caputo & Yount, 1993; Giroux, 1983). Assumptions can remain invisible and unspoken if the disciplinary principles of the discipline are considered normative. Usher (1993) aptly describes educational psychologists as "enfolded" in an implicit understanding of the discipline as a scientific, neutral body of knowledge. Discourse in this sense can be dangerous in that it can "work behind our backs in powerful and constraining ways" (Gitlin, 1990, p. 444). Yet when assumptions are made explicit and we pose serious questions, we can transform the way we think about the discipline.

A problematic exists in the understanding of discourse itself. From a positivist-empiricist perspective, a discourse is regarded as a neutral body of knowledge, produced through scientific practice; it "refers to what is said and written and passes for more or less orderly thought and exchange of ideas" (Cherryholmes, 1988, p. 2). This understanding becomes problematic when we highlight the social constructionist character of discourse. A critical perspective recognizes a discourse as an artifact of culture (Apple, 1991; Aronowitz & Giroux, 1991) and the result of "historically situated interchanges among people" (Gergen, 1985, p. 267). A discourse expresses through its "content and form, particular constructions of reality, particular ways of selecting and organizing the vast universe of possible knowledge" (Apple, 1991, p. 49). Discourses develop from specific social and political locations and are as much the product of social negotiations as they are scientific processes (Gergen, 1985).

Textbooks as primary expressions of discourse present an illustration of this problematic. Because they are generally written in a matter-of-fact, dispassionate style (Gage & Berliner, 1991), they portray the characteristic of "narrative realism"; it is as though they are "reporting already existing ready-made reality" (Usher & Edwards, 1994, p. 150). A statement such as "It became possible during the twentieth century to measure individual differences in intelligence" (Gage & Berliner, 1991, p. 50) exemplifies this characteristic in that it appears as though a neutral scientific fact is being reported. With this move, the scientists who developed these measurement procedures become invisible, along with their own ideological, political, and cultural biases. In this way the discourse casts the issues surrounding the measuring of intelligence as a technical question, and at the same time masks the political struggles that plague the discipline's history in regard to this question.

A critical reading of the discourse must be undertaken not to ascertain the discipline's knowledge claims or its neutral "truths." Rather, a critical reading is necessary because discourses are sites of social struggle (McNay, 1994) and the discipline's "truths" are understood as embedded in those struggles. In contrast to a positivist-empirical perspective, a critical analysis recognizes the active and social functions of the discourse of a discipline and a discourse's constructing character (Luke, 1995). The "truth" of a discourse is understood as the product of social activity imbued with power relations. And yet educational psychologists seem to forget that they do not discover but invent the knowledge they apply (Caputo & Yount, 1993, p. 7). Discourses are social practices that "systematically form the objects of which they speak" (Foucault, 1972, p. 49).

SOCIALIZATION OR NORMALIZATION

Foucault's (1995) contention is that the knowledge and power of modern disciplines are intimately connected with the managing and regulating of populations. This disrupts our commonsense understanding of the scientific knowledge of a discipline, giving people power to act in more progressive ways. The power of a discourse develops gradually over time. The discourse of educational psychology, for example, did not appear on the educational scene self-contained and coherent; rather, the discipline developed as practices aimed at managing students were collected from various local sites. Universal schooling, the industrial revolution, shifts in demographics, and the like prompted schools to determine efficient procedures for handling and bringing order to their burgeoning populations. Specific practices were "invented and organized from the starting points of local conditions and particular needs...in piecemeal fashion" (Foucault, 1980b, p. 159). Later these local strategies were gathered to form a generalized and unified discourse (Fraser, 1989).

A review of the history of educational psychology illustrates this point. Hilgard (1996), for example, notes that in the latter part of the nineteenth century, before educational theory and teacher education became centralized in institutions of higher learning, "most of the adaptions of education...were made by school administrators" (p. 992). Distinctive procedures such as graded classes or keeping records of student attendance and progress provided both a sense of "order" and the precise methods to govern students in local situations (Hilgard, 1996). Another well-known example is the work of Binet and Simon in France at the turn of the century. With the mandate of universal education, the need to sort students was thought to be a way to bring order to an educational system in transition. Binet's charge was to "construct an instrument for classifying unsuccessful school performers" (Mensh & Mensh, 1991, p. 23). Thus the standardized testing industry had modest beginnings growing out of a very specific local need. Gradually the implementation of these and myriad other ordering and governing practices were formally established and generalized.

By 1910 Edward L. Thorndike, later known as the father of educational psychology, could produce one of the nascent discipline's first textbooks. In it he aligns the discipline with the purpose of education by asserting: "The aim of education is...changing [the student] for the better—to produce in him the information, habits, powers, interests and ideas which are desirable" (Thorndike, 1910, p. 4). Ninety years later, eminent educational psychologists have a message akin to Thorndike's:

> Because education is aimed at *causing* wanted changes in people—in their knowledge, skills, and attitudes—the discovery of ways to cause these changes has practical importance. (Gage & Berliner, 1991, p. 14)

The "discovery" of the means of changing students is found in the discourses and sanctioned practices provided by educational psychology texts; it is the substance of educational psychology. The authoritative discourse of the discipline does not recognize its humble beginnings at particular and local sites developed first as a means of managing students; the contextual complexity of the discursive community is invisible.

Thorndike, Gage, and Berliner would probably categorize the discipline's work as contributing to the socialization of students. However, when read against other texts, socialization is seen as "normalization," the "gentle way" (Foucault, 1995) of ordering and governing populations through modern sciences.

Foucault's "gentle way" is the result of his contention that every society has had a way of controlling its population. In *Discipline and Punish*

(1995), Foucault traces the overt control of monarchs over the bodies of their subjects. Although there is a shift in modern times to a more subtle, covert control, it is every bit as corporeal. The modern form of power expressed in disciplines such as educational psychology is accomplished through the increased "ordering of all realms" of the education situation along with the students themselves. Through the modern science of educational psychology, "wanted changes" in students' knowledge, skills, and attitudes (Gage & Berliner, 1991) can be effected; the production of "desirable" habits, interests, and ideas can be accomplished (Thorndike, 1910). As Foucault (1995) says, the aim is to render the student "docile" and "useful."

TECHNOLOGIES OF POWER

The work of rendering students docile and useful is accomplished through the work of specific technologies of power (Foucault, 1995). These are appropriated from Foucault's description of the prison; they are conspicuous and pervasive in educational psychology's discursive practices. Technologies of power are introduced as simple yet controlling instruments the discipline uses to impose homogeneity and docility. They also have the simultaneous effect of constructing individuals as normal or abnormal. By becoming critically conscious of these technologies in the mainstream discourse of the discipline, educational psychologists can see assumptions, once taken for granted, as "strange" (Foucault, 1995). When practices seem strange, they may be more easily interrogated and disrupted.

Foucault (1995) explicates three interrelated technologies of power: hierarchical observation, normalizing judgment, and examination. The following examples that illustrate these are far from exhaustive, as only a brief exposition is possible here.

Through *hierarchical observation* supervisors assume an aloof and objective position from which they see students more clearly in both a figurative sense and a literal one. This technology is a kind of "optics of power" (Dreyfus & Rabinow, 1982) that signifies the alliance between visibility and power (Smart, 1985). Once students are seen, they are able to be known; when they are known, they can be controlled. In a literal sense surveillance techniques are recommended to teachers. "With-it-ness" is an attribute students of educational psychology are commonly encouraged to cultivate. "With-it" teachers, they are told, have developed "the knack of seeming to know what is going on all over the room...of having 'eyes in the back of your head'" (Gage & Berliner, 1991, p. 512). This promises increased order and focus by students on their work, as students understand that they are continually being monitored. To increase the economy of surveillance, teachers are encouraged to "teach students to monitor themselves" (Woolfolk, 1995, p. 420).

Hierarchical observation thus becomes a very efficient and effective form of super-vision as the gaze of authority becomes internalized and students begin to watch themselves, each other, and the teacher. Teachers, too, internalize the gaze of those in authority over them, that is, administrators and the public. A web of supervision is constantly being woven. Foucault (1995) explains that what is set in place is a

> network of relations from top to bottom, but also to a certain extent from bottom to top and laterally; this network "holds" the whole together and traverses it in its entirety with effects of power that derive from one another: supervisors, perpetually supervised. (pp. 176–177)

Hierarchical observation renders students and the teaching-learning situation visible and thus allows for evaluation and judgment. Judgments are based on the norm (Jones, 1990), a standard, a comparison "with a favored paradigm real or imagined" (Prado, 1995, p. 61). Foucault refers to this evaluation as normalizing judgment, which he names as lying at the heart of any system of disciplinary power (Foucault, 1995). Any performance of a student—any behavior or response—can be judged and ranked as it falls between two poles (good and bad) based on the norm. In this way the modern sciences have opened the possibility of differentiating, or "objectively" separating and ranking, students.

Normalizing judgments become obvious in describing student behavior. The educational psychologist knows what "proper" behavior looks like, although it often is recognized that this judgment is embedded in cultural contexts and power relationships. Woolfolk (1995) provides a pertinent illustration in a popular educational psychology textbook. She acknowledges that American schools "typically reflect the white, Anglo-Saxon, Protestant, middle-class, male-dominated values that have characterized mainstream America" (p. 155). This bias is explicitly mentioned in the text, along with a statement of the necessity of embracing the values of diverse cultures. However, the orientation that judges nonmainstream behaviors as inferior resists displacement. For instance, teachers are urged to "teach students directly about how to be students...the courtesies and conventions of the classroom...how to get a turn to speak...how to whisper" (Woolfolk, 1995). What needs to be highlighted is that while "how we do it in school" is recognized in this textbook and others as exhibiting the values of the dominant culture and is regarded as problematic, it is never disrupted or replaced as the norm. Standards of the Anglo, middle-class, male culture retain a favored position, and they are used as a universal norm for judging behavior as proper or not. These are the "desired changes" that the discipline is aimed at effecting. Children are judged on their compliance to these norms.

What a behavior may mean to a student is ignored or marginalized as unimportant, and yet oppositional behavior may be a "proper" response to an oppressive educational system (Kohl, 1994). Through their "misbehavior," students may be expressing an attempt to reappropriate some control over their work in school (Everhart, 1983). However, "misbehavior" is not seen as an act of student agency embedded in political and social contexts; it is simply categorized as too many unwanted behaviors or too few wanted behaviors (Gage & Berliner, 1991).

The *examination* combines hierarchial observation and normalizing judgment. Foucault (1995) considers this technology of power a slender and modest yet widespread "ceremony of objectification" (p. 187). Through the multiple forms of examination (Hanson, 1993) students are subjected to (read objectified by) the "gaze" of those with power, that is, those who exercise supervision and are keepers of the "norm." The vision of the educational psychologist is extended and endlessly enhanced through this technology of examination. As Haraway (1991) explains: "Vision in this technological feast becomes unregulated gluttony" (pp. 188–189).

Through examinations—standardized tests being the prototype—students are assigned places along the infamous "bell curve." This "curve" has become the backbone of the discipline, as it represents the arithmetic of normalization. It yields a measure that is ordinal, yet this measure is presented as metric in the discipline's discourse. Gage and Berliner (1991) have helped to create the illusion that both metric and ordinal systems are measuring in the same way by insisting that "one reason for the popularity of tests is that they give us a quantitative estimate of ability or achievement; *they tell us how much*" (p. 570, emphasis added). Woolfolk (1995) tells her readers that "the bell-shaped curve [is] the most famous distribution because it describes many naturally occurring physical and social phenomena" (p. 519).

Educational psychologists know better than to misconstrue metric and ordinal measurements, i.e., the metric measure of physical characteristics (e.g., height or weight) and the ordinal placement of social phenomena (e.g., intelligence) along a distribution curve. There certainly have been numerous critiques leveled against such distortions (e.g., Mensh & Mensh, 1991; Lewontin, Rose, & Kamin, 1996). Educational psychologists know that testers create tests in such a way that the bell curve appears; in other words, "the test items and instructions have been tried out to make sure they work and then rewritten and retested as necessary" (Woolfolk, 1995, p. 517). Tests are made to "work" in terms of their ability to differentiate students; they provide and extend the "normalizing gaze" of their makers. Their norm, seen as neutral, unbiased, and unproblematic, is conflated with relevance; as Gage and Berliner (1991) explain, for "tests of intellectual abilities useful in modern American society, a 'middle-class'...orientation may not constitute bias but relevance" (p. 90).

Students are compared and ordered in ever finer degrees of "normal" and "abnormal," which the technologies of the modern sciences have made available; they have become "calculable and manageable" (Rose, 1989, p. 129). On the basis of their behavior and their scores, students are sorted and selected in and out of programs, receiving unequal and unjust opportunities to learn high-status knowledge that is unsurprisingly akin to the perspective of the test-makers. Teachers are assigned the position of "gatekeepers" (Gage & Berliner, 1991) as they become skilled in using the technologies of the discipline. The discourse embeds its users in its rationality, which misconstrues socioeconomic privilege as evidence of intelligence and socioeconomic marginalization as ineptitude.

There is an irony here in that as the visibility of the student is increased, the examination's social constructionist and productive characteristics often are overlooked (Foucault, 1995). Educational psychologists must not forget that they have constructed the categories and the technologies they apply. Students are inscribed by the discipline's technologies even as they are described by them. As the discipline maintains its narrow focus on the learner or teacher, it "factors out" the world of contextual complexity.

CONCLUSION

Let us return to a question posed at the beginning of this chapter: Who benefits? (Star, 1991). Whom does the discourse serve? I suggest that the discourse of educational psychology serves all students, but not equitably. The discourse serves to marginalize some students and privilege others.

Students are rewarded as their experiences and understanding of the world approximate a particular and idealized norm of mainstream schooling in this country, or as they are able to internalize this norm. Through our uncritical consumption of the discourse of educational psychology, through our effort to extend a disciplinary base of theory and knowledge built on unexamined assumptions, and through "teaching" that is more akin to "training" newcomers, we have become oppressors even while we remain oppressed (Freire, 1970) by the discipline's discourse.

A critical literacy regarding the discipline of educational psychology is our ethical imperative. Understanding (and teaching) that the text and the talk of the discipline are embedded in historical, political, and social contexts allows us to read against mainstream texts. We can then recognize the discipline's "ideological inheritance" (Kincheloe & Steinberg, 1993) and its intertextual complexity. Thus critical literacy opens the possibility of a postformal thinking and more reflexive practice. Perhaps critical educators can return the discipline's normalizing gaze with a critical one and begin to question and redress the harm done daily to children in the name of our discipline.

REFERENCES

Apple, M. W. (1993). *Official knowledge: Democratic education in a conservative age.* New York: Routledge.

Apple, M., & Christian-Smith, L. K. (1991). *The politics of the textbook.* New York: Routledge.

Aronowitz, S., & Giroux, H. A. (1991). *Postmodern education: Politics, culture, and social criticism.* Minneapolis: University of Minnesota Press.

Berliner, D. C., & Calfee, R. C. (Eds.). (1996). *Handbook of educational psychology.* New York: Macmillan.

Caputo, J. D., & Yount, M. (1993). "Introduction." In J. D. Caputo & M. Yount (Eds.), *Foucault and the critique of institutions* (pp. 3–23). University Park, PA: Pennsylvania State University Press.

Cherryholmes, C. H. (1988). *Power and criticism: Poststructural investigations in education.* New York: Teachers College Press.

Doyle, W., & Carter, K. (1996). "Educational psychology and the education of teachers: A reaction." *Educational Psychologist, 31* (1), 23–28.

Dreyfus, H. L., & Rabinow, P. (1982). *Michel Foucault: Beyond structuralism and hermeneutics.* Chicago: University of Chicago Press.

Everhart, R. B. (1983). "Classroom management, student opposition, and the labor process." In M. W. Apple & L. Weis (Eds.), *Ideology and practice in schooling* (pp. 114–142). Philadelphia: Temple University Press.

Foucault, M. (1972). *The archeology of knowledge.* New York: Pantheon.

Foucault, M. (1980a). "Power/knowledge." In *Power/knowledge: Selected interviews and other writings* (pp. 109–133). Ed. C. Gordon. New York: Pantheon.

Foucault, M. (1980b). "The will to truth." In *Michel Foucault: The will to truth* (pp. 113–134). Ed. A. Sheridan. New York: Tavistock.

Foucault, M. (1980c). "Truth and power." In *Power/knowledge: Selected interviews and other writings* (pp. 109–133). Ed. C. Gordon. New York: Pantheon.

Foucault, M. (1995). *Discipline & punish: The birth of the prison* (2nd ed.). New York: Vintage.

Fraser, N. (1989). *Unruly practices: Power, gender, and discourse in contemporary social theory.* Minneapolis: University of Minnesota Press.

Freire, P. (1970). *Pedagogy of the oppressed.* New York: Seabury.

Freire, P., & Faundez, A. (1992). *Learning to question: A pedagogy of liberation.* New York: Continuum.

Freire, P., & Macedo, D. P. (1987). *Literacy: Reading the word and the world.* South Hadley, MA: Bergin & Garvey.

Gage, N. L., & Berliner, D. C. (1991). *Educational psychology* (5th ed.). Boston: Houghton Mifflin.

Gergen, K. J. (1985). "The social constructionist movement in modern psychology." *American Psychologist,* 40 (3), 266–275.

Giroux, H. A. (1981). *Ideology, culture, and the process of schooling.* Philadelphia: Temple University Press.

Giroux, H. A. (1983). *Theory and resistance in education: A pedagogy for the opposition.* South Hadley, MA: Bergin & Garvey.

Giroux, H. A. (1987). "Introduction: Literacy and the pedagogy of political empowerment." In P. Freire & D. P. Macedo, *Literacy: Reading the word and the world* (pp. 1-27). South Hadley, MA: Bergin & Garvey.

Giroux, H. A. (1988). *Teachers as intellectuals.* New York: Bergin & Garvey.

Gitlin, A. D. (1990). "Educational research, voice, and school change." *Harvard Educational Review,* 60 (4), 443–466.

Hanson, F. A. (1993). *Testing testing: Social consequences of the examined life.* Berkeley: University of California.

Haraway, D. (1991). "Situated knowledges: The science question in feminism and the privilege of partial perspective." In D. Haraway (Ed.), *Simians, cyborgs, and women: The reinvention of nature* (pp. 183–202). New York: Routledge.

Harding, S. G. (Ed.). (1996). *The racial economy of science: Toward a democratic future.* Bloomington: Indiana University Press.

Hilgard, E. R. (1996). "History of educational psychology." In D. C. Berliner & R. C. Calfee (Eds.), *Handbook of educational psychology* (pp. 990–1004). New York: Macmillan.

Houtz, J. C., & Lewis, C. D. (1994). "The professional practice of educational psychology." *Educational Psychology Review,* 6 (1), 1–23.

Jones, R. (1990). "Educational practices and scientific knowledge: A genealogic reinterpretaion of the emergence of physiology in post-revolutionary France. In S. J. Ball (Ed.), *Foucault and education: Disciplines and knowledge* (pp. 78–104. New York: Routledge.

Kincheloe, J. L. (1993). *Toward a critical politics of teacher thinking: Mapping the postmodern.* Westport, CT: Bergin & Garvey.

Kincheloe, J. L., & Steinberg, S. R. (1993). "A tentative description of post-formal thinking: The critical confrontation with cognitive theory." *Harvard Educational Review,* 63 (3), 296–320.

Kohl, H. (1994). *I won't learn from you: And other thoughts on creative maladjustment.* New York: New Press.

Kuhn, T. S. (1970). *The structure of scientific revolutions* (2nd ed.). Chicago: University of Chicago Press.

Lenzo, K. (1995). "Validity and self-reflexivity meet poststructuralism: Science ethos and the transgressive self." *Education Researcher,* 24 (4), 17–23.

Lewontin, R. C., Rose, S., & Kamin, L. J. (1996). "IQ: The rank ordering of the world." In S. Harding (Ed.), *The racial economy of science.* Bloomington: Indiana University Press.

Luke, A. (1995). "Text and discourse in education: An introduction to critical discourse analysis." In M. Apple (Ed.), *Review of Research in Education* (pp. 3–48). (Vol. 21). Washington, DC: American Education Research Association.

McNay, L. (1994). *Foucault: A critical introduction.* New York: Continuum.

Mensh, E., & Mensh, H. (1991). *The IQ mythology: Class, race, gender, and inequality.* Carbondale: Southern Illinois University Press.

Prado, C. G. (1995). *Starting with Foucault: An introduction to genealogy.* Boulder, CO: Westview.

Rose, N. (1989). "Individualizing psychology." In J. Shotter & K. Gergen (Eds.), *Texts of identity* (pp. 119–132). London: Sage.

Scholes, R. (1985). *Textual power.* New Haven: Yale University Press.

Smart, B. (1985). *Michel Foucault.* New York: Routledge.

Soyland, A. J. (1994). *Psychology and metaphor.* London: Sage.

Star, S. L. (1991). "Power, technology, and the phenomenology of conventions: On being allergic to onions." In J. Law (Ed.), *Power, technology and the modern world* (pp. 26–56). Oxford: Blackwell.

Thorndike, E. L. (1910). *Education psychology.* New York: Teachers College, Columbia University.

Usher, R. (1993). "Re-examining the place of disciplines in adult education." *Studies in Continuing Education,* 15 (1), 15–25.

Usher, R., & Edwards, R. (1994). *Postmodernism and education.* New York: Routledge.

van Dijk, T. A. (1993a). *Elite discourse and racism.* Newbery Park, CA: Sage.

van Dijk, T. A. (1993b). "Principles of critical discourse analysis." *Discourse & Society,* 4 (2), 249–283.

Woolfolk, A. (1995). *Educational psychology* (6th ed.). Boston: Allyn Bacon.

Chapter 5

Eugenics, Evolution, and Deaf Education

Lana Krievis
and Karen Anijar

Ideology is in everything and every*body*. Reading the body as an ontological entity (resisting essentialist biologisms) reconstructs the body as a text that begins with a political process of reconstructing our bodies in relation to other bodies. The political body as a semiotic text is a body that coalesces both the metaphor and the material. It is a body laden with discursive and practical modifications that emerge from economic, political, and historical exigencies. Thus the body is a process; it is always becoming. The body is both a pedagogical practice and an educative process, for it remains a contested terrain, a terrain of presentational conflicts. Because bodies are culturally and historically constituted, they do not ever exist outside the realm of power relationships.

The location in which the word deaf is inserted into the language creates, shapes, and sustains tacit assumptions about those whom the word describes. The word deaf is misplaced, distorted, and misconstrued. Deaf is both an adjective and a state of being ("I don't want this to fall on deaf ears; what's the matter with you, are you deaf?").

Deafness, in the same manner as any other socially constructed phenomenon, does have historical, political, and material consequences. "The terrain of the flesh" remains the site in "which meaning is inscribed, constructed and reconstituted" (McLaren, quoted in Haymes, 1995, p. 194). The body/subject of deafness remains encased in a semiotic symphony of signifiers and does represent how "ideological elements (re)combine on the surface of an objective feature to embody tremendous subjective meaning. That is, the body [must be] conceived as the interface of the individual and society, as a site of embodied or enfleshed subjectivity which also reflects the ideological sedimentations of the social structure inscribed into it" (McLaren, quoted in Haymes, 1994, p. 144).

No word or concept comes to us devoid of the ideological. There is no such thing as a neutral concept or a neutral word (Bakhtin, 1984). No adequate critique of any disabling discourse can proceed without paying attention to the ways that disability, abnormality, disease, and handicap linguistically develop in multiple contexts and contingencies within a variety of complex appropriations. The language used in deafness and deaf education camouflages its contentious codes. Signification and coding present in the language used regarding the deaf body (a negative body) are hegemonic, producing prosaic rhetoric that invites deconstruction (invalidating the language prior to the language invalidating—turning people into invalids). Poststructuralism offers a vigorous and compelling critique concerning the deaf and deaf education. By radically engaging everyday assumptions, poststructuralism offers a profound possibility for transforming the continuing relations of domination, exploitation, and oppression that are endemic in discussions surrounding the deaf, deaf education, and the deaf community—a community forged by educative practices that are described by advocates in terms of "impoverished models of communication", "unnatural languages" (Supalla 1990), "biological predisposition's" (Supalla, 1991), "the lack of language" (Mylander & Meadows, 1991), and "neurological atrophy" (Bochner & Albertini, 1990). The modernist managerial paradigm that uses tautological, spurious scientistic correlations to devalue those whom the researchers and experts profess to serve has a real effect of the bodies on the deaf.

The continued use of the dominant dualistic model of deafness remains caught in a fossilized web, "an endless oscillation between dead abstractions" (Morson, 1986, p. xi). *The Mask of Benevolence* (Harlan, 1992), a work that informs perceptions of deafness, research on deafness, and deaf education, never "break[s] out of the dialectical trap between...oppositions" (Kristeva, 1988, p. 95). Deafness is positioned as the opposite of hearing. Deaf education is an excellent example of what Pierre Bourdieu refers to as the "hegemony of symbolic violence" (quoted in Bartolome & Macedo, 1997, p. 225).

TIRED OLD DIALECTICS: VULGAR SCIENTISMS AND THE DEAF BODY

> According to Descartes...our physical organs are so internally interrelated that when any one of them is removed, that renders the *whole body defective.* (Leder, 1990, p.109)

> The same goes for an organ that does not function, with the exception of my appendix. (a physician interviewed for this chapter)

Modern vernaculars of rationality, hygiene, and bureaucratic order made the sorting of people into categories an "imperative of life scientists as well as of lawmakers and the police" (Urla & Terry, 1995, p.1). Rigidly unyielding binary dialectics are at the core of and are fundamental to this peculiar structuralist approach to reality. This binary system of classification is a model that operates on several levels, continually oppressing those who fall within any of its parameters in a multiplicity of manners. For example, the deaf body is always set in relation to and against the normal body (the hearing body) and thus becomes a diseased body, an invalid body. The medical model framing disability and disease is especially disabling. First, the model suggests a cure exists or can be found (part of the American religion of the scientific). Second, the medical model carries traces of "other sorts of etymology suggesting the not valid" (see Herndl, 1993, p. 12).

Abbé de l'Epée, who has often been considered the founder of deaf education, understood the deaf to be people similar to "us." However, with tremendous patriarchal privilege, and with no small amount of altruistic colonialist compassion, he also understood the deaf to be reduced (essentialized) by their condition to the level of beasts. It was incumbent upon the hearing world to free the deaf from their silent slavery so that the deaf could join the family of men. What was problematic and what remains problematic is that deafness is constructed as a disability only in relation to the hearing world.

As any high school student who has taken a class in biology can explain, what is thought to make us human is our capacity for spoken language. This worldview, (historically) stemming from Cartesianism and the positivistic sciences such as Darwinistic biology, advances an esoteric scientific ideology that transforms deafness into a colonialized, orientalized space.[1]

One of the leading French philosophers of the nineteenth century, Hippolyte Taine, created a taxonomy of humanity. A colonial-bodily geography that still maps the terrain on which deafness is constructed, Taine's language scale (naturally) firmly placed the languages of the Aryan nations at the pinnacle of his linguistic taxonomy. Sign language was classified as primitive and closely related to the Chinese language (which he deemed incapable of abstraction). In other words, sign language was an Oriental language, far removed from the Eurocenter. Certainly the assumption was that the further one moves from the Eurocenter, the more primitive and natural people become. Closer to nature is closer to the world of the plants and animals, implying a greater distance from civilization and mankind.

L'Epée's self-chosen mission was to deliver the deaf from the shackles of their Orientalized savagery, bestowing upon them the gift of normal speech. L'Epée would turn the deaf beasts into civilized men. Not unsurprisingly, l'Epée's attempts at rescue were extraordinarily unsuccessful. In his frustration, he felt he had no choice but to cross-reference deafness with the terminology of mental illness. The deaf were unrepentantly unredeemable. He could not make them hear.

Philip Pinel, who invented the terminology of mental illness, concurred. For him it was quite apparent the deaf were not like "us." It was observable; it was scientific; it could be measured. Deafness was thought to be symptomatic of idiocy; if the deaf had any brains at all, they would learn to speak.

By framing deafness within medicalized, deviant, or pathological categories, deafness became reconstructed as a somatic essence in which (anomalious) anatomical features were and continue to be imbued with social consequences. This remains one of the many problematic features within the entire dominant mode of psychological-pathological medicalized thought. Value is continually excluded from the realm of research; this reductionist approach to science and to research always describes, focusing solely on *how* events exist from a singular position that is pompously understood to be universal. More fundamental questions never emerge. We never ask *why* something is, or *what* purpose it serves, or what political, social, or economic conditions brought about the situation's appearance.

In an article entitled "Home Sign Systems in Deaf Children: The Development of a Morphology Without a Conventional Language Model" (Mylander & Meadows, 1991), the authors suggest the deaf cannot *naturally* acquire oral language (the highest mode of language on the enlightened/eugenic/evolutionary scale). Mylander and Meadows suggest that despite the deaf's inability to learn a real language, they do develop a gestural communication system. The word *gestural* is significant, because animals (who are part of nature) gesture. Mylander and Meadows's findings also suggest that the gestural communication system of the deaf has some of the same properties of language systems used and developed by very young children. However, according to the researchers, young children eventually develop the ability to use more conventional language models.

The use of the words *some, young,* and *conventional* reveals far more in the slippages, spaces, and silences than is concealed by the quasi-scientific, algorithmic language used. *Young* on a Piagetian developmental trajectory invariably signifies something unable to construct significant knowledge; young people's understandings of the world are trivialized. Young people cannot own property, cannot get married, cannot go to work, and cannot vote. *Young* signifies somebody in the process of growing toward becoming human, but not quite there yet. *Conventional* language models indicate that there are presupposed absolutes. There are recipes, methods, and practices for learning language. There is a norm (the prevailing model) and a normal way to learn—a standard by which all language (and therefore all reality) is imparted. The use of the word *some* suggests partiality and incompleteness. So the deaf remain not quite fully human, outside the boundaries of the norm, able only to partially partake in the human experience.

The dominant model of deaf education and deaf research retains both Cartesian and eugenicist roots. The deaf, according to this model, do have a primitive form of communication that has several of the features of language but is not really a language because it is only partial.

According to the dominant research paradigm, the deaf merely "mimic" the properties of language. *Mimicry* is a term that remains synonymous with *parroting, aping, imitation,* and *travesty* but not with what is sentient and human. Other researchers and bodies of research in the canons of the acritical suggest that the deaf do mature physiologically but that their language remains retarded. The consistent use of the words "retarded language" in the literature has profound political, economic, and social consequences on deaf bodies.

The deaf body remains a body that transgresses the limits of normality, for it is not normal. So it is incumbent on the deaf themselves to demonstrate their normalcy to the hearing world. It is up to the deaf themselves to prove that their dreams and their desires are the same as "ours." The continuing focus of deaf research authoritatively pronounces:

> The mastery of a first language in childhood, it would seem, establishes the neurological basis for language learning in adulthood. When mastery of a first language has not been attained by the onset of adolescence, as typically occurs in the deaf population, progress in acquisition is inhibited or supressed. Because the neurological foundations for language processing have not been sufficiently developed to support the intake of a first language by the onset of adolescence, the neurological and cognitive substrates of language processing will fail to develop. (Bochner & Albertini, 1990, p. 28).

Human beings are far more than collocations of observable, objective (and objectifiable) categories and characteristics. The world becomes split into the dialectical categories of public and private. The in-valid (which includes the old, the infirm, and the disabled, as well as women and children) are relegated to the private sphere. The public world, where the nondisabled body resides, is situated on an ontological map as "the world of strength, the positive (valued) body, performance and production" (Wendell, 1996, p. 24). The negative (devalued body) remains

> private, generally hidden, and often neglected. Coming into the public world with…a devalued body, people encounter resistance to mixing the two worlds; the split between disability and illness goes underground, because there is no socially acceptable way of expressing it and having the physical and psychological experience acknowledged. (Wendell, 1996, p. 40)

Prominent features contained in the body of scientific (medical, psychological, audiological) literature reveal the ideological elements contained in the social world regarding deafness. The construction of categories for the disabled entails a complex set of negotiations among professionals, the general public, and "afflicted" individuals, and it is continually mediated by broader cultural ideologies. Alternative cultural and biological capital is reduced to morphological essence, as deafness is abased to an opprobrious pathology, as something lower on a taxonomy of classifications in/on a hierarchy of biological capital.

IDEOLOGY AS ENUMERATION: KNOWING THE WORLD OBJECTIVELY

In a peculiar twist on the word *capital*, human beings have become the gold standard in a symbolic political economy via a series of measurements that are part of a multimillion-dollar industry. The measures themselves are part of a focus on enumeration, a focus whose impact is so pervasive that we seem to relate to our entire world through quantification. Numbers continually intervene in the relationship between our minds and our bodies. How tall are you? How much do you weigh? What is your IQ? How much disposable capital have you accumulated? How much can you hear? We experience the world via a bell curve of normalized existence.

The same nexus of capital defines at what point a person is not psychologically suited, academically prepared, or physically able to hold claim to normalcy. The audiology machine's gradations in deafness determine the standard deviations of the disabled from the normal or "real" world. However, the primacy attached to speech and the confusion of speech with language throughout the modern era have ensured that deafness remains a pathological construction.

In the postmodern universe of slippery signifiers, a post-Fordist economic framework emerges in which images are purchased. Deafness (re)presents a silent screen on which images are played out. It is a field mapped by an immobile mountainlike formation in which the deaf can be seen and understood only through their deafness.

On one hand, the idea of pathology, dis-ability, and in-validity "unites the romantic ideology of woman as body (as opposed to man as mind) and the bourgeois consumerist construct of the deaf (and all the disabled) as conspicuous consumer (who passively, unreflectively constantly consumes)." Standing in "specific relation to both money and productive labor," the disabled are "expected to consume (by the turn of the century even the word 'consumption' had moved from describing a disease to describing a cure). The disabled (which include the deaf) become the ultimate consumers in the process of being consumed by" their specific disability, condition, disease, and/or pathology (Herndl, 1993, p. 10).

Deaf children (we are told) accept and internalize a passive stance through life. Deaf children are frequently described as seeing themselves as under the control of caregivers. Under this rubric, the research tells us that the most critical consequence surrounding deafness currently is a consumer crisis. The research suggests deaf consumers do have a right to the best services that assiduously trained professional care givers are able to provide. The incommensurablity of the words *training* (which implies *rote*) and *professional* are never addressed. The absurdity of a social construction created under the rubric of pathology is never addressed. The horrors of human beings subjectively attempting to negotiate a pathologized terrain are never addressed. But then again, with the use of the word *best*, clearly a subjective judgment is being framed as a goal. A descriptor emerges as a noun whose relative value is constructed in direct relation to its emptiness. "Best" according to whom and for what purpose is never discussed. Consumption and consumerism are central to this deformation, or deaf-formation. Deafness becomes swept up into the symbolic political economy. But nobody asks why.

Hearing loss, we have heard, may interfere with and intervene in parent-child interactions. So it becomes necessary, according to professional pundits, to provide access to experts who can help facilitate the development of effective parent-child interaction. What determines effective parent-child interaction resides on the shoulders of the "expert" rather than the parent or the child. The very people who are being affected by administrative and professional practices do not have a say in the definition of what constitutes intimate human bonds.

The professional care–capital nexus is commodified in ever-greater concentric circles as the afflicted individual's private life is increasingly mediated by the public sphere:

> The Individuals with Disabilities Education Act—Part H, as amended...has mandated development of an IFSP for each infant and toddler and his or her family eligible for early intervention services. (ASHA, 1994, p. 36)

The individual profiles (the IFSP) are quantified in relation to what is deemed as normal.

What remains obscured in this deaf-formation are the prolific debates in the philosophy of medicine regarding the relationship between illness and disease. This has always been an uncertain relationship at best. The illness-disease couplet is complex, complementary, and contradictory. This has always been an artificially imposed dialectic, an either/or situation.

Illness (within the philosophy of medicine) is seen an evaluative concept. Nevertheless, disease is seen as a neutral term. There is no such thing as a neutral concept or word; all words have power, all words are politicized. Diseases, within the philosophy of medicine, are related to disturbances in an organism or some atypical functional deficiency. Since deafness is constructed as the opposite of hearing, it invariably becomes a functional deficiency, a deviation from the biological constructed (albeit enumerated) norm.

In the space between disease and illness another paradoxical relationship emerges between nature and culture. The connection between nature and culture invariably is connected to the institutionalization of power and knowledge. Foucauldian analysis extends this concept further, for the body is used as an object of and for technologies of control and normalization.

REACH OUT AND DEHUMANIZE SOMEONE: PAPA BELL MEETS THE EUGENICISTS

Science cannot be separated from the domain from which it emerged; it does not reside outside of history. Eugenics and statistics emerged from the mind of Francis Galton (Charles Darwin's number-obsessed cousin). Galton counted and measured everything from the number of petitionary prayers done in church in relationship to the number of times they were answered, to the flavor and freshness of his tea in correlation with the amount of tea used. Galton insisted that behavioral measures fit into a neat and symmetrical distribution, which we call a bell curve. Galton's entire life was devoted to his quest to investigate hereditary influences and breed a better strain of human being; he could not find a singular trait that was too trivial or obscure to trace to an antecedent member of a family, and he created the equations to prove it. The Galtonian legacy openly influenced social policy and science in the United States during the first three decades of the twentieth century (with the lives of tens of thousands of people affected by exclusion, experimentation, and sterilization). At one point eugenics contests were held all over the United States to encourage familial fitness. School textbooks gave the characteristics of the differing races of people (which at that time included Slavs, Italians, Greeks, Jews, Appalachian mountain folk, and the Irish, to name a few) Eugenics in many circles was seen as a progressive science. Nazi Germany regularly acknowledged the significant contribution of America in the development of political biology. After the Final Solution for "genetically inferior" people, eugenics went underground, but it did not go away.

Alexander Graham Bell was a progressive proponent of eugenics (he also invented the telephone and was a founder of the National Geographic Society: he was as complicitious in the eugenicist ordering of the world as Herrnstein and Murray). According to Bell who presented a paper to the National Academy of Sciences in 1883 entitled "Upon the Formation of a Deaf Variety of the Human Race," the deaf ought not be granted the right to marry, thus preventing the birth of progeny who carried the disability.

> Bell took the data, which he himself admitted was incomplete, subjected them to a worst case scenario and was able to produce a graph that demonstrated that: "the indications are that the congenital deaf mutes of the country are increasing at a greater rate than the population at large; and the deaf-mute children of deaf-mutes at a greater rate than the congenital deaf-mute population." Mapped on the graph the deaf children of the deaf seemed to be dramatically outbreeding the hearing...[leading eventually to] a deaf variety of the human race. (Mirzoeff, 1995, p. 70)

An interesting position considering that Bell had married a deaf woman. Bell also argued that the use of sign language (as opposed to oral communication) caused "the intermarriage of deaf-mutes and the propagation of their physical defect" (Bell, 1883, p. 216).

Bell's clarion call resounded in the minds of the hearing community. It certainly reached out and touched the Royal Commission on Deaf Education, which accepted Bell's perniciously persuasive arguments advising oral education. The commission, recognizing the "natural savagery" of the deaf (a eugenicist and Eurocentric construct) also advocated segregation of the sexes, since the passions among the deaf were thought to be strong. Certainly, as enlightened (Eurocentric) eugenicists, it would be unthinkable to permit hot-blooded degenerates to breed and pass their devolutionary seed on to subsequent generations, thus allowing a deaf sub-species to emerge.

Over one hundred years have passed since Bell's statements, but not much has changed. Ideology cannot be extricated from the conditions that brought about its emergence. The deaf community may speak of deafness as a culture (and has for almost twenty years now), but, professionals who minister to the deaf still speak of deafness in terms of biological deviance, essence, and morphological opposition to the hearing world. Evolutionary conjectures connect the social to the biological and confuse the social with the biological. The social thus is legitimated as the biological. What emerges from the technologies and machinations are systems of classification that conveniently place groups of people on a hierarchical ladder of relative worth and value, thus maintaining gender, class, ethnic, and racial oppressions.

PIAGETIAN PORNOGRAPHIES
AND VULGAR PSYCHOLOGISMS

Special education follows the Piagetian model, which utilizes developmental stages "embedded in the dominant political, economic and religious ideologies" (Braginsky, 1985, p. 88). Basic social structures, such as what is the underlying basis for the assumption of deafness as affliction, are never questioned. Piaget's theories emerged by interpreting a *normal* child's answers to esoterically formulated questions, and of course Piaget determined just who and what was normal. The frame of the questions was constructed in and determined by the hearing community.

Developmental psychology's unreflective, uncritical stance perpetrates a myth as absolute and universal reality. The attempt to overdetermine everything and everybody acts as an apology for the existing social order. What Macedo (1994, p. 6) would term a process of "stupidification," one of the many "linguistic games that disfigure reality," emerges as a guiding and guileful force within empirical psychological research that informs practice in deaf education.

Piaget depicted a universal subject who was irrevocably isolated, remaining outside history, time, and society (Riegal, 1976; Broughton, 1981; Burman, 1994). A Cartesian reductionism informs a poisonous pedagogy "designed to impart from the beginning false information and beliefs that have been passed on from generation to generation even though they are not only unproved but are demonstrably false" (Macedo, 1994, p. 66).

The Piagetian model remains central to contemporary deaf education. It assumes that the development of deaf children runs parallel to the development of (a historically specific group of) hearing children. Positing aurally spoken words as the norm while continuing to construct the deaf body as inefficient and in-valid is an act of "learned ignorance," for the "unwillingness to unpack the...ideology gives rise to a plethora of approaches presented as panaceas that are destined to failure" (Macedo, 1994, p. 154).

Piagetian cognitive psychology continues to blame the child. Adopting the defect model, applied Piagetian cognitive approaches ignore the social contexts out of which the defect emerged. The essentializing traditional practices of referral, testing, placement, and remediation do not address the larger environment, socially or educatively. Rather, school psychology quite conspicuously exonerates deaf education by focusing attention on the individual rather than on the larger structures that constructed the deaf child as abnormal in the first place.

Scientific studies continue to point to the cognitive, developmental, and linguistic superiority of hearing children in comparison to deaf children (see Bebko, Lacasse, Turk, & Oyen, 1992; Gaines & Halpern-Felsher, 1995; Hadadian & Rose, 1991; Kluwin, 1993; Schirmer, 1993). In preparation for this chapter, we decided to review the literature on deafness and psychology. What we found was a focus grounded in essentialist, utilitarian, positivistic research, which maintained an agentic hierarchy of deficits. For example:

> Two experiments compared signed and written stories by deaf 7- to 15-year-olds with oral and written stories by hearing age-mates. Researchers found that the signed and oral stories had similar discourse structures as indicated by patterns of causal goal-action-outcome episodes. The grammatical and lexical character of deaf students' written stories lagged behind that of hearing children. (Marsharck, 1994, p. 89)

Who determines what adequate grammar and lexical patterning are? Who determines what "behind" is? Does the lack of lexical character signify that the deaf children's processes are less sophisticated—or that the units of measure utilized are based on that of the hearing students? The Orwellian research model in which the questions and parameters of the problem already prescribe the results have a profound impact on all of our worldviews. More important, this same research paradigm prescribes, describes, and affects the life of the targeted group. Another research paper constructed within this tautology implies that deaf children cannot answer directive questions as accurately as hearing children, as seen in its abstract:

> Fifteen deaf and eleven hearing children (ages 8–10) witnessed slides depicting a wallet theft and were interviewed using a free recall approach followed by increasingly directive questions. Although accuracy of the two groups did not differ in free recall, deaf children provided less accurate responses to directive questions, whereas accuracy of the hearing children declined only slightly. (Porter, 1995, p. 51)

The construction of the problem stated in this particular study is based on incommensurablities. The meaning of this form of research is highly political, and the ideological elements embedded in it do have profound consequences. As we will suggest in the next section, if in the abstract we were to substitute for the word *deaf, black, Hispanic, Jew, Italian, Greek,* or any other cultural identifier, we would be appalled. Lou Fant, a Native American signer, author, and American Sign Language teacher, said in referring to teacher training programs for the deaf, "They make them study everything about the ears that do not work, and nothing about the eyes that do." Calling attention to a singular anatomical anomaly and then connecting it to capability and intelligence is as perverse as Herrnstein and Murray's *The Bell Curve.* (1994)

Fifty profoundly deaf adolescents in a residential school were given a battery of psychological tests. Unsurprisingly, the researchers found that deaf students have a significantly higher incidence of depression and tend to be more bored in classroom settings (see Watt & Davis, 1991). If any of us were treated and educated in terms of absolute deficits, we would be depressed, too. Considering the level of what is taught to deaf students and how it is taught, it does not take government grants, research projects, or much conjecture at all to figure out why deaf students are bored. The training of most deaf educators consistently returns to traditional theories and assumptions. There is safety in numbers, there is security within the essentialist matrix, which encompasses undertheorized techniques that do not ask questions but seek out answers, disconnected recipelike methods that remain focused on a singular statistical goal, and complexities, contingencies, and contradictions that are never placed into the training pot.

Another "psychological" study on deaf students examined

the social adjustment of deaf adolescents enrolled in segregated (n=39), partially integrated (n=15), and mainstreamed (n=17) settings. Partially integrated students reported better adjustment than mainstreamed students with deaf peers; mainstreamed students reported better adjustment than partially integrated students with hearing peers. Segregated students showed the lowest levels of adjustment overall. (Mussleman, 1996, p. 52)

This is so because understanding emerges in interaction. Students who have an opportunity to intermingle with members of their community, as well as the larger social order, are more socially well adjusted because they get to retain that which is unique to them. The students who are not culturally isolated but can engage in relationships with hearing students fare better than those who are isolated and marginalized. The students who are able to engage in a relationship with the hearing world but also learn in sign have better attitudes. Why wouldn't they? Human beings are social; we exist in relation to others. Oppression, subjugation, and enforced segregation do not foster happy social relationships.

Psychologist Nicholas Rose (1985) argues that psychology arose specifically to sort and classify people, fulfilling the surveillance role on which this pyramid of hierarchical comparative potential rests. For the measured, tested, psychologically enumerated person remains a highly studied, highly specific, administered, and managed entity always set in relation to a statistical norm. Knowledge of both the individual body in society and the general body of society were understood to be the same; each required the other. Definitions resided in comparison.

The division of the insane from the sane, the deaf from the hearing, and the educable from the ineducable, transformed what are fundamentally judgmental moral and political subjective understandings into scientific evaluative decrees—which are still no more or no less than judgments.

Developmental psychological models are dependent on the testing industry, (a growth industry, to be sure). The testing industry itself is dependent on fixed dualities. The dialectical model becomes a perverse hermeneutic circle of intensified consumption and commodification. As Haraway aptly observes, "The testing industry is central to the production of social order" (1989, pp. 236–237). Testing relies heavily on social institutions to permit its administration.

Special education is constructed as something outside the parameters of normal schooling for normal children (see Burman, 1994). Indeed, special education is constructed in opposition to "mainstream" classrooms. The dualistic, modernist, colonial school, "which reduces both teachers and students to mere technical agents who are destined to walk unreflectively through a labyrinth of procedures" (Macedo, 1994, p. 36), represents (in terms of the education of the deaf) the social Darwinists' revenge, their ultimate victory.

In this psychological context, students who hear are constructed as more literate than those who cannot hear. Students who hear a little are more literate than those who are completely deaf. Of course, English remains the standard of literacy, even in deaf education. In this context English becomes the unit of measure by which all real communication is judged. Philosophical discussions in deaf education concerning language focus only on a singular narrow parameter: whether or not sign language is a real language. After all, sign is not a written language, nor is it spoken (in the normalized sense of the word).[2]

One of the authors of this chapter rhetorically posed a question to a teacher of deaf children: "Why do hard-of-hearing children learn more English than the deaf?" "Because they can hear more English," the teacher replied. "Yes, but why should that mean they learn more English?" The teacher rolled her eyes and replied, "Because English is a hearing language." The ideology is quite apparent. Utilitarian logic notwithstanding, when language must be spoken, the deaf child is still seen as not having a language. Thus disingenuous practices conceived in a reality of essentialist missionary paternalism (Macedo, 1994, p. 181) continue to shape and sustain tacit assumptions concerning those whom the word *deaf* describes.

Teacher training, as opposed to critical professional education programs for deaf educators, continues to perpetuate a deficit-and-deterioration model, speaking to ludicrous reductionist psychologisms such as left-brain or right-brain modalities. As one example of research explains, "The left hemisphere of the brain if not lateralized for language prior to pubescence will deteriorate, thus precluding the acquisition of a spoken verbal system" (Christensen, 1990, p. 223). The brain has two hemispheres; that is a descriptive reality. The politics attached to this mode of thinking is the significant issue here, not the description in and of itself. In interviewing teachers of deaf children, one of this chapter's authors met with responses that conceived of the brain as a muscle that could atrophy if not used. Nothing implies that the brain's capacity to think is lessened, even if a particular portion of the brain does atrophy. However, those who teach the deaf assume that because the deaf cannot hear, they have a diminished capacity to create a language for naming the world. Unpacking the not-so-hidden agenda, the deaf therefore cannot be expected to learn what the hearing person can know. As our conversations with teachers suggest: What proof do we have that the deaf cannot learn to read? Because there is an inordinately high illiteracy rate in the community. Because they cannot read, that must mean they cannot learn to read. The arguments become circular, not grounded in anything but their own maze.

Since the capacity for communication is one of the things that distinguish human beings from nonhumans, the narrow model of what signifies communication continues to shape the content of what the deaf learn and the context in which deaf education occurs. As one teacher of the deaf commented: "They have no language." If they have no language, then how can they become literate? This sort of language play reproduces the existing social order, undermining critical thought and perspective while presenting an attack on the very people that the system professes to serve. The problem remains one of inncomensurablity and inequity administered under what Donaldo Macedo would term as a "pedagogy of lies" (1994, p. 137) inflicted on the body of the powerless.

GENOCIDAL METAPHORS, THE COCHLEAR IMPLANT, AND CONCLUSION

The military metaphor, in which science will finally annihilate (cure) deafness once and for all, may seem innocuously directed at a "thing." But ultimately the violent metaphors are targeted at human beings who reside in their own cultural milieu. The development of artificial technologies of hearing can eliminate and eradicate deafness—and the deaf—once and for all.

The deaf who understand their deafness through a cultural model and speak about technologies of artificial sound (cochlear implants) as destructive to their community often are seen as anachronistically suffering from a form of false consciousness (a vulgar scientistic construct). Why would anyone not want to be "normal"? Why would anybody want to remain deaf?

Physicians maintain that their professional obligations and responsibilities mandate action; they cannot stand by and allow deaf people to remain deaf. The deaf community, however, distinguishes between deafness and the deaf. The deaf differentiate themselves in terms of a community, unified by a common history, a common language (signing), and a shared cultural tradition of oppression and appropriation. Such actions allow the deaf to break out of the dialectical Ping-Pong of modernist dualistic logic; they demand "the right to live Deaf" (Mirzoeff, 1995, p. 72). Tragicomically, the hearing community cannot hear what the deaf are saying.

If I tell you I belong to a cultural group, who are you to tell me that it is not a group, that it is a handicap? Who determines my right to live as a deaf person? What gives you the right to annihilate my culture?

(Clearly, this has been tried before.) But as eugenics once again emerges, this time under the sign of the gene pool (as opposed to blood plasms), genetically "superior" people see fit to control the right of genetically "inferior" people to determine the course of their own existences. Recolonization is a worldwide new-eugenicist phenomenon:

> We are already beginning to see it in journals such as *Foreign Affairs* the notion of "failed states"; that is, Third World nations which have had their experiments with self-determination, sovereignty and democracy and failed in them. Now it is up to the United States to re-colonize and re-impose some level of what will be called in the press "civil society." Somalia is only the first example. Paul Johnson makes [this] all too painfully clear in the April 18, 1993 issue of the *New York Times Magazine*. His article is called "Colonialism's Back—and not a moment too soon." His thesis is simply: "Let's face it: some countries are just not fit to govern themselves." (Merrill, 1993, p. 46)

As matters are conceived now, some people are considered not politically ready to govern themselves. Some people are not genetically fit to govern themselves. If they were they would realize that they were handicapped. After all, if the deaf had any common sense, they would want to live like "us." They are not normal if they don't want to hear. It should seem only "natural" that social Darwinism be selected to remain at the forefront of deaf education at the close of this millennium.

Hitler noted, "What good fortune for those in power that people do not think" (Macedo, 1994, p. 36). Good thing, too, for if and when people do think, what they say might fall on deaf ears.

NOTES

1. In an extraordinary chapter on the deaf, Nicholas Mirzoeff historically analyzes the placement of the deaf within the harem (in which the deaf were favored by the sultans). He argues that the cannibalized cultures (see Root, 1996) created by Western consumption of Eastern ways of being constructed a visual discourse framing the deaf and women in the harem within a sexualized exotic pathology.
2. The Cherokees created a written language in order to prove their "civilized nature." Alas, the written language did not prevent the genocide that subsequently took place.

REFERENCES

ASHA (1994). "Service provision under the Individuals with Disabilities Education Act—Part H, as amended (IDEA—Part H) to children who are deaf and hard of hearing ages birth to 36 months. Joint Committee of ASHA and Council on Education of the Deaf." *ASHA* 36(8).

Bakhtin, M. (1984). *Problems of Dostoevsky's poetics.* Ed. and trans. by C. Emerson. Minneapolis: University of Minnesota Press.

Bartoleme, L., & Macedo, D. P. (1997). "Dancing with bigotry: The poisoning of racial and ethnic identities." *Harvard Educational Review,* 67 (2), p. 222–246.

Bebko, J. M., Lacasse, M. A., Turk, H., & Oyen, A. S. (1992). "Recall performance on a central-incidental memory task by profoundly deaf children." *American Annals of the Deaf,* 135: 271–276.

Bell, A. (1883). "Upon the formation of a deaf variety of the human race." *Memoirs of the National Academy of Sciences,* 2: 216.

Bochner, H., & Albertini, J. (1990). "Language varieties in deaf populations and their acquisition by children and adults." In M. Strong (Ed.), *Language learning and deafness* (pp. 3–48). New York: Cambridge University Press.

Braginsky, D. D. (1985). "Psychology: Handmaiden to society." In S. Koch & D. E. Leary (Eds.), *A century of psychology as science* (pp. 880–891). New York: McGraw Hill.

Broughton, J. (1981). "Piaget's structural developmental psychology III: Logic and psychology." *Human Development,* 24: 195–224.

Burman, Erica. (1994). *Deconstructing developmental psychology.* New York: Routledge.

Bysshe, J. (1994). "Deafness in childhood: Diagnosis and treatment of deaf babies and children." *Professional Care Mother and Children,* 4:6, Sept–Oct 180–183.

Christensen, K. (1990). "Thinking about thinking: A discussion of the development of cognition and language development in deaf children." *American Annals of the Deaf,* 135:3, 222–225.

Gaines, R., & Halpern-Felsher, B. L. (1995). "Language preference and communication development of a hearing and deaf twin partner." *American Annals of the Deaf,* 140: 47–55.

Hadadian, A., & Rose, S. (1991). "An investigation of parents' attitudes and the communication skills of their deaf children." *American Annals of the Deaf,* 136: 273–277.

Haraway, D. (1989). *Primate visions: Gender, race, and nature in the world of modern science.* New York: Routledge.

Harlan, L. (1992). *The mask of benevolence.* New York: Knopf.

Haymes, S. (1995). *Race, culture and the city.* New York: State University of New York Press.

Herndl, D. (1993). *Invalid women.* Chapel Hill: University of North Carolina Press.

Herrnstein, R., & Murray, C. (1994). *The bell curve: Intelligence and class structure in American life.* New York: Free Press.

Kevles, D. (1984). *In the name of eugenics.* New York: Knopf.

Kluwin, T. N. (1993). "Cumulative effects of mainstreaming on the achievement of deaf adolescents." *Exceptional Children,* 60: 73–81.

Kristeva, J. (1988). *Etrangers à nous-mêmes.* Paris: Fayard.

Macedo, D. (1994). *Literacies of Power.* Boulder: Westview.

Marschark, M. (1994). "Discourse rules in the language productions of deaf and hearing children." *Journal of experimental child psychology,* 57: 1, 89–107.

Merrill, R. (1995). "Simulations and terrors of our time." In D. Brown & R. Merrill (Eds.), *The politics and imagery of terrorism.* Seattle: Bay Press.

Mirzoeff, N. (1995). "Framed: The deaf in the harem." In J. Terry & J. Urla (Eds.), *Deviant Bodies.* Indiana: University of Indiana Press.

Morson, G., & Emerson, C. (1986). *Mikhail Bakhtin: Creation of a prosaics.* California: Stanford University Press.

Mussleman, C. (1996). "The social adjustment of deaf adolescents in segregated, partially integrated, and mainstreamed settings." *Journal of deaf studies and deaf education,* 1:1, 52–63.

Porter, S. (1995). "A comparison of the eyewitness accounts of deaf and hearing children." *Child abuse & neglect: The international journal,* 19:1, 51–62.

Prittlenisky, I. (1994). *The morals and politics of psychology.* New York: SUNY.

Riegal, K. (1976). "The dialectics of human development." *American Psychologist,* 698–700.

Rose, N. (1985). *The psychological complex: Psychology, politics and society in England, 1869–1939.* London: Routledge & Kegan Paul.

Schirmer, B. R. (1993). "Constructing meaning from narrative text: Cognitive processes of deaf children." *American Annals of the Deaf,* 138, 397–403.

Urla, J., & Terry, J. (Eds.) (1995). "Introduction, Mapping Embodied Deviance." *Deviant bodies.* Bloomington: University of Indiana Press.

Watt, J., & Davis, F. (1991). "The prevalence of boredom proneness and depression among profoundly deaf residential school adolescents." *American Annals of the Deaf,* 136:5, 409–413.

Wendell, S. (1996). *The rejected body: Feminist philosophical reflections on disability.* New York: Routledge.

Chapter 6

Teaching as Sacrament

Aostre N. Johnson

Modernist psychological paradigms restrict our understanding of what it means to be human by excluding spiritual dimensions of being, a limitation not shared by most cultures throughout history. Cognitive developmental theories narrowly confine the vision of human possibility by positing the individual rational mind as the critical organizing force in human development and functioning. While constructivist metaphors are a vast improvement over mechanistic behavioristic models, they still inhibit our ability to comprehend the sacred dimensions of each person, and indeed, of all of life. This finite view severely constricts the liberatory potential of educational systems based on these models. The field of curriculum theory is beginning to include religious and spiritual perspectives; Pinar (1995) suggests that "the scholarly project to understand curriculum as theological text which is developing now might challenge the modern worldview of salvation by material progress and scientific technology, a salvation seriously imperiled by ecological limits" (p. 626).

I use *spiritual* as "the immaterial, intelligent or sentient part of a person"; as the "animating or vital principle held to give life to physical beings"; and as "relating to sacred matters," with *sacred* derived from the Latin *sacrare,* meaning "holy," from the Old English *halig* or *hal*—"more at whole." To accept the spiritual dimensions of being is to strive to become "more at whole." Further, *sacred* means "entitled to reverence, honor and respect," according to popular usage. If we respect the sacred nature of being human, then teaching becomes a sacramental action that honors and symbolizes the reality of our existence as nondualistic embodied spirits. Berryman (1987) suggests that *sacrament* means both "mystery" and "sign." While much about the spiritual dimension of life is destined to remain a mystery, understanding teaching as sacrament and honoring the sacred nature of the profession is a symbolic act that transforms dominant positivistic developmental and educational paradigms, allowing us to reclaim the original meaning of both *educate*, "to lead out," and *profess*, "to affirm, to declare faith, to accept a calling." Sacramental educators are responding to a deep inner voice calling them to a life of dedication to students, a love of learning and knowledge, and a struggle for faith in the potential for beauty, truth, and goodness in each person and in the world. Accepting the mystery of the spiritual nature of being and the sacred nature of the education profession radically changes our views of students, of curriculum and teaching, and of ourselves as teachers.

Although *religious* and *spiritual* both intimate questions of origin, purpose, and ultimate meaning, *religious* usually implies a point of convergence on specific established religions organized around particular deities in some form of community, whereas *spiritual* is used in a more general sense, reaching across and outside of particular religions. *Moral* refers to principles, ideas, and rules having to do with beliefs about how human beings should relate with each other and the world, and moral beliefs are often associated with both religious and spiritual perspectives. While I will emphasize the spiritual dimensions of the person and of education, *spiritual* cannot really be separated from *religious* or *moral* any more than it can be isolated from anything else. *Spiritual* can be seen as the essence or heart of all of life, as inherent in every aspect of living and educating as the moral. And although I emphasize spiritual possibilities potentially available in any context, rather than any specific religious perspective, religion's emphasis on a particular faith community is critical. Indeed, the spirit is always present in a specific time, place, and social context. Cajete (1994) illustrates the interconnections of these concepts in speaking of an aspect of sacred knowledge shared by most Indian tribes: "Knowledge and understanding of morals and ethics are a direct result of spiritual experiences. Sacred traditions and the elders who possess special teachings act as bridges to spiritual experiences and as facilitators for learning about spiritual matters" (p. 44).

For most of human history, teaching and learning were intricately bound with religious institutions and contained explicit moral and spiritual perspectives. The separation of church and state is a relatively recent historical phenomena. As Robert Ulrich (1968) says: "All early education was religious, and all early religion was also educational. Both elements were inherent in the rites and ceremonies of birth and death, war, hunting, and harvesting. Even in highly developed civilizations, the priests were the educators..." (p. 42). When these functions separated, teaching was still seen as a religious calling or vocation. To a large degree, this was because the intellectual and academic aspects of education were not understood as separate from moral and spiritual aspects. Education was not viewed as a private, individually centered, competitive endeavor but as a religious, moral, and public activity.

Elements of this attitude still exist, and the current groundswell of interest in spiritual and religious perspectives may be signaling a return to this view. For example, Schwehn (1996) reports that when adults are asked to describe the teachers who have been most important in their lives, they depict people with strong qualities of character. "Even today, and against some of the most powerful impulses of modernity, people quite spontaneously connect the vocation of teaching more firmly to the arts of moral and spiritual formation than to the rigors of academic speculation" (p. 7). And Lickona (1993) suggests that because increasing numbers of people "across the ideological spectrum" believe the United States is in moral crisis, education for moral character is finding its way back into schools.

To allow teaching to become a sacrament is to accept the mystery of spiritual presence and the intense meaningfulness that presence gives to human experience. Rather than a particular set of skills or understandings, it implies a way of being intent on overcoming the duality between sacred and secular, a faith that we encounter the divine in every moment, in every place, and in every person—and indeed, that we ourselves are instruments of the divine. Understandings and interpretations of sacramental education will be as diverse as are perspectives on spirituality. The following reflections are not intended as a comprehensive or universal list or system but as one personal offering.

THE SACRAMENT OF SELF-KNOWLEDGE

Schon's *The Reflective Practitioner* (1983) initiated a significant dialogue about the importance of educators integrating theory and practice through constant inner reflection-in-action. In *The Contemplative Practitioner,* Miller (1994) suggests that reflection must move to a deeper level, to that which

Miller calls "Being," accessed by contemplative practice. This practice can take many forms, based on the practitioner's religious path or spiritual inclinations. Whatever form it takes, accessing spirit in ourselves allows us to be more fully present to the spirits of others.

In "A Transcendental Developmental Ideology of Education," James Macdonald (1995) refers to the process by which we gain access to our inner selves as "centering," a well-known concept in both Eastern and Western religious traditions. "Centering is the fundamental process of human being that makes sense of our perceptions and cognitions of reality" (p. 88). The aim of education in the transcendental developmental ideology is centering in both self and world. The teacher who would nurture the centering of students must be deeply engaged in his or her own centering, simultaneously exploring both "inner" and "outer" worlds.

Martin Buber (1958) wrote: "The simple truth is that the wretchedness of our world is grounded in its resistance to the entrance of the holy into lived life" (p. 39). The word *holy* is derived from the word *whole*. How can we as educators help make our students whole if we are not committed to becoming whole ourselves? We have to ask ourselves what stands in the way of each of us becoming wholly ourselves. This means confronting our fears and asking for help in overcoming them, seeing ourselves as we really are, with all of our imperfections, and overcoming the addictions we use as screens. We become more ourselves by letting go, discovering the holy working in and through us as we live with others. It is this willingness to engage deeply and honestly in the process of self-discovery and personal change in community with others that is sometimes called "spiritual growth." Parker Palmer (1993) suggests that the classical spiritual virtues of "humility and faith, reverence without idolatry, love and openness to grace" are also the natural virtues of the educator or professor:

> The true professor of a faith is one who affirms a transcendent center of truth, a center that lies beyond our contriving, that enters history through the lives of those who profess it and brings us into community with each other and the world. (p. 113)

Theology literally means "knowledge of God" and is understood to be intellectual, affective, and intuitive in nature. It can be seen as both content, the system of beliefs of a particular religious tradition, and process, a living act of continually wrestling with issues of meaning, developing a living faith that continues to change. The sacramental educator functions as a theologian of sorts, continually engaging in and modeling a process concerned with bringing spirit into everyday life. As Nelson (1984) expresses this:

> Educators who are living examples of persons struggling for faith in order to find meaning in life are a great inspiration to their students. Educators who refuse to think about faith and simply retell preformulated statements about what people thought in former times are stunting the spiritual life of their students. (p. 16)

Opportunities to model this informal theologizing might appear in any discipline or subject of the curriculum. For example, the Nobel prize winning biologist George Wald began his introductory biology course at Harvard University with a testimony about how his scientific engagement with the evolution of life inspired him with such wonder and awe about the extraordinary patterning of the universe that it led him to become a believer in God. However, explicit reference to divinity is not necessary for mentor modeling of deep engagement with issues of meaning and faith.

THE SACRAMENT OF COMMUNITY

The sacrament of self-knowledge always takes place within the context of community. The Catholic theologian Bernard Cooke suggests that friendship is the most basic human sacrament. The ways in which we encourage students to care for each other and the ways in which we care for them result in various kinds of community at the heart of each classroom and each school. The ideal of schools as communities of friendship in which each member is loved and supported for who he or she is, as well as challenged to become him- or herself more fully, must be the most fundamental goal of sacramental education. Noddings (1993) suggests that schools can become supportive and caring communities without displacing churches.

So much has been written about the Western obsession with individualistic preferences and desires. Yet Western educational practices do not truly affirm either the individual or the community. Individual wills learning to work in harmony can be seen as the most pressing goal of human existence, and educational communities can correct for egotistic tendencies of the individual. A community is constructed by individuals with diverse talents and interests, all working together for the common good. The composer Bach envisioned well-functioning human communities as symphonies, with each person playing her part in a harmonious whole—he saw his music as an illustration of a heavenly order on earth. The educator of spirit constantly orchestrates a community of students, seeing them not only as individuals but as parts of the whole, guaranteeing the basic harmony, respect, and concern for others that allows individual creativity to become joint creativity.

One hopes that this vision will expand beyond the classroom as educators become, in Aronowitz and Giroux's (1985) term, "transformative intellectuals," blending the political with the pedagogical in an effort to overcome injustice in the wider society. However, Purpel (1989) warns that

> it does not seem to be in the interest of those currently in power to encourage and empower the education profession to seek that intellectual and moral authority. On the other hand, there are those educators who believe strongly that it is very much in the interest of those who struggle for a culture of love, joy and justice to demand that our profession develop such a vision. These educators also believe that members of our profession have a basic right to pursue their calling (vocation) with integrity and pride and to seek to fulfill their responsibilities to participate in the struggle to achieve those conditions. (p. 103)

Thus a sacramental vision of education as caring community begins with a friendship between educator and students and ripples out into ever-widening circles that include groups of students, classrooms, schools, local communities, nations and the world. Sacramental educators nurture this ideal in their students.

THE SACRAMENT OF APPRECIATING EACH BEING

In the context of community, each individual *is* a different message of the spirit—the spirit speaks to us through each being. Teachers of spirit understand the nature of their relationship with each individual student as sacramental and search for the incredible potentials of each particular manifestation of spirit. Dropping roles and categories in order to directly confront the being of another person can be an awe-inspiring experience, and it is certainly in direct opposition to the deficit model prevalent in many modernist educational systems. Rather than a conglomeration of facts and skills not yet attained, each student becomes a unique and sacred gift of the universe with valuable gifts to offer the community.

Sacramental teaching is committed to developing these divine offerings. The musician Pablo Casals (1970) expressed this attitude:

> Each second we live in a new and unique moment of the universe, a moment that never was before and will never be again. And what do we teach our children in school? We teach them that two and two make four, and that Paris is the capital of France. When will we also teach them what they are? We should say to each of them: Do you know what you are? You are a marvel. You are unique. In all of the world there is no other child exactly like you. In the millions of years that have passed there has never been another child like you. And look at your body—what a wonder it is! Your legs, your cunning fingers, the ways you move. You may become a Shakespeare, a Michelangelo, a Beethoven. You have the capacity for anything. Yes, you are a marvel. And when you grow up, can you then harm another who is like you, a marvel? You must cherish one another. You must work—we must all work—to make this world worthy of its children. (p. 295)

Kovel (1991) further suggests that "all human beings have the spiritual capacity of a Buddha or Saint Francis, yet all save a tiny few squander these powers beyond measure" (p. 71). If we could see each of our students as a potential Buddha or Saint Francis or Mother Teresa and give them that kind of reverence as beings of spirit, perhaps we can help this potential to emerge.

This deep respect for each student leads to a nonhierarchical way of relating and understanding teaching. While each educator has a sacred duty to teach particular knowledge and skills, each also functions as a catalyst for "leading out" the wisdom and knowledge already embodied in each student. From this perspective, our students become our teachers. Young children might inspire in us their immense capacity for faith, trust, wonder, joy, honesty, and simplicity, helping us once again to "enter the kingdom of heaven." Adolescents might reawaken our idealism, our sense of outrage at injustices that many adults have become inured to. Students of all ages have much to teach us about human qualities as well as skills and knowledge.

THE SACRAMENT OF LEARNING

The essence of learning, of coming to know, is a feeling of deep meaningfulness. Learning in this sense is *agape,* suffused with wonder and love. Learning as sacrament seeks the purpose of existence and supports the

revealing of the truths of the spirit in the universe. Enlightenment thinking separated reason from faith and feeling, and the challenge now is to
restore them. Reason informed by faith can be called contemplative thinking, which Macdonald (1974) describes as "an openness to the mystery of
existence," perpetually engaged in "examining the fundamental meaning
of things....We must encourage the young to say both yes and no to culture and to probe the ground from which our culture arises" (p. 110).

Sacramental learning is based on the faith that we are not duality but
incarnated spirit beings in the world and that the sacred world is not different from the secular. This belief leads to the faith that we can find a
divine pattern in the world, that the source and meaning of life commu-
nicates itself to us through the natural world. It also leads to the faith that
we can learn from human history and, despite evidence to the contrary,
can come to understand how to work together to bring dignity and justice to all people.

If we accept the spirit in the person and in the world, we will want
our students to be directly in touch with the world, to be engaged in a
process of meaningful discovery themselves. This means that sacramental
educators will want to get out of the way, imparting the knowledge,
skills, and inspiration necessary for optimal engagement, but continually
examining our own egoistic tendencies to stand as idols between our students and their quest for knowledge.

Throughout history most peoples have raised existential and metaphysical questions. Noddings (1993) reminds us that rather than embracing students' questions about God and existence, about the meaning of
life and death, our educational institutions have deliberately excluded
them. She suggests that these questions can be included, even in the public schools, at a "meta-level" of curriculum planning, enriching the standard curriculum. While there are many potential approaches, both direct
and indirect, to including these fundamental concerns, as well as many
potential concerns and challenges concerning their inclusion, the sacramental educator will be committed to the project of salvaging education
from a trivial pursuit agenda, restoring its value as a profound and worth-
while human endeavor.

THE SACRAMENT OF TIME: PRESENT, PAST, AND FUTURE

The experience of sacred presence and the changed meaning that it gives
to human experience highlights the present moment. Many spiritual

paths attest to the powerful presence inherent in the concrete moment: Everything takes place in the now, and there is no place to go but here. If we encounter the divine everywhere and in every moment, nonsacred times and places do not exist.

In order to experience the power of the present moment, we have to be able to be receptive, to listen for presence, to pay attention to what is here. The grace of the spirit is continually operating through us when we are fully present in the moment, leading to the healing nature of personal presence. When we live in the power of present presence, we are more able to help our students to become fully present in the moment and thus to use their senses, their bodies, and their minds more fully as they come to know themselves and the world.

Therefore we should be talking less about future outcomes or standards and more about the possibilities in the present moment, or at least we should be aware when our concern for the outcome is obscuring the sacredness of entering fully into the present moment. Huebner (1974) asks, "How can one plan educational futures via behavioral objectives when the mystical literature emphasizes the present moment and the need to let the future care for itself?" (p. 215). While the importance of students becoming skilled and knowledgeable in order to fulfill themselves and contribute as much as possible to the community should not be minimized, still, when fears of the future engulf the living present, education becomes spiritless and the future is diminished.

The present can be understood only by seeing the underlying process revealed in the pattern of historical unfolding in any discipline or subject. We must return to the past to test our memory, to remember those things, both ugly and beautiful, that we have forgotten about how to create a more just and beautiful world. Our relationship to the past becomes sacramental when it is seen as a powerful source of information for bringing spirit into the present. Huebner (1974) suggests that we make curriculum decisions by asking: "what is valuable enough to be conserved as part of the past and made present to the young?" (p. 49). The young of our culture are too often surrounded by crass, materialistic, commercial images; by unworthy role models and oddly distorted views of history. Worthy of only our very best, they get our very worst. Sacramental educators strive to reverse this tendency, creating a curriculum drawn from that which is most true, honorable, beautiful, and worthy of emulation—and making sure that students are able to critically examine sources of information about and lessons from the past so that they will be able to create a better present and future.

The tendency of traditional premodern religious theologies to postpone salvation and justice until some future time has been increasingly challenged by various forms of theology, including liberation and feminist theologies. As more religions turn their attention to present inequities, valid questions about future sacramentality arise. However, this tendency is taken to the extreme in a despiritualized modern culture that rejects the delay of gratification and locates all hope in a materialistic present. Whitehead (1933) warned that if the future is cut away, the present collapses; this observation may be increasingly descriptive of the moral and spiritual bankruptcy of Western culture.

In order for human communities to change, they must be shaped by visions of future possibility. Within the sacramental tradition is a deep history concerned with shaping the future by means of imagination. The imagination allows us to hold an image of something other than what is before us in the present moment, either remembered from the past or not yet created. Thus imagination allows both past and future to have an impact on the present moment.

Allowing for the possibility of an imagined better future is an act of faith. A belief in the future is perhaps the best gift we can give to despairing youth. The gift of mature adulthood is a belief in the future despite a multiplicity of experiences that might lead us to abandon that belief. This is not a naive belief, based on looking the other way at human tragedy, but a seasoned belief, based on living through difficult times, having one's faith shattered again and again "on the rock of truth" and yet emerging from difficulty and despair to hope. Freire (1992) reminds us that

> the idea that hope alone will transform the world, and action undertaken in that kind of naiveté, is an excellent route to hopelessness, pessimism and fatalism. But the attempt to do without hope in the struggle to improve the world is a frivolous illusion. (p. 8)

Perhaps more than anything else, the sacramental educator embodies hope for the world as she renews herself again and again through the sacraments of personal spiritual work, commitment to and participation in caring communities, deep appreciation for each individual student as a unique gift of spirit, learning as a profoundly meaningful endeavor, and participation in a sacred present embracing both past and future.

REFERENCES

Aronowitz, S., & Giroux, H. (1985). *Education under siege: The conservative, liberal and radical debate over schooling.* South Hadley, MA: Bergin & Garvey.

Berryman, P. (1987). *Liberation theology.* Bloomington, IN: Random House.

Buber, M. (1958). *Hasidism and modern man.* New York: Horizon. p. 39.

Cajete, G. (1994). *Look to the mountain: An ecology of indigenous education.* Durango, CO: Kivaki.

Casals, P. (1970). *Joys and sorrows.* New York: Simon & Schuster.

Freire, P. (1992). *Pedagogy of hope: Reliving pedagogy of the oppressed.* New York: Continuum.

Huebner, D. (1974). "Towards a remaking of curricular language." In W. Pinar (Ed.), *Heightened conciousness: Cultural revolution and curriculum theory.* Berkeley, CA: McCutcheon.

Kovel, J. (1991). *History and spirit: An inquiry into the philosophy of liberation.* Boston: Beacon.

Lickona, T. (1993). "The return of character education." *Educational Leadership, 51* (3), 90–93.

Macdonald, J. (1974). "A transcendental developmental ideology of education." In W. Pinar (Ed.), *Heightened consciousness, cultural revolution, and curriculum theory* (pp. 85–116). Berkeley, CA: McCutchan.

Miller, J. P. (1994). *The contemplative practitioner.* New York: Bergin & Garvey.

Noddings, N. (1993). *Educating for intelligent belief or unbelief.* New York: Teacher's College Press.

Nelson, C. E. (1984). "Theological foundations for religious nurture." In M. J. Taylor (Ed.), *Changing patterns of religious education.* Nashville, TN: Abingdon.

Palmer, P. (1993). *To know as we are known: Education as a spiritual journey.* San Francisco: Harper.

Purpel, D. (1989). *The moral and spiritual crisis in education.* New York: Bergin & Garvey.

Pinar, W. F. (1996). *Understanding curriculm.* New York: Peter Lang.

Schon, D. A. (1983). *The reflective practioner.* New York: Basic Books.

Schwehn, M. R. (1996). "The spirit of teaching." *Conversations, 10,* 4–18.

Ulrich, R. (1968). *A history of religious education.* New York: New York University Press.

Whitehead, A. N. (1933). *Adventures of ideas.* New York: Macmillan.

Chapter 7

Practicing Eternity:
Socialization, Development,
and Social Life

Paul Stein

Critiques of developmental psychology have originated from four grounds: ideology, reproduction, resistance, and postmodern epistemology. The ideology critiques expose the naturalism of both development and psychology as cultures of false solidarity that dissolve differences in litanies of normalization. The reproduction critiques work to interrupt the pedagogical services of developmental psychology, circulations of power and knowledge that repeat the evidential legitimacy of economic and class practices by disclosing the symbolic violence of inculcating the contingent but dominant exercises of reason as obligatory. The resistance critiques have taken the necessary failures of hegemonic developmental psychology, the dislocations of subjects by the imperfections of incorporation, and the contradictions of domination that bear "other" possibilities as the basis for emancipatory practices. Lastly, the postmodern epistemological critiques have indisposed the representational logic of developmental order, the transcendence of cognition, and the neutrality of methodology with the afflictions of immanence, of language performances that constitute the pragmatic contingency of any psychology and any teleological order of processes or development.

Social life is, generally, unperturbed by these strong and persistent critiques, in part because such critiques reinstate the "affirmative culture" of developmentalism that "uses the soul as a protest against reification only to succumb to it in the end" (Marcuse, 1969, p. 108). The "professional ideology" of developmentalism, now harmonizing a new evolutionary psychology to the marketplace melody of biotechnics, remains consistent with Mills's appraisal: "Social and normal elements are masked by a quasi-biological meaning of the term 'adaption' with an entourage of apparently socially bare terms like 'existence' and 'survival,' which seem to draw prestige from the vogue of evolutionism. Both the quasi-biological and the structureless character of the term 'adjustment' tend by formalization, to universalize the term, thus again obscuring specific social content" (Mills, 1970, p. 139). Biopower blends into a psychosocial evolution that culturally fulfills the market and history as nature.

The "fresh synthesis" of developmental science, a "recognition of the complexity of development as a first step toward understanding its coherence and simplicity" (Cairns, Costello, & Elder, 1996, p. 1) merely reasserts the cultural value of complexity as a calibration of already prescribed coherence and simplicity, a continuous adjustment of contingencies without other possibilities. Similarly, the millennium of developmental psychology is projected as "putting the whole child back together again after recent retreat to the minitheories of biological, biochemical and social levels of inquiry" (Parke, Ornstein, Rieser, & Zahn-Waxler, 1994, p. 50). But that millennium evades the primary and historical question of creating the existential conditions of fully living in this, a first time that is possibly other than more and more, time and time again. Problems of living evade the work of all the king's men occupied with putting their problems back together again.

The need for developmentalism resides in "the substrata of the construction of life and [is] valued as ultimate in lived life," and it mediates between the conditions of living and knowledge about living, legislating the relational politics that enact how life is lived and experienced (Mannheim, 1982, p. 38). Developmentalism is a formalism relative to life processes, the working ultimates that make it up. "That which presents itself as origin and beginning in the system produced by thought and which there falls beyond any theoretical justification, receives its warranty within the historical life-process from the collective conciousness present at a time, and it can be kept unproblematic only by this" (ibid., pp. 38–39). In order to make life processes problematic and reach the infrastructural roots of containment and contentment, a "radical transvaluation of values" that "involves a break with the familiar, the routine ways of seeing, hearing, feeling, understanding things so that the organism may become receptive to the potential forms of a nonaggressive, nonexploitative world" is needed (Marcuse, 1969, p. 6). "Insofar as in Western thought culture has meant affirmative culture, the abolition of its affirmative character will appear as the abolition of culture as such" (Marcuse, 1969, p. 130).

"A radical revolution—a revolution that goes to the root of the exploitation—is concerned with the production of a new subjectivity that addresses the origin of the radical alienation making up the structure of the world" (Santamaria & Manville, 1992, p. 409). A presently thinkable, revolutionary sense of development requires a "critical utopianism" (McLaren, 1994, p. 206) that produces an imaginative, seriously playful epistemology of living (Melucci, 1996); not methodological objectivity nor ironic rhetorical authority, but instead an objectivity emergent from the transformative, intersubjective relations of embodied politics of knowing (Fabian, 1994). Sensuous, social poesis may negate the real and the ideal and inspire an imaginative social materialism, refusing the "facism of representation" that forecloses the social place, the "broken middle" (Rose, 1996, p. 54) of life.

Such socially sensuous imagination of alternative ways of knowing, of incarnate belonging, is suppressed by the existential motives for developmental psychology and sociology that permutate historically to create an interdependence of psychosocial needs and desires—authoritative knowledge and ethics or powers (Wexler, 1996a; Pfister & Schong, 1997; Herman, 1995; Morss, 1996; Prilleltensky, 1994; Walkerdine, 1988). Developmental psychology (I include developmental sociology in the designation) is a systematic theodicy that explains our suffering, a "secularized theodicy" that entails a theodical solution to problems of living historically (Robertson, 1978, p. 77). As an ethic, developmental psychology surveys the "road to salvation," mapping and guiding a successive social and personal immortality by constituting childhood as a recapitulatory becoming of what adulthood requires and the depository of what adulthood denies (Jenks, 1996; Morss, 1990).

Lastly, as an everyday practice, developmental psychology is a practice of "self-perfection": an autogenesis of self and the social by the same processes, split into complements of development and socialization. The co-contingency of development and socialization composes a practice of eternity, a specific, historical sort of endless repetition of becoming infinitely more human by the amplification of the principles of capitalist exchange: living for the prescience of life everlasting—death for knowledge passed on. First going in one way and then the other on this busy two-lane road to and from nowhere, both self and social realization are "liberations" from the conditions of living, obtaining the normalcy of not being alive as "liberation from the most dysfunctional disturbances of capitalist society for the sake of its normal pathology" (Lichtman, 1982, p. 267).

The traffic in this eternity is policed by the concepts of socialization, development, and internalization. The issue is not the precedence or weight of this or that dimension (social, cultural, developmental) in human becoming. Such logic already forfeits becoming differently human by changing nothing but the positionality, the traffic of the terms of being. The radical human desire is about being itself, as possibilities of the productive relations of living. This requires producing conditions to know "universal original multiplicity, which makes us so variegated that others become accessible and imaginable to us through some aspect of our own complex self" (Shweder, 1996, p. 24; 1991) and practicing the social revelatory experiences in the world that realize the play of becoming different.

IN AND OUT

The dominant approach to socialization is to theorize the existential condition (social life) as a problem of specific sociohistorical formulations of regenerativity or reproduction (formulations such as identities, families, roles, classes, institutions, society) that are realized internally in the developmental forms of subjects. Regenerativity entails induction, the incumbency of order and control: the integration of structural concerns of differentiated recruitment and of coordinated interactions, various allocations of functions and sanctions relevant to socialized performances (Giddens, 1979). Development takes place by the same logics and practices by which the subject becomes a space of social order and control—the internal forms of self-perpetuation, celebrated as socialization for the former and identification for the latter. Problems of social life are, then, problems of adjusting needs and satisfactions between the consumption requirements of development and the production requirements of social structure. Developmental psychology and sociology mediate this market space between the nature of development and the nurture of the social, middle-managing developmental demand and societal supply. Regeneration of social life becomes a principle, not a problem, and social relations become regulatory and inferential—the currencies of exchange between development and socialization for collective and individual futures. The existential conditions of social life are spaces of exchange, relatively valued and measured by contributions to development and socialization, promissory of induction into self and community and finally, civilization.

Order and control, proposed as the social foundation of regenerativity, may be addressed as a less structural-functional issue: as the "good society" derived from sociomoral epistemology and sentiments, integrating knowledge and will into common morality (Durkheim, 1961; Bellah, Madsen, Sullivan, Swidler, & Tipton, 1991; Alexander, 1995). Both entrances to social life, interaction and morality, are ramps from American Protestantism (Smith, 1970; Mills, 1970), which presents social life as preparation for an exit, as an attempt to systematize an ethics of "good works" by social perfecting, thereby consecrating the collective social entity in anticipation of eventual immortality (Weber, 1964; Bauman, 1992, pp. 7–8).

If there is presently an "end of sociological theory" and an evacuation of "the quest for foundations and for a totalizing theory of society" (Seidman, 1991, p. 131), the new beginning is simply at another end-beginning of the sociological tradition—the self. Regenerativity becomes the problem of perfecting an order and control of "'self' able to "live strongly in a weakly measured world" (Lemert, 1995, p. 95). The reciprocity of social structure and character reinstates order and control as discipline of the self, which realizes and reoriginates the problem of a productive social order from an alternative position. "Hence, the character structures of the people of a given epoch, or of a given social system are not only a mirror of this system. More significantly, they represent its anchoring" (Reich, 1972, p. xxiv). The interchangeability of subject and object, in constant supersession, so that the acquisition of subjectivity through the other completes in the subject being other, constitutes socialization. Socialization is the metabolism of referentiality. "By 'successful socialization' we mean the establishment of a high degree of symmetry between objective and subjective reality (as well as identity, of course)...socialization...may be defined as the comprehensive and consistent induction of an individual into the objective world of a society" (Berger & Luckmann, 1966, pp. 163, 130).

Socialization, then, is theorized as social technology, an exercise of structured action obtaining an internalization of values and motives constitutive of a social subject and the conditions of knowledge and knowing. In the same moment, socialization is an evocation of social transcendence, ever re-creating the objective world that allows the self and social orders to enter a more perfect future. Socialization is posited as necessary and contingent. The necessity appears twice for "good reason": in the sense of justification by the need to reproduce good subjects and good society and, second, as developmental potentiation of the capacities of reason to know the world and oneself objectively. The contingency appears as "good reason" in the costume of progress and transformation, in that "good reason" (aka science, logos, development) accumulates and propels knowledge phylogenetically and ontogenetically. Piaget's formulation of genesis ("simply a form of development")—"a relatively determined system of transformations comprising a history and leading in a continuous manner from state A to state B, state B being more stable than the initial state and being an extension of it" (1996 p. 144)—combines such appearances of necessity (a history) and appearance or contingency (transformations) into the dynamism of equilibrium. Equilibrium, "an intrinistic and constitutive property of organic and mental life," is Piaget's "fourth factor" (the others being maturation, physical environment, and social environment) that allows reason, "which expresses the highest forms of equilibrium," to compensate for the "external intrusions" of existence by the relatively autonomous activities on mind (ibid., pp. 102, 103, 70, 113).

Accordingly, socialization provides the necessary conditions that development must surpass to secure an "extratemporal structure," a necessary "*a priori* which is constituted only at the end not at the point of departure, as a resultant and not as a source and hence retains only the concept of necessity and not that of preformation" (Piaget, 1968, p. 157). While development requires socialization, socialization also needs development for a future, a "mobile equilibrium" (ibid., p. 4). The social is, for Piaget and developmentalism, analogous to the "essential difference between the life of the body and that of the mind." The development of the social or body and the mind both consist "essentially of activity directed toward equilibrium," but while the organic social or body reaches a static and unstable final form, "no sooner has ascending evolution terminated than a regressive evolution automatically starts"; the "dynamism inherent in the mind" is life eternal, genesis "emanating from structure and culminating in another structure" (ibid., pp. 3, 147).

Socialization and development induct and regenerate life as logos via this onward genesis, this animating mobility of reason, outside the presence of the flesh and the external intrusions of death. The fatal flaw of such genesis is living, for, as premodernist and postmodernist cosmologies propose, the metaphysics of mind are ways of being in place, or, in this case, out of place. "In the concept of mind-in-itself, consciousness has

ontologically justified and perpetuated privilege by making it independent of the social principle by which it is constituted" (Adorno, 1994, p.
132).

However, the importance of situated cognition has fostered a wave of
"person-centered" theory in developmental psychology, stressing context
and agency of self-narrativity during interpretative practices (Tappan and
Packer, 1991; Cole, 1992; Corsaro and Miller, 1992; Corsaro, 1996;
Damon, 1996; Poole, 1994):

> The interpretative approach views development as reproductive rather than
> linear. Children do not merely internalize individually the external adult
> culture. Rather, they become part of adult culture—that is, they contribute
> to its reproduction—through their negotiations with adults and their cre-
> ative production of a series of peer cultures with other children. (Corsaro,
> 1996, p. 420)

From these approaches, stressing the indeterminacy of individual distinctions, enculturation is formulated as "population-specific codes of
conduct" (LeVine, 1990, p.113) that are individualized by utility—use in
specific contexts of learning—thereby obtaining socialization in practice.
The subject becomes the analogue of multiple contexts, "person-self-
individual" (Poole, 1994), translating the role divisions of structuralism
into processual divisions of the subject.

> Developmentalists today typically wish to describe and analyze *as process* the
> sequence of changes that take place *within the individual* who participates in
> a particular set of practices; or, as a concession to environment, to under-
> stand development as a process taking place in the individual and her imme-
> diate interpersonal systems....Context bears much of the burden of post-
> positivist social science to understand human phenomena as historically sit-
> uated, and to interpret the meanings with which individuals carry on their
> daily lives, reproducing society but with unpredicatable inflections.
> (Modell, 1996, p. 493–494).

The moving picture of context becomes a developmental phenakisto-
scope (the deceptive appearance of action by rapid sequences of variant
positions); methodological animation substitutes for the life of the social
in action. "What is absent is a sense of social action.... Personality is a
resultant quality....Context is there, but it is not engaged" (Modell,
1996, p. 495). Context is postulated as a problematic environment to be

solved by cognitive constructions while the solutions already completed by context are occluded. Context, understood as embodiment-in-place and relationality-in-time, is the denied social unconscious that returns in theory and practice as a symptom: a problem of interaction.

As development becomes cognitively processual in events and contexts, socialization parallels with internal referentiality as "the line of development": "the only significant connecting thread is the life trajectory as such. Personal integrity, as the achievement of an authentic self, comes from integrating self-experiences within the narrative of self-development: the creation of a personal belief system" (Giddens, 1991, p. 80). The principle of the market—"Free dependence" (Lichtmann, 1982, p. 219)—releases the subject to what is left inside: an ideational private property. "The destiny made of subjectivity...has become the equivalent to its suppression" (Santamaria & Manville, 1992, p. 415).

This internal destiny of the subject—completion in an autogenetic project of internalization—is a moment of fating the social in the historical, "cultural drama of parturition" (Bordo, 1987, p. 59), which is at once bearing evolution as a holism of cultural development and bearing "the human being...as a decisively separate entity, no longer continuous with a universe which has now become decisively 'other' to it" (Bordo, 1987, p. 70). No longer at home in the world, the social emerges through its "inwordness"—by self-conscious referentiality that depends on the the co-location of same-selves likewise self-referential—to an "outwardness" of knowledge. The social construal, then, becomes both things out there, appearances of socializing language and symbolic action, and things in there, intentions/meanings/consciousness behind the appearances. Being known is being saved from the mortality of existence out there; being known is, finally, being safely self-conscious in the analogical minds of others while aware of being oneself. The immortality of consciousness requires ceaseless telepathic bi-location: "life in the late capitalist era is a constant initiation rite. Everyone must show that he wholly identifies himself with the power which is belaboring him" (Horkheimer & Adorno, 1993, p. 153).

Both the self and the social become monological (Taylor, 1995). Socialization presents the co-destiny of chicken and egg, as Piaget (1968, 41, 42) describes the (non-) "transformation" to "logic that constitutes the system of relationships which permit the coordination of points of view corresponding to different individuals":

Reflection is nothing other than internal deliberation, that is to say, a discussion which is conducted with oneself just as it might be conducted with real interlocutors or opponents. One could say that reflection is internalized social discussion (just as thought itself presupposes internalized language)....Contrariwise, socialized discussion might also be described as externalized reflection. Since all human conduct is both social and individual, this problem, like all analogous questions, comes back to whether the chicken appears before the egg or the egg before the chicken.

The co-completion of internal and external—of self-reflection twice—of inside-outside social referentiality produces the organism of development. Growth of knowledge fulfills maturity and is progenitively permanent, while failure is entropic ignorance: a death of representational animation, of likeness and a death of the "onword" order of time. Difference becomes regression, pathology, retardation, or death of self and of a social future. Difference, whether inchoate or terminal, is primitive. Immaturity is the inability to survive (Horkheimer & Adorno, 1993, p. 83). Genocide colludes with ontogenetic and phylogenetic classification, the complement of psychic and social dissociation (Brantlinger, 1995; Vitebsky, 1993; Gilman, 1985). The "great chain of being" (Lovejoy, 1964) of developmentalism—the necessary plentitude of classifiable beings and the complementary graduation of ontological order—is alloyed with modern "diversitarianism" (ibid., 294) in the synergy of romantic capitalism. The Romantic "evolution of the individual" (Wilshire, 1968) is crucial to the establishment of self-consciousness as the conduit and realization of knowledge regarding self and the world, as both process and product of socialization and development:

> The disenchantment of the external world required as a parallel process some "enchantment" of the psychic, inner world....The growth of self-consciousness had, as one of its many consequences, the effect of severing any remaining necessary connection between man's place in the world and his reaction to it. Objective reality and subjective response were now mediated through consciousness in such a way that the individual had a wide degree of choice. (Campbell, 1989, p. 73)

The constituted oppositions of knowledge/ignorance, nature/culture, and self/other present difference as outside or peripheral and the inherent periphery as temporally, spatially and, ontologically primary (Ortner, 1974). Distance from difference becomes the position of knowledge and safety; the panoptic center view from no place becomes, telescopically, most certain. The "bomb's-eye view" of intelligent technology, in the classroom as satellite, is the propaedeutic position of the elevated self, returning to autogenetic mastery of both informational creation and social relationality: "Since technology is already a crystallization of selfhood—of the constitutive, transcendental framework of subjectivity itself—identification is not just a discovery but a rediscovery. This finding thus mimics the propaedeutic experience of acquiring the object of desire, which psychoanalysis shows us is always a return to an earlier, lost object" (Broughton, 1996, p. 148). Hide and seek becomes both the internal and external structure of relationality and motivation.

The full colonizing implications of this "ego-ocular-verbocentrism" (Romanyshyn, 1993, p. 340) are examined elsewhere. (Bordo, 1987; Levin, 1985; Buck-Morss, 1992; Lowe, 1982; Dwyer, 1996). The implications concern the co-formation of evil (as defilement and servility of will) and of uniformity of knowledge (as good and salvational). Development and socialization practice eternity in deference to a past and a future, in part by transportation of the saved into safe knowledge, constantly correcting the different facts of existence by socializing the present into uniformity with a past and a future.

Ricoeur (1969, pp. 155–156) describes a triple schema of evil as defilement (as suggested above, difference is indicative of defilement): "positiveness" in the sense of a posited force to be removed; "seduction" in the sense of active, outside enticement; "infection" in the bad choice of contact, entailing "that seduction from the outside is ultimately an infection of the self by the self, an autoinfection, by which the act of binding oneself is transformed into being bound." The excitement for making safe schools, for the glory of canon, for disciplinary seclusion, for early enrollment in custody, for model teachers, for standards, for excellence, for the educational priority can be partly understood as a crusade of good against evil, of knowledge against embodiment, rational regulation against the peripheral.

Similarly, the excitement for brain-wiring education (intervening in "primal nature") is partly the "fascination for the elementary modes of matter," "a desire for deliverance from the weight of dead forms" (Eliade, 1976, p. 17), in an occult nostalgia for a domestication of the genome—the recovery of a better beginning or first nature; "from sociobiology to biosociality" (Rainbow, 1992), the new millennium is approached in reverse, redoing creation.

The popular, positive conceptual heroes of "developmental plasticity" and "resilience" require developmental destinations (Toulmin, 1981) in order to qualify for the Olympics of the human. Generational, racial and gendered differences are measured by analogical universals that are unchanged by an inclusion that requires the directionality—a measuring up. The "verdict of reality" remains while the site of failure shifts in context (biopsychosocial); the complexities of contexts are titrated to evolving standards of development molded to inclusive ideals but not contrary possibilities.

The commodification of knowledge, separated from the places and performances of living and being used as an abstract value of exchange, permits development in both Piaget's genetic epistemology and Vygotsky's evolutionary history: Knowledge negates ignorance through the necessity of experience over time and accumulates as development, in terms of solvency and sovereignty from differences in experience. Experience needs to be added up involutionally and evolutionally, in order to be the basis (product) of development and socialization. Knowledge, the simultaneous reification of experience and concept, circulates between consumption and production, creating needs of its own perpetuity in and for the owners. Knowledge, as the annuity of development and socialization over lifetimes and over "human-time," places the present as a "pernicious chasm" to be crossed, but not to become different from what it is. "But reality is not, it becomes.... The truth of becoming is the future that is to be created but has not been born.... For a possibility to be realized, for a tendency to become actual, what is required is that the objective components of a society should be transformed" (Lukas, 1971, p. 204). Transforming reality into a present becoming is a transformation of the productive conditions of knowing, not the state of knowledge or the distributional allotments among modalities and shareholders. The social relations of consciousness, as processes of becoming real, are materially active. "The only way to think of consciousness without separating it from the organism or banning it to some kind of forum internum is to insist on its sensuous nature" (Tyler, 1987, p. 161).

SAFE CARNILITY: THE RHYTHM METHOD

The logic definitional of developmentalism—universality, unidirectionality, sequentiality, telos, irreversibility, qualitative or structural change, optimality, endogenous motive (Lerner, 1976; Damon, 1996)—is the "policy science" (Bruner, 1986b, p. 20) of a "logic of domination": "between the beginning and the end is the development of reason as the logic of domination—progress through alienation...in the idea and in the ideal" (Marcuse, 1962, p. 107). Dealienation is degenerative of this historical destruction of social life: "The consummation of being is, not the ascending curve, but the closing of the circle: the re-turn from alienation" (ibid.). The perpetuity of alienation is premised on the unity of development and socialization in a denial of life and death, securing safety from the social politics of sensual existence in the present. The alienated present cannot become but only convey as the transaction of a past and future.

Giddens (1979, pp. 120, 128–130) attempts to "connect together" the subject and object as a "duality of structure" in a way avoidant of determinacy but regenerative of social order:

> The reflexive monitoring of action draws upon and reproduces forms of tacit and discursively available knowledge: continuity of social reproduction involves the continual "regrooving" of established attitudes and cognitive outlooks holding down potential sources of anxiety in the basic security system. "Socialization" should be understood as an element of the continuity of social reproduction—of the inherent temporality of social process...as the succession of the generations.

The critical insight of Giddens is the existential, gravitational meaning ("holding down anxiety in the basic security system") of socialization. Bernstein makes it clear: "In a sense then socialization is a process for making people *safe*" (1972, p. 162; emphasis added). Making safety is obtained by emptying the social of life while identifying living with internal-external perpetuity, with sharing secrets over generations. The safety of false contradiction, the facade of possibility between the egg and the chicken, development and socialization, creates the social space for a plausible denial of becoming.

Developmental science is an "ontic device" (Bruner, 1986b) for systematically forgetting origins in the sufferance of possibilities in history, a promise that converts into a contract. "The loss of memory is a transcendental condition for science. All objectification is a forgetting" (Horkheimer & Adorno, 1993, p. 230). Theorization of development and socialization is both a product of a historical social order and the perpetuation of a historical order and control, deferring demise in the assurance of immortality by fetishizing the commodity of socialization: the reproduction of human likeness in the endurance of social order. Fate is reassured as need.

Socialization theories may be regarded as creation myths, as "expressions of a mode of being in the world" (Eliade, 1960, p. 24), by which the origin and ending of being human are teleologically composed into practices of life. The creation myth of socialization motivates a need, in the "middle-time" of living, for noncontamination, to purify feeling-seeing-touching, to avert diseases of living and so complete life's projects.[1] The recitation of the species distinctions made to recall special mythological purpose in human creation to put nonhuman to the past in time, to put nonhuman to use for a human future.[2] The union of the human with the social is known against the negativity of nature (Eder, 1990; Alanen, 1990; James, 1995; Jenks, 1996). The succession of nature by social ontology combines with propositions of order and progress to construct "open, quantitative growth models" of both individual and societal development.[3]

In contrast to the cyclic presence of being-in-time based on the existence of an eternal return of the rebeginning of cosmic creation ("to relive the psychic shock and bring it into consciousness" [Eliade, 1959, p. 53]), the social psychology of "present-time" is that of being in the historical middle of nature-past and human-future. This is the image of what Kermode (1966, p. 17) terms the "middest":

> Men in the middest make considerable imaginative investments in coherent patterns which, by the provision of an end, make possible a satisfying consonance with the origins and with the middle. That is why the image of the end can never be permanently falsified. But they also, when awake and sane, feel the need to show a marked respect for things as they are; so that there is a recurring need for adjustments in the interest of reality as well as of control.

Social space between generations is the middle-time of regenerativity wherein socialization operates to deny finality of the present. Time lived in the "middle" and the spent life become exchange value for immortality. The social space of self-consciousness exists as self-socialization—progenitive reflective time to "achieve" an "ego-integrity," to integrate an interior order of meaning with the superordinate transfer of reproductive control. Erikson (1963, p. 268) describes this "ripening of the fruit" of "him who has taken care of things and people and has adapted himself to the triumphs and disappointment [that] adhere to being":

> It is the acceptance of one's one and only life cycle as something that had to be, and that, by necessity permitted not substitutions.... For he knows that an individual life is the accidental coincidence of but one life cycle with but

one segment of history; and that for him all human integrity stands and falls with the one style of integrity of which he partakes. The style of integrity developed by his culture or civilization thus becomes the "patrimony of his soul," the seal of his moral paternity of himself. In such final consolidation, death loses its sting.

The final consolidation or socialization of oneself is personal maturation of what was assigned by necessity, accepted as self-generation, and which in turn is consolidated by life's placement in the successive coherence of civilization. Becoming finally socialized is experiencing integrity by creatively having "infantile conflicts...sustained by the firm support of cultural institutions and the special leader classes representing them...the individual must know how to be a follower of image bearers in religion and politics" (ibid., p. 269). Common culture is modeled as the "good-enough" mother to wean the self to eternity (Kotre, 1996, p. 261). Social value is ultimately divorced from life itself and becomes the obligation of self; social value in living "lets go" of times and places and nicely resigns itself to thereafter (Lichtman, 1987).[4]

HEADS AND MOUTHS

The mobile transposition of subject and object, proceeding from conversations to self-reflexive monologues or self-consciousness, is a bidirectional synthesis: "The study of language development in general and semantic development in particular is basically a problem in the acquisition of culture" (Nelson, 1985, p. 250), and "language acquisition appears to be a by-product (and a vehicle) of culture transmission.... The engine that drives the enterprise is not language acquisition per se, but the need to get on with the demands of the culture" (Bruner, 1983, p. 103). Development and socialization progress by the subject becoming the other that is acquired and is, thereby, acquired by the other. From the acquisition of the developmental capacity to know oneself as the object of another and others as objects of oneself, socialization is transposed into social cognition, as representational processes of socially relevant legislative and regulative meanings attributable to inner states of the other (Astington, 1993; Damon, 1978; Uzgiris, 1979). The development of a theory of mind (Astington, Harris, & Olson, 1988) is the development of role-taking capacity or mind reading, which influences understanding of social interaction (Flapan, 1968). The Kantian postulate of Piagetian psychology of transcendental structures of reason,[5] which, in utilization of experience, equilibrate the resistance of life's vagaries into ever more formal and abstract laws of logic, submits the social life to cooperation and reciprocity while ensuring that reason escapes the concrete, particular imperfections of experience.[6] Reason becomes the abstract exchange-value proxy of eternity (Buck-Morss, 1979). Cooperation and reciprocity are contingent on decentration: "The more he can decentrate himself the more active is the subject, or, to say it better, his decentration is the very measure of his effective activity on the object" (Piaget, quoted in Battro, 1973, p. 45). The conditions for cooperative sociability are "the *sui generis* product of a life lived in common" so that, reason notwithstanding, the reciprocity of the subject depends on his/her grouping ("to decenter means 'to group'" [ibid.]) with the social order:

> But for true equality and a genuine desire for reciprocity there must be a collective rule which is the *sui generis* product of life lived in common. There must be born of the actions and reactions of individuals upon each other the consciousness of a necessary equilibrium binding upon and limiting both "alter" and "ego" (Piaget, 1965, p. 318).

The immanent circularity (the social originates out of itself) (Horkheimer & Adorno, 1993, p. 21) of decentration and the autonomy of reason yield the regenerative vertigo of development and socialization. Socialization, from these premises, is the *simulation* of relationship in that the unification of the subject and object is already the substance of relation. Social order and control reappear in the development of reason, which re-creates a like-mindedness, an intermental literacy or Meadian conscience. Reason changes nothing because the productive social relations are unchanged:

> Reason is supposed to create the universality and community in which the rational subject participates with other rational subjects. This is the basis of the possiblity that, beyond the encounter of merely self-sufficient monads, a common life develops in a common world. But even this achievement does not lead beyond what already exists. It changes nothing. For the constitution of the world has always been effected prior to the actual action of the individual....In a world without reason, reason is only the semblance of rationality; in a state of general unfreedom, freedom is only the semblance of being free. (Marcuse, 1989, pp. 60–61)

The redundancy of development and socialization effectuates a semblance of social life: "imitation enters into the service of domination inasmuch as even man is anthropomorphized for man.... The striking unity of the microcosm and macrocosm presents men with a model of their culture: the false identity of the particular and the general" (Horkheimer & Adorno, 1993, pp. 57, 121–122). Continuity of culture and continuity of self are alloyed, so changes of either are developments (or regressions) based on the connectivity with co-order (Kagan, 1983); therefore advancement of either culture or self complements what already is indexed in the relations of origination.

The communicative pragmatism of sociocultural mediation of mind (Wertsch, 1991) offers a heterogeneity of situationally indexed practices that facilitate various uses of mediational means or languages in social action so that setting, voice, and mediated action are synthetic and not predetermined by genetic, hierarchical need. But appropriateness of speech and speech genre convert the legislation of language practices into improvisational regulation. Difference is reduced to what is talked about; change reduced to how we talk about it; freedom reduced to a forum. Discourse epistemologies put our lives where our mouths are, deconstructing signification only to reintroduce communication as humanization. Social learning is merely rerouted, without behavioristic mechanics, but as a generic, ontogenic, practical value, as in Tomasello and colleagues' "cultural learning" and in Bugental and Goodnow's depiction of socialization:

> Cultural learning is a uniquely human form of social learning that allows for a fidelity of transmission of behaviors and information among conspecifics not possible in other forms of social learning, thereby providing the psychological basis for cultural evolution. (Tomasello, Kruger, & Ratner, 1993, p. 485)

> In the course of experience with others, people develop competencies in living and working together. They come to share—or at least to anticipate—each others' ways of acting, thinking and feeling. Socialization is the term used to describe the process by which these accomplishments occur....Socialization may be defined as the continuous collaboration of "elder" and "novices," of "old hands" and "newcomers" in the acquisition and honing of skills important for meeting the demands of group life. (Bugental & Goodnow, in press)

The ideals of development are replaced with an abstract propensity for a reskilling, collaborative culture, a retraining design in the shifting evolutionary-cultural job market. Situated practice and contextualized development are the temporary services of postindustrial employment of social relationality without contract, as job- or task-specific.

LOVING ONE'S SELF

Developmentalism formalizes a historical lifestyle that "learns to love what...reason recognizes to be a fact" (Horkheimer, 1992b, p. 101), that is, to love internal domination as self-determination (Lichtman, 1987). The integrity of the self is the interiorization of this social reality, which denies any need for the self to exist except as the execution of the principle of fulfillment. There is only the accommodation of decentering the self into the center of the social object, which refutes the self's presence and life except as part of the object's identity (of course, this also creates the illicit as a field of transgressive desire, siphoning pleasure into alternative industries). At this point, the self is "autonomous" and exists in the consciousness of its representation or is an object to its consciousness. The paucity of vital social poesis and the illegitimacy of a predicative social imaginary that colludes with experience *requires self-conscious alienation to be social experience.* Social life is spectatorial. The character structure is the ready regression of *internalized* love (relearning to love oneself over and over as subjective reproduction) and mobilized, *externalized* hate (relearning to hate the rejected selves/others, which are projective negations of identification or which are unsocialized).[7] The character structure is felt psychologically as an interior life and thought of therapeutically as self-management, while the externalized social is projected as unrequited desires for possessive knowledge and control. The social is contracted into an increasingly idealized culture of self, taking refuge in an interior formed by externalizing its demons. Such projective relationality is also the productive characterological anchor of such reality by fetishizing the self's social production.[8] Demons and dreams, severed from imaginable originations in social relations, work as alienated desires, consuming excitements of social relations. Consolidations of self and social order are hygienic of each—sanitizations that clean the past and sterilize the present by producing private symptoms and public entertainments.

The prevailing need is to outlive the incipient incineration of the providence of history threatened with the next dissolute moment and appearance of difference—the loss of momentum and positional order. It is a specific sort of desire for "ontological security" premised on a specific sort of "existential anxiety" that impels the "lifestyle" of late modernity to dispel both fate and risk by ceaseless interpretation, touristic self-expeditions (Giddens, 1991, pp. 34–143; Bauman, 1992). Generational positionality becomes preparation for immortality by the interactive, simultaneous developmental identifications of subjects: parent/child, young/old, and so on. In this socialized opposition, each position is perpetuated by the succession and excesses of the other. By obtaining adaptation on the systematic levels and adjustment on the individual levels, social reproduction surpasses itself.

Socialization, from this view, is a mode of social regeneration by which the historical character of the mortality of social relationships works to produce a specific need for safety, and the character of such safety works to redetermine the nature of immortality as social necessity. Developmentalism, in turn, is a culture of immortality for the timed being, ending history by endless hegemonic transferral of knowledges. Self-perpetuation requires a legacy of recollective and corrective self-perfection; social perfection requires a history of progress, a necessary future. The social relations of mind-culture are anonymously universal:

> The human social ideal—the ideal or ultimate goal of human social progress—is the attainment of a universal society in which all human individuals would possess a perfect social intelligence, such that all social meanings would each be similarly reflected in their respective individual consciousness—such that the meanings of any one individual's acts or gestures (as realized by him and expressed in the structure of his self, through his ability to take the social attitudes of other individuals toward himself and toward their common social ends or purposes) would be the same for any other individual whatever who responded to them. (Mead, 1934, p. 310)

The predominant theoretical premises of socialization and development duplicate the *loss* of the social in the conditions of living, eternally returning as natural the absences of places and experiential times in which and by which social imagination may constitute and reconstitute social life. Despite the valuable efforts involving the interpretive processes of socialization (Gaskins, Miller, & Corsaro, 1992, p. 9; Miller, 1994), the processes are miniaturized and maintain "productive-reproductive" (Gaskins, Corsaro, & Miller, 1992, p. 7) currents of socialization and development.[9] Social imposition is replaced with situated intimacy. Meaning serves as the advertisement of knowledge, offering personalization of the commodity and diversification of the market.

In reproductive socialization and development, the order and coherence of social experience is dependent on the mediation of representational signs to a transcendental reality: the production of language references meaning both to and from a common mind. Intersubjectivity is predicated by the common denomination of subjectivity and subjection. That which is silent, sensual, and unspeakable is unsociable. Once, however, the cosmic split between mind and body, formal and material, history and spirit, and past and future is closed, intersubjectivity is opened to an alchemy of differences, to a performativity of social presence that is incarnate in acts of life.[10] A negation of socialization, as the mode of social reproduction of a priori conditions of subjectivity and objectivity, needs to affirm the ecstatic, agonized generation of intersubjectvity, an embodied betweeness and fullness of imagination (Hastrup, 1995; Berger & Mohr, 1982, pp. 99–100). The ineffable betweenness is a decentered verb of full plurality that is neither one thing nor the other but is embraced by the differences between what is and resists the bliss of containment and preservation (Tyler, 1987).

Ecologies of life-times and cohabitations of life-places know a tranversal unification of presence in now-time. "The concept of transversal unification...illustrates a dynamic and open-textured process of unifying that allows for plurality and difference and neither seeks the metaphysical comforts of stable beginnings and universal telic principles nor displays an epistemological enchantment with zero-point epistemic foundations" (Scrag, 1997, p. 129). The project of social imagination is "a new kind of holism, one that is emergent rather than given...neither a theoretical object nor an object of theoretical knowledge...nether evoked by explicit methods nor the derivational source of practices. It does not motivate or enable practice in the expected manner of the usual theory-practice correlation.... It aims not to foster the growth of knowledge but to restructure experience" (Tyler, 1987, pp. 209–210, 212). "The unity of time is no longer guaranteed by our roots in the past and our memories nor by projects for the future; it is secured only by our capacity to be present in the now-time" (Melucci, 1996, p. 22).

The basis of this embodied primary social imaginary is the sensual constitution of relational knowing in the world itself. Emerging in negation of developmentalism as a way out to eternity are ways in, practices in eternity.

NOTES

Philip Wexler kindled and tended this work. I am grateful.

1. Lévi-Strauss (1969, 162) describes myths about the loss of immortality as having two very different sensual relations with existence: "In the set of myths dealing with the loss of immortality, the mortality of man is viewed from two different angles; it is looked at prospectively and retrospectively.

Is it possible to avert death—that is, to prevent men from dying sooner than they want to? And conversely, is it possible to restore men's youth once they have grown old, or to bring them back to life if they have already died? The solution to the first problem is always formulated in negative terms: do not hear, do not feel, do not touch, do not see, do not taste.... The solution to the second problem is always expressed positively: hear, feel, touch, see, taste. On the other hand, the first solution applies only to men, since plants and animals have their own method of avoiding death, which is to become young again by changing their skins. Some myths consider only the human state and can therefore be read in one direction only—prospective continuance of life, negative injunction; others contrast the human state with that of creatures or entities that grow young again and can be read in both directions—prospectively and retrospectively, negatively and positively."

2. "The patterns of humanity's way of looking at nature finally reflect on and determine the imaging of humans in the human mind and eliminate the last objective goal that might motivate the process.... The entire universe becomes a toll of the ego, although the ego has no substance or meaning except in its own boundless activity" (Horkheimer, 1992a, p. 108).

3. "Quantitative growth models imply a continuous progression toward an abstract achievement ideal.... Growth consists in the acquisition of bits and pieces of information, habits or experiences that are being accumulated in the subject's repertoire, making him or her increasingly more able. If, at a given time, problems cannot be resolved, the individual will have to acquire more information so that he finally will be able to succeed" (Riegel, 1976, p. 76–77). See also Bauman, 1992, pp. 1–25.

4. Eliade is insightful here in regard to the interiorization of space and time in "irreversible time": "The primordial could only mean one's earliest childhood, the true individual initium.... For modern man...when the psyche comes to a crisis, it is to infancy that he must return in order to relive, and confront anew" (1960, p. 53).

5. Bernstein (1983, p. 8) describes this as "objectivism": "the basic conviction that there is or must be some permanent, ahistorical matrix or framework to which we can ultimately appeal in determining the nature of rationality, knowledge, truth, reality, goodness, or rightness."

6. "Mind builds its knowledge structures by taking external data and interpreting them, transforming them, and reorganizing them. It does meet with the environment in the process of constructing its knowledge, and consequently that knowledge is to a degree 'realistic' or adaptive for the organism....The mind meets the environment in an extremely active, self-directed way—more than halfway, as it were" (Flavel, 1977, p. 6). Furth (1987) is insightful in comparing Freud, who "psychologized" biology, with Piaget, who "biologized" logical reason with his dynamic of equilibrium so that knowledge is a needful desire, prefiguring its object.

7. This process is instanced in Anderson's work on nationalism (1983) and in Western desocialization of nature and woman (Ortner, 1974; Mills, 1987; O'Flaherty, 1988). See also Diamond, 1967.

8. "The contradiction between a high degree of self-representation and a negotiated socially sensitive field-dependent self is a modern psychological version of the classic contradiction between private ownership and social production" (Wexler, 1996a, p. 132). As self becomes more bio-nature and states of self-ownership less private, being chemically prescribed and, hence, less ideal and more securable (diagnosable as bio-psychosocial *effect*, not production), subjectivity becomes self-touring, a dynamic of postmodern replacement of history with rationalized simultaneity (Bauman, 1992).

9. "The interpretive approach views development as a process of children's appropriation of their culture. Children enter into a social system and, by interacting and negotiating with others, establish understandings that become fundamental social knowledge on which they continually build. Thus, the interpretive model refines the linear notion of stages by viewing development as a productive reproductive process of increasing density and reorganization of knowledge that changes with the children's developing cognitive and language abilities and with changes in their social world" (Corsaro & Rizzo, 1988, pp. 880–881).

10. Presence, as Wexler (1996b, pp. 123–132) indicates, is a potentially redemptive socialization that imaginatively revises sacred revelations, a "collective uncovering," which (unlike the usual conception of ritual as integrative and regulative social restatements of what is) is both "shattering" and "gathering" of what appears to be—presence is iconoclastic and receptive. Presence, in this social ontological sense, denies the necessity of historical repitition by recognizing histories that are hidden, silenced, or unheard while vitalizing or "renewing" the possibilities of historical being. There is here a transcendence of context as a situational environment or "zone of proximal development" or experiential experiment in the relationality of recognition, even as limited as the instance of eyes meeting in betrayal of the logic of what is being done to each other. The cultural incitements possible from numinal experiences has a deep complex history in charismatic, often revolutionary movements. "Inner-worldly mysticism" (Wexler, 1996b) is contrasted anthropologically as "spirit" to "gods" (Mageo & Howard, 1996; Weber, 1964, pp. 1–31). The crucial point is that "what is primarily distinctive in this whole development is not the personality, impersonality, or superpersonality of these supernatural powers, but the fact that *new* experiences *now play a role in life*." (Weber, 1964, p. 6; emphasis added). My argument for a different understanding of socialization responds to such experiences as both insurgent in contemporary culture (including sociological theory) and primary to social life. Presence describes the nascent experience of intersubjectivity that is also the analytic space composed to

allow account of it. The concept does not deconstruct the typical terms of socialization—internalization, communication, learning—into a generic transaction, as psychoanalytic poststructuralism tends to with the interpellation or reflux of desire into idealogy. Presence is not transparent to psychic desire or social power. Presence is sociotropy in the sense of turning toward being in relationship and the literary sense of a trope calling to an experience beyond literal meaning.

REFERENCES

Adorno, T. W. (1974). *Minima moralia*. New York: Verso.

Adorno, T. W. (1994). *The stars down to earth*. New York: Routledge.

Alanen, L. (1990). "Rethinking socialization, the family and childhood." *Sociological Studies of Child Development*, 3, 13–28.

Alexander, J. C. (1995). *Fin de siècle social theory*. London: Verso.

Anderson, B. (1983). *Imagined communities*. London: Verso.

Astington, J. W. (1993). *The child's discovery of the mind*. Cambridge, MA: Harvard University Press.

Astington, J. W., Harris, P. L., & Olson, D. R. (Eds.). (1988). *Developing theories of the mind*. New York: Cambridge University Press.

Battro, A. M. (1973). *Piaget: Dictionary of terms*. New York: Pergamon.

Bauman, Z. (1992). *Morality, immorality and other life strategies*. Stanford, CA: Stanford University Press.

Bellah, R. N., Madsen, R., Sullivan, W. M., Swidler, A., & Tipton, S. M. (1991). *The good society*. New York: Alfred A. Knopf.

Bercovitch, S. (1993). The rites of assent. NY: Routledge.

Berger, J., & Mohr, J. (1982). *Another way of telling*. New York: Pantheon Books.

Berger, P. L., & Luckmann, T. (1966). *The social construction of reality*. New York: Anchor Books.

Bernstein, B. (1972). "Social class, language and socialization." In P. P. Giglioli (Ed.), *Language and social context* (pp. 157–178). London: Penguin.

Bernstein, R. J. (1983). *Beyond objectivism and relativism*. Philadelphia: University of Pennsylvania Press.

Bloom, H. (1992). The American religion: the emergence of the post-christian nation. New York: Simon and Schuster.

Bordo, S. (1987). *The flight to objectivity*. Albany: State University of New York Press.

Brantlinger, P. (1995). "'Dying races': Rationalizing genocide in the nineteenth century." In J. Nederveen Pieterse & B. Parekh, *The decolonization of imagination: Culture, knowledge and power* (pp. 22–42). London: Zed.

Broughton, J. (1996). "The bomb's-eye view: Smart weapons and miltitary TV." In S. Aronowitz, B. Martinson, & M. Menser (Eds.), *Technoscience and cyberculture* (pp. 139–166). New York: Routledge.

Bruner, J. (1983). *Child's talk.* New York: W. W. Norton.

Bruner, J. (1986). "Value presuppositions of developmental theory." In L. Cirillo & S. Wapner, (Eds.), *Value presuppositions in theories of human development* (pp. 19–28). Hillsdale, NJ: Lawrence Erlbaum.

Buck-Morss, S. (1979). "Socioeconomic bias in Piaget's theory." In A. R. Buss (Ed.), *Psychology in social context* (pp. 349–364). New York: Irvington.

Buck-Morss, S. (Fall, 1992). "Aesthetics and anaesthetics: Walter Benjamin's artwork essay reconsidered." *October, 62,* 3–41.

Bugental, D. Blunt, & Goodnow, J. (In press). "Socialization processes." In W. Damon (Ed.), *Handbook of child psychology* (5th ed.). New York: Wiley.

Cairns, R., Costello, J., & Elder, G. Jr. (1996). "Developmental science: A collaborative statement (The Carolina consortium on human development)." In R. Cairns, G. Elder, & J. Costello, (Eds.), *Developmental science* (pp.1–6). New York: Cambridge University.

Campbell, C. (1989). *The romantic ethic and the spirit of modern consumerism.* Oxford: Blackwell.

Cole, M. (1992). "Context, modularity, and the cultural constitution of development." In L. T. Winegar, & J. Valsiner, (Eds.), *Children's development within social context,* Volume 2 (pp. 5–32). Hillsdale, NJ: Lawrence Erlbaum.

Corsaro, W., & Rizzo, T. (December, 1988). "Discussion and friendship: Socialization processes in the peer culture of Italian nursery school children." *American Sociological Review, 53,* 879–894.

Corsaro, W. (1996). "Transitions in early childhood: The promise of comparative, longitudinal ethnography." In R. Jessor, A. Colby, & R. Shweder (Eds.), *Ethnography and human development: Context and meaning in social inquiry* (pp. 419–458). Chicago, IL: University of Chicago Press.

Corsaro, W., & Miller, P. (Eds.). (1992). *Interpretative approaches to children's socialization.* San Francisco: Jossey-Bass.

Damon, W. (1996). "Nature, second nature, and individual development: An ethnographic opportunity." In R. Jessor, A. Colby, & R. Shweder, (Eds.), *Ethnography and human development: Context and meaning in social inquiry.* (pp. 459–478). Chicago, IL: University of Chicago Press.

Damon, W. (Ed.). (1978). *New directions for child development: Social cognition.* San Francisco: Jossey-Bass.

Diamond, S. (1967). "Primitive society in its many dimensions." In K. Wolff, & B. Moore, Jr. (Eds.), *The critical spirit* (pp. 21–30). Boston: Beacon.

Durkheim, E. (1961). *Moral education.* New York: The Free Press,

Dwyer, P. (1996). "The invention of nature." In *Redefining nature: Ecology, culture and domestication* (pp. 157–186). Oxford: Berg.

Eder, K. (1990). "The cultural code of modernity and the problem of nature: A critique of the naturalistic notion of progress." In J. Alexander, & P. Sztompka (Eds.), *Rethinking progress* (pp. 67–88). Winchester, MA: Unwin Hyman.

Eliade, M. (1960). *Myths, dreams, and mysteries.* New York: Harper & Row.

Eliade, M. (1976). *Occultism, witchcraft, and cultural fashions.* Chicago: University of Chicago Press.

Erikson, E. H. (1963). *Childhood and society.* New York: W. W. Norton.

Fabian, J. (1994). "Ethnographic objectivity revisited: From rigor to vigor." In A. Megill (Ed.), *Rethinking objectivity* (pp. 81–108). Durham, NC: Duke University Press.

Flapan, D. (1968). *Children's understanding of social interaction.* New York: Teachers College Press.

Flavell, J. (1977). *Cognitive development.* Englewood Cliffs, NJ: Prentice-Hall.

Furth, H. G. (1987). *Knowledge as desire.* New York: Columbia University Press.

Gaskins, S., Miller, P., & Corsaro, W. (1992). "Theoretical and methodological perspectives in the interpretive study of children." In W. Corsaro & P. Miller (Eds.), *Interpretive approaches to children's socialization* (pp. 5–24). San Francisco: Jossey-Bass.

Giddens, A. (1979). *Central problems in social theory.* Berkeley: University of California Press.

Giddens, A. (1991). *Modernity and self-identity.* Stanford: Stanford University Press.

Gilman, S. (1985). *Difference and pathology: stereotypes of sexuality, race, and madness.* Ithaca, NY: Cornell University Press.

Hastrup, K. (1995). "The inarticulate mind: The place of awareness in social action." In A. P. Cohen & N. Rapport (Eds.), *Questions of consciousness* (pp. 181–197). New York: Routledge.

Herman, E. (1995). *The romance of American psychology: Political culture in the age of experts.* Berkeley: University of California Press.

Horkheimer, M., & Adorno, T. W. (1993). *Dialectic of enlightenment.* New York: Continuum.

Horkheimer, M. (1992a). *Critical theory: Selected essays.* New York: Continuum.

Horkheimer, M. (1992b). *Eclipse of reason.* New York: Continuum.

James, A. (1995). "On being a child: The self, the group and the category." In A. P. Cohen & N. Rapport (Eds.), *Questions of consciousness* (pp. 60–76). New York: Routledge.

Jenks, C. (1996). *Childhood.* New York: Routledge.

Kagan, J. (1983). "Developmental categories and the premise of connectivity." In R. Lerner, (Ed.), *Developmental psychology: Historical and philosophical perspectives* (pp. 29–54). Hillsdale, NJ: Lawrence Erlbaum.

Kermode, F. (1966). *The sense of an ending.* London: Oxford University Press.

Kotre, J. (1996). *Outliving the self.* New York: W. W. Norton.

Lemert, C. (1995). *Sociology after the crisis.* New York: Westview Press.

Lerner, R. (1976). *Concepts and theories of human development.* Reading, MA: Addison-Wesley.

Levin, D. M. (1985). *The body's recollection of being.* Boston: Routledge and Kegan Paul.

Lévi-Strauss, C. (1969). *The raw and the cooked.* Chicago: University of Chicago Press.

LeVine, R. (1990). "Enculturation: A biosocial perspective on the development of self." In D. Cicchetti & M. Beeghly (Eds.), *The self in transition* (pp. 99–118). Chicago, IL: University of Chicago Press.

Lichtman, R. (1982). *The production of desire: The integation of psychoanalysis into Marxist theory.* New York: Free Press.

Lichtman, R. (1987). "The illusion of maturation in an age of decline." In J. M. Broughton (Ed.), *Critical theories of psychological development* (pp. 127–148). New York: Plenum.

Lovejoy, A. (1964). *The great chain of being.* Cambridge, MA: Harvard University Press.

Lowe, D. (1982). *History of bourgeois perception.* Chicago: University of Chicago Press.

Lukas, G. (1971). *History and class consciousness: Studies in Marxist dialectics.* Cambridge, MA: MIT Press.

Mageo, J., & Howard, A. (Eds.). (1996). *Spirits in culture, history and mind.* New York: Routledge.

Mannheim, K. (1982). *Structures of thinking.* New York: Routledge.

Marcuse, H. (1962). *Eros and civilization.* New York: Vintage.

Marcuse, H. (1969). *An essay on liberation.* Boston: Beacon.

Marcuse, H. (1989). "Philosophy and critical theory." In S. E. Bronner & D. M. Kellner (Eds.), *Critical theory and society* (pp. 58–76). New York: Routledge.

McLaren, P. (1994). "Postmodernism and the death of politics: A Brazilian reprieve." In P. McLaren & C. Lankshear (Eds.), *Politics of liberation: Paths from Freire* (pp. 193–215). New York: Routledge.

Mead, M. (1934). *Sex and temperament in three primitive societies.* New York: W. Morrow & Company.

Melucci, A. (1996). *The playing self.* New York: Cambridge University Press.

Miller, P. (1994). "Narrative practices: Their role in socialization and self-construction." In U. Niesser & R. Fivush (Eds.), *The remembering self: Construction and accuracy in the self-narrative* (pp. 158–179). New York: Cambridge University Press.

Mills, P. J. (1987). *Woman, nature and psyche.* New Haven, CT: Yale University Press.

Mills, C. W. (1970). "The professional ideology of social pathologists." In L. T. Reynolds & J. M. Reynolds (Eds.), *The sociology of sociology* (pp. 129–151). New York: David McKay.

Modell, J. (1996). "The uneasy engagement of human development and ethnography." In R. Jessor, A. Colby, & R. Shweder (Eds.), *Ethnography and human development: Context and meaning in social inquiry* (pp. 479–504). Chicago: University of Chicago Press.

Morss, J. (1990). *The biologising of childhood: Developmental psychology and the Darwinian myth.* Hillsdale, NJ: Lawrence Erlbaum.

Morss, J. (1996). *Growing critical: Alternatives to developmental psychology.* New York: Routledge.

Nelson, K. (1985). *Making sense: The acquisition of shared meaning.* New York: Academic Press.

O'Flaherty, W. D. (1988). *Other peoples' myths.* Chicago: University of Chicago Press.

Ortner, S. (1974). "Is female to male as nature is to culture?" In M. Zimbalist Rosaldo & L. Lamphere (Eds.), *Woman, culture and society* (pp. 67–88). Stanford: Stanford University Press.

Parke, R., Ornstein, P., Rieser, J., & Zahn-Waxler, C. (1994). "The past as prologue: An overview of a century of developmental psychology." In R. Parke, P. Ornstein, J. Rieser, & C. Zahn-Waxler (Eds.), *A century of developmental psychology* (pp. 1–75). Washington, DC: American Psychological Association.

Pfister, J., & Schnog, N. (1997). *Inventing the psychological: Toward a cultural history of emotional life in America.* New Haven, CT: Yale University Press.

Piaget, J. (1965). *The moral judgment of the child.* New York: The Free Press.

Piaget, J. (1968). *Six psychological studies.* New York: Vintage.

Poole, F. J. Porter. (1994). "Socialization, enculturation and the development of personal identity." In T. Ingold (Ed.), *Companion encyclopedia of anthropology* (pp. 831–860). New York: Routledge.

Prilleltensky, I. (1994). *The morals and politics of psychology: Psychological discourse and the status quo.* Albany: State University of New York Press.

Rabinow, P. (1992). "Artificiality and enlightenment: From sociobiology to biosociality." In J. Crary & S. Kwinter (Eds.), *Incorporations* (pp. 234–252). New York: Zone.

Reich, W. (1972). *Character analysis.* New York: Touchstone.

Ricoeur, P. (1969). *The symbolism of evil.* Boston: Beacon.

Riegel, K. (1976). *Psychology of development and history.* New York: Plenum.

Robertson, R. (1978). *Meaning and change: Explorations in the cultural sociology of modern societies.* New York: New York University Press.

Romanyshyn, R. (1993). "The despotic eye and its shadow: Media image in the age of literacy." In D.M. Levin (Ed.), *Modernity and the hegemony of vision* (pp. 339–378). Berkeley: University of California Press.

Rose, G. (1996). *Mourning becomes the law.* New York: Cambridge University Press.

Santamaria, U., & Manville, A. (1992). "Marx and the Question of Anthropology." In C. Ward Gailey (Ed.), *The politics of culture and creativity* (pp. 407–426). Gainesville: University Press of Florida.

Scrag, C. (1997). *The self after postmodernity.* New Haven, CT: Yale University Press.

Seidman, S. (1991). "The end of sociological theory: The postmodern hope." *Sociological Theory, 9(2),* 131–146.

Shweder, R. A. (1991). *Thinking through cultures.* Cambridge, MA: Harvard University Press.

Shweder, R. (1996). "True ethnography: The lore, the law, and the lure." In R. Jessor, A. Colby, & R. Shweder (Eds.), *Ethnography and human development.* (pp. 15–52). Chicago: University of Chicago Press.

Smith, D. L. (1970). "Sociology and the rise of corporate capitalism." In L. T. Reynolds & J. M. Reynolds (Eds.), *The sociology of sociology* (pp. 68–84). New York: David McKay.

Tappan, M., & Packer, M. (Eds.). (1991) *Narrative and storytelling: Implications for understanding moral development.* San Francisco: Jossey-Bass.

Taylor, C. (1995). "The dialogical self." In R. Goodman & W. Fisher (Eds.), *Rethinking knowledge.* (pp. 57–68). Albany: State University of New York Press.

Tomasello, M., Kruger, A. C., & Ratner, H. H. (1993). "Cultural learning." *Behavioral and Brain Sciences, 16,* 495–552.

Toulmin, S. (1981). "Epistemology and developmental plasticity." In E. Gollin (Ed.), *Developmental plasticity* (pp. 253–267). New York: Academic Press.

Tyler, S. (1987). *The unspeakable: Discourse, dialogue, and rhetoric in the postmodern world.* Madison: University of Wisconsin Press.

Uzgiris, I. C. (Ed.). (1979). *Social interaction and communication during infancy.* San Francisco: Jossey-Bass.

Vitebsky, P. (1993). "Is death the same everywhere? Contexts of knowing and doubting." In M. Hobart (Ed.), *An anthropological critique of development* (pp. 100–115). New York: Routledge.

Walkerdine, V. (1988). *The mastery of reason.* New York: Routledge.

Weber, M. (1964). *The sociology of religion.* Boston: Beacon Press.

Wertsch, J. V. (1991). *Voices of the mind.* Cambridge, MA: Harvard University Press.

Wexler, P. (1996a). *Critical social psychology.* New York: Peter Lang.

Wexler, P. (1996b). *Holy sparks: Social theory, education and religion.* New York: St. Martin's Press.

Wilshire, B. (1968). *Romanticism and evolution: The nineteenth century.* New York: Capricorn.

Chapter 8

Postformal Thought as Critique, Reconceptualization, and Possibility for Teacher Education Reform

Gaile Cannella

For the past seventy-five years scholars have engaged in attempts to improve teacher education. These reform efforts have included such programs as the Commonwealth Teacher Training Study (Charters & Waples, 1929), which systematically described what teachers should be taught; Competency/Performance-Based Teacher Education (C/PBTE) of the 1960s and 1970s; developmentalism, focusing on the scientific study of children from the work of Lucy Sprague Michell (1931) to programs framed by Piagetian constructivism; and teacher education grounded in the work of John Dewey and notions of reflective inquiry and social change (Giroux & McLaren, 1986; Shor, 1986). Field experiences working in schools with children, performance assessment, and national and state guidelines have all, at one time or an other, been components of reform. While espousing diverse philosophies and beliefs about education, the various reforms have either not been accepted by the general teacher education community or, when embraced, have had little influence on the overall functioning of schools. Education in general, and teacher education specifically, has remained patriarchal in nature, a form of cultural inscription in which elite "superior" groups use their power to control others (e.g., teacher educators and classroom teachers over those who are learning to teach, adults over children, state departments and principals over female teachers, one socioeconomic group over another). Further, the technicist perspective is quite common; it reifies and deskills teaching and learning as a set of pedagogical methods, classroom management techniques, predetermined objectives and lesson plans, psychological "truth" applied to all human beings, and judgment of others (Beyer, 1988).

"Teacher education" as a modernist regime of truth has been questioned only recently and by a very few scholars (Kincheloe, 1993; Gore, 1993). Even when labeling teacher preparation practices as the technicist denial of the social, most writers and teacher educators have not applied a postmodern critique to the construction of teacher education as an Enlightenment or modern creation. The value assumptions that construct a belief in teacher education are not questioned. When reform movements are designed and implemented, the regimes of truth, knowledge, language, and power that are fostered by teacher education are not generally analyzed. Further, the construction of reform efforts themselves represent the modernist progressive belief that "we can get it right"; the most legitimate and best practice will prevail (Lyotard, 1993). As long as we, as educators, function with this belief in ultimate "truth," the power generated through teacher education will privilege and legitimate the knowledge of some and disqualify the knowledge of "others," increase opportunities for those who are in control, and disempower those who do not or cannot accept the dominant philosophy.

As postmodern researchers in the arts, literature, linguistics, philosophy, various academic disciplines, feminism, and multicultural education have demonstrated, human beings function within the context of multiple, diverse, and complex views of the world that are historically, politically, and socially grounded. Universal truths that are applicable to all people(s) have been called into question. Dominant ways of thinking that have characterized Western thought have been challenged. Teacher education and any reform efforts tied to it require a continuous postmodern critique if the goals of education are to include equity, justice, possibility, and increased opportunity.

Postformal thought as a type of postmodern analysis provides a perspective from which both teacher education and reform efforts can be critiqued. Further, the values that are intrinsic within postformal perspectives generate new possibilities and the potential for reconceptualization of teacher education overall and the notion of reform specifically. I admit to my own interpretation of postformal thinking and accept the notion as going beyond concepts of formal operational and psychological thought. Just as *postmodern* does not mean the next hierarchical step above modern, but rather a break with totalizing, universalistic "modern" perspectives (Lather, 1991), I interpret postformal thought to be a break with psychology and modernist notions of thought. The postformal provides a different way of analyzing and conceptualizing possibility in the area that we have traditionally called teacher education.

POSTFORMAL THOUGHT: THE CRITIQUE
OF TEACHER EDUCATION

Joe Kincheloe and Shirley Steinberg (1993) have described postformal thinking as "a dialogue between critical theory and post-modernism" (p. 298) that expands the boundaries of human emancipation, dignity, respect, social justice, and social responsibility. The goal of postformal thought is to actively engage in the struggle for social justice, with the recognition that there can be no predetermined outcome. The emphasis is on multiple perspectives that would include those human beings who have been traditionally excluded, challenge the tyranny of dominant ideologies, and unveil the limits that reason and science have placed on human beings. For example, modernist grand narratives such as the concept of "intelligence" have excluded people of color, the poor, and females as not logical or rational, not able to employ abstract, linear thinking, and too emotional. Other grand narratives that have excluded various groups of people in both education and teacher education include the regime of science as representing universal truth (e.g., psychological testing, universalized human change and development), the privileging of linear, sequential thought, Cartesian dualism that constructs separation and opposition (e.g., adult/child, experience/inexperience, appropriate/inappropriate, abstract/concrete), a focus on predetermined "truth" as defined by one group for another (e.g., behavioral objectives, competencies, outcomes), and the belief in progress (e.g., constructing superiority for those who are older, more educated, and/or more experienced). Additionally, postformal thought appreciates, uses, and draws from feminisms and African-American epistemologies in an attempt to see, hear, and understand subjugated knowledges, ways of knowing that have not traditionally been accepted in education (Kincheloe & Steinberg, 1993).

The four features of postformal thought are etymology, pattern, process, and contextualization. These features, in various forms, can be used (and have been used by some) to critique teacher education as a modernist construction. *Etymology* addresses the validation of knowledge by the culture. Regarding teacher education, of issue are the historical origins of the practice of teacher education, as well as the cultural sites of power that have produced teacher education as an accepted practice. An additional component of the critique is the examination of the ways that societal values limit human beings through the discourse and practice of education and teacher education. *Pattern* refers to human connections, relationships, and boundaries. The hidden assumptions that underlie the conceptualization and implementation of teacher education are a major issue. The physical, social, and political worlds are seen as parts of an interconnected and related whole. Teacher education as an institution is addressed from the unique perspective of those who have not benefited or been part of it, such as teachers who have left the classroom, children whose knowledges have not been accepted by teacher education, and lay persons. *Process* is making sense of society and ourselves through new ways of reading and knowing the world. At issue for teacher education are the "myths of truth" generated by dominant societal perspectives that limit human possibilities. Postformal thought becomes action that reveals people and ideas that have not been heard, that have been rendered invisible or disqualified as "not good enough." Taken-for-granted authority (of people or ideas) and simplistic literalisms (dominant discourse and bandwagon language) are challenged in attempts to uncover hidden meanings. *Contextualization* is the recognition of the historical, political, social, and cultural embeddedness of people and knowledge, including those that play a part in teacher education. Concepts such as "learning theories" are considered constructions of a technicist culture, rather than universals appropriate for all education. The role of power in determining how the world is represented and the production of power through dominant language and ideologies are examined. The teacher's "place" within this context is recognized as embedded within autobiographical and cultural constraints.

True to their critical perspective, Kincheloe and Steinberg present postformal thought neither as a grand narrative nor as a universal guide for thought and decision making in a new age. Postformal thought is represented as a possibility within a struggle to maintain modernist features of social justice and democracy while drawing on postmodern insights that would address dominance, power, privilege, and subjugation. They propose this way of thinking as one of multiple opportunities for postmodern critique, as a possibility that would always include self-analysis and humility, as a way of thinking that would serve as a double-voiced dialogue between acceptance and critical analysis. Postformal thought accepts teacher education (and reform efforts) as cultural ways of functioning while critiquing both its existence and the hidden assumptions that construct it.

TEACHER EDUCATION AS REGIME OF PEDAGOGY

Although not acknowledged in teacher education reform literature, the field has recently undergone various forms of postmodern critique. The analyses most relevant to this discussion are the postformal representation of teacher education constructed by Joe Kincheloe (1993), the discussion of teacher education as "meta"-pedagogy by Jennifer Gore (1993), and the work of such social reconstructionists as Ken Zeichner (1991, 1993).

The history of teacher education can be traced to beliefs in social regulation and patriarchal dominance over women. As Grumet (1988) has clearly explained, "teaching took up women" (p. 33). Supported by the belief that women should teach because they could be paid less, teaching in the nineteenth century was constructed as a gendered field. In the name of motherhood, and because they were assumed to possess the characteristics of domesticity, self-sacrifice, patience, silence, and self-denial, women were declared best suited to educate children. As women became the majority in the field, outside control emerged. Male administrators and university professors constructed education as a profession in which women were placed under the hierarchal control of male superintendents and school boards. The profession was grounded in a "scientific truth" that would be revealed through teacher training. Consistent with the belief in the medical profession that women could be told what to do by male physicians, this education was constructed as nonintellectual and based on technical training in management, lesson planning, learning content, and teaching methodologies. Further, the field has continually undergone criticism as academically lacking, a position that has recently been recognized as having more to do with categorizations of "women's work" than with intellectual inferiority (Ginsburg, 1988; Lanier & Little, 1986).

Teacher education continues to enculturate future teachers into a world of passivity in which they are to welcome surveillance and supervision, accept what they are told is "correct," and internalize the notion that complex tasks can be broken into small, simple units (Kincheloe, 1993). The teacher education student begins to construct views of him- or herself as a "good" or "bad" teacher, accepting societally based disciplinary powers that label one as normal or abnormal (Foucault, 1980). Knowledge is viewed as the transmission of dominant cultural forms determined by superiors (whether university professors, principals, or cooperating classroom teachers). Conformity, mastery of predetermined teaching skills, technical competence, and individual survival undergird the preservice teacher's professional world. The message is to learn to do what "good" teachers do—model good teaching and reject poor teaching (whatever that is). Good teaching is clearly established as the production of correct answers by one's students on standardized achievement tests.

Missing from the discourse of teacher education is the possibility that the practice of educating future teachers is a socially constructed modernist notion that does not foster multiple ways of reading the world and is limited by particular voices and adherence to particular truths. Teacher education is the embodiment of a regime of pedagogy. From whatever philosophical learning perspective, a pedagogical truth is perpetuated in the separation of teacher and student, in the belief that learning transforms individuals, and in the regulatory power of pedagogy (Gore, 1993). Teacher education represents institutionalized pedagogy, a societal "myth of truth." In many ways, teacher education inhibits new possibilities for reading and knowing the world. Within the truth-oriented, technological context in which teacher education has been conceptualized, could we really expect multiple voices to be heard, multiple knowledges to be accepted as legitimate, or complex sites of power to be analyzed? Teacher education functions as if independent of context, as if there were teaching truths to be learned, as if all voices had been heard. From within this context, the notion of reform has emerged.

POSTFORMAL THOUGHT AND TEACHER EDUCATION REFORM

Most recent teacher education reform efforts include the dominant assumptions of the past. However, the new reforms are posited within the context of a "new language," a discourse of outcomes, collaboration, and empowerment. These recent reforms can be categorized as efforts to (1) increase regulatory requirements, (2) establish the legitimacy and necessity of authentic field experience in schools, and (3) develop reflective thinking in teachers (Zeichner, Melnick, & Gomez, 1996). Postformal analysis provides a unique perspective from which these reform movements can be analyzed. Although there is no one method of postformal critique, I will examine each reform category based on the postformal values of human emancipation, social justice, and multiple perspectives that would challenge dominant ideologies within the context of a more specific analysis that uses the features of etymology, pattern, process, and contextualization.

Regulation through Accreditation and Licensure

Regulating teacher experiences, skills, and qualifications is not a new idea. In 1855 Horace Mann used the notion that women could be told how and what to teach as part of his rationale for their employment in the Iowa system (Morain, 1980). Further, Apple (1987) has shown that as a particular form of labor has been identified with women, those jobs have been increasingly proletarianized and regulated. Control in teacher education has been exhibited mainly by the imposition of "standards" through program accreditation or approval and through individual certification or licensing. The concept of standards has been used in two ways, either to imply agreement concerning a particular set of experiences and requirements or as an assessment of quality, usually in terms of what is minimally acceptable (Andrew, 1997). The dominant avenues for the imposition of regulatory standards on teacher education have been government requirements (determined and controlled by individual states in the United States) and national professional requirements determined by the National Council for Accreditation of Teacher Education (NCATE). In the United States, a long history of teacher regulation by the state can be traced from written examinations taken by individuals in the nineteenth century, through state teacher education program approval during the twentieth century, and to the return of individual exit assessment during the past twenty years (Tom, 1996). Individual evaluation has included both content examinations and performance assessment. Established in 1952 as an equal and formal collaboration with public schools, colleges of education, and state departments of education, NCATE has generally had the purpose of evaluating individual teacher education programs.

Through recent reform efforts, an even greater emphasis has been placed on standards. The centerpiece of the recent report by the National Commission on Teaching and America's Future (1996) illustrates this notion: "How can we have competent and caring teachers in every classroom? With standards and assessment" (Andrew, 1997, p. 167). Since the 1980s (long before the commission's report) individual states and

NCATE have continuously worked to redesign the requirements for those who would enter teaching. Beginning with the push in the 1980s by various state governors, departments of education (often guided by legislation) constructed and implemented teaching performance examinations (called "competency-based performance" by some in the 1970s) and various exit tests to determine a teaching candidate's knowledge in particular content areas. In 1988 NCATE implemented a newly designed method of accrediting teacher education programs that was to be more rigorous and less expensive, yet was to insure that institutions of higher education used a sound knowledge base in the construction of programs (Tom, 1996). Upon completion of its report, the commission moved to work with state policy makers and national officials, not teacher educators, to again "improve" the standards in teacher education.

Regulation through the imposition of standards is easily indictable through postformal analysis. Implicit in the constructions of the notions of accreditation and licensing are cultural perspectives that validate knowledge as a truth to be revealed through research, as unidirectional, and as something that can be imposed on others. Good teaching (often termed "effective teaching" in this context) is treated as a universal truth that applies to everyone—hence the obvious appropriateness of expecting all programs to include particular components and all individual teachers to exit teacher education with particular characteristics. Further, the patriarchal notion that some groups are superior and can legitimately judge others is apparent in the notion of gatekeeping and in the disqualification of those who do not meet the standards. Human subjectivities are shaped based on the willingness to conform and the ability to meet the standards; otherwise the program or individual is not good enough, is deficient, is inadequate.

The overall message in efforts to reform teacher education standards is that people cannot be trusted and that particular superior groups must regulate others to control quality. Based on the assumption that "raising" everyone to a minimum standard will improve the whole of education, the message is "regulate, regulate, regulate" (Tom, 1996, p. 24). Just as those with money and resources have historically established the educational agenda for teaching the poor how to live, the "standards" are set by a particular group whose understanding of the world is imposed on others. The hegemonic role of the culture of those in power (Delpit, 1993) and the suffering imposed by institutional regulation is not examined. Those who are regulated become increasingly more passive as they learn to expect new sets of standards as new forms of control, as they accept their own disempowerment, or (in a few cases) as a form of resistance to regulation.

New ways of reading and knowing the world as part of understanding ourselves and society are not compatible with efforts to reform standards in teacher education. Standards, licensing, and accreditation are concepts that impose the Enlightenment or modernist view of the world. The notions of social justice, multiple perspectives, and diversity (of peoples, ideas, cultures, concepts, ways of experiencing the world, ways of teaching and learning) are in conflict with ideas of professional standards as historically and currently practiced. The modernist belief in human objectivity, efficiency, and the ability to predetermine outcomes is used to reinforce hierarchal structures of authority and hegemony in society. Oversimplified terms such as *national standards, high quality, excellence, best practices,* and *research findings* are presented as concern for the education of children, like the use of *motherhood, God,* and *apple pie* by middle-class Christian culture in the United States. The language is used to mask the self-interest and political agendas of those who would control others, generate professional and/or political authority for themselves, and construct capitalist power bases (e.g., testing businesses, technology resources, funding for grants). The standards of reform are put forth as if apolitical, as if independent of institutional and societal power structures. The use of more and/or higher standards as the method of reform in teacher education will most likely generate greater social injustice and decrease opportunities for those future teachers and children who do not fit the dominant perspective, those who either will not or cannot be controlled.

Authentic Field Experience

The notion of field experiences in classrooms with children can be traced to multiple points in history: student teaching tied to normal schools in the mid-1800s (Andrews, 1964); field observations and work in laboratory schools that emerged during the first half of the twentieth century (Lindsey, 1969); and early field experiences in public schools that developed after World War II and resulted in as many as three-hundred contact hours before student teaching (McIntyre, 1983). Zeichner (1996a) has described three dominant types of field experience. The apprenticeship experience is a practicum in which the classroom teacher (an individual mentor) demonstrates teaching and advises the novice. In the applied-science practicum, preservice teachers are expected to directly use academic content and educational research knowledge in the classroom. In the inquiry-oriented practicum, the novice is expected to reflect on her/his own theories of learning, with the source of expertise located in the experiences of currently practicing classroom teachers. While teachers have consistently identified classroom field experience, especially student teaching, as the most valuable component of teacher education, the belief is problematic. Student teachers tend to display fleeting involvement with individual children, usually related to the specific learning task, and function within a narrow range of mostly mechanical activities (Tabachnick, Popkewitz, & Zeichner, 1979).

Recent reform efforts have generally included the notion of "authentic" field experience, the kind that naturally occurs in "real-world" classrooms. The reforms include field experiences located in professional development schools, practice schools, and/or partnership schools (Abdal-Haqq, 1991; Darling-Hammond, 1993; Levine, 1992) and may be tied to collaborative activities such as the National Network for Educational Renewal (Goodlad, 1994; Smith, Gottesman, & Edmundson, 1997).

Most reform activities contain elements found in the three types of field experiences. Knowledge is validated by declaring the primacy of real-world classroom activity. Teachers decide whom they will include and exclude from experiences in their schools. Principals and teachers plan activities that socialize preservice teachers to conformity in the school environment. Classroom teachers and university professors are collaborating to determine expectations for future teachers as they work with children. There is an underlying belief, or perhaps hope, that collaboration and listening to the voices of individual teachers will result in improved, democratic, renewed schools.

This universalization of the concepts of "experience" and "collaboration" serves as an excellent example of the way in which dominant ideologies perpetuate themselves and support the status quo. Classroom experience becomes the "right answer" for teacher education, the right way to improve teaching. Davis and Sumara (1997) have noted the "cultural arrogance underlying the belief that the formal educational setting is the principal location for the study of cultural knowledge" (p. 123). Postformal thinking would challenge the privileging of any one cultural view, whether that view is located in the academic perspective of university environments, in the psychological focus on learning theories, or in the classroom experience of practicing teachers. Further, although the discourse of collaboration would build the expectation that multiple voices would be heard, the "imposition" of collaboration on the way that all are to function serves as both an individual disciplinary power and a group regulatory power (Foucault, 1980). Consensus becomes a silencing, regulatory vehicle. As with site-based management, the power of the system over teachers and children (and even over university professors, parents, and community members) is denied. Classroom teachers and university teacher educators have already demonstrated their unwillingness to generate controversy (Zeichner, 1996b; Corwin, 1973); the collaborative mission easily becomes the legitimation of this disposition. Dominant cultural forms, representations of the status quo, are perpetuated.

The overall message of field experience reform efforts is that teaching and learning are school-based, truth-oriented endeavors. There are no new or subjugated knowledges included. Institutional analysis of education as contributing to the disqualification of poor, minority, or otherwise diverse children is not part of the endeavor. Analysis of the institution of teacher education is conducted basically from the perspective of classroom teachers only. Teacher realities represent the boundaries of "truth"; if everyone (generally meaning classroom teachers, principals, and university faculty) works together, the truth will be revealed. In fact, increased teacher power has resulted in the reduction of community-based experiences for preservice teachers and a smaller role for parents and community in educational decision making (Zeichner, 1991). Although the work of such individuals as Shirley B. Heath (1983) has demonstrated the power of community knowledge, teachers want those who are learning to teach to spend time in classrooms, not in other cultural learning environments. The place of classroom teachers as mostly white, educated, middle-class females who attempt to function with children in a gendered, deskilled, regulatory environment and the role that this positioning plays in teacher interpretations of experience and "truth" are invisible. Controversial, institutionalized ways that education disempowers children through ageism, racism, sexism, and classism are not generally addressed (Gillette, 1990; Zeichner, 1996a). There is no avenue for such concerns. Who benefits from the reform? Those who already have power.

Reform movements that would foster authentic field experience use new terminologies that allow those involved to fool themselves into thinking that social justice, equity, and increased opportunity are intrinsic to the process. This new language uses phrases and words such as *tripartite collaboration, democratic classrooms, stewardship of schools, moral dimensions of teaching, development, professional,* and *partnership.* The discourse actually adheres to modernist beliefs in progress and the expert (in this case the classroom teacher) and even clings to the language of Christianity in the use of words such as *stewardship, tripartite,* and *morality.* The notion that "we are all working together" generates a disposition in which participants believe that access is equally available to everyone—children, parents, and teachers who represent multiple diverse groups and perspectives about the world. The status quo again prevails.

In the flurry to create partnerships with public schools and to give teachers a voice concerning their own classrooms, the cultural context in which education has been constructed is denied. These "new" field-based collaborative reform efforts intensify the work of educators to an even greater degree (e.g., collaboration meetings, paperwork), resulting in conditions in which we are even less likely to be able to see the imprisonment of children by the education that we offer to them. Further, without critique, field experience reform perpetuates social injustice by reducing and essentializing education to "what works" (whatever that means, and subject to the judgement of whoever is in a position to define it), giving voice to the views of those who are already part of the system. The voices of children, their families, and their communities remain silenced. Even those who are to become teachers are usually excluded, are not heard.

Reflective Thinking
Inspired by the work of John Dewey (1933), teacher educators have taken up the notion of the "reflective practitioner" or "reflective thinking," generating a reform movement that represents multiple philosophical perspectives on teacher education. Dewey distinguished between reflection and routine practice by defining reflection as "active, persistent, and careful consideration of any belief or supposed form of knowledge in light of the grounds that support it and the further consequences in which it leads" (p. 9). Routine practice is primarily tradition-based and authoritative. Zeichner and Tabachnick (1991) have stated the obvious reason why teacher educators appear to agree with the notion of reflective thinking: "Thoughtful teachers who reflect about their practice are more desirable than thoughtless teachers" (p. 2). This construct has been appropriated by educators who believe that teachers should learn to reflect on subject matter (Shulman, 1987), educators who would have teachers reflect on research-based appropriate teaching strategies (Ross and Kyle, 1987), educators who believe that good teaching is reflection on the needs, interests, and development of children (Duckworth, 1987), and educators who

value teacher reflection about social justice, equity, and the social and political context of schooling (Beyer, 1988).

At first glance, at least teacher reflection on social justice in education would appear to address issues that are of concern in postformal thinking. For that very reason, and because teacher reflection has been taken up in reaction to the view of teachers as technicians whose work must be controlled, analysis is an absolute necessity. Lest we accept reflective thinking as a "universal" and desirable reform movement (a notion that contradicts a postmodern, critical perspective) in the struggle for justice, human dignity, and the appreciation of diversity, postformal analysis is required.

Knowledge in the reflective thinking reform movement is grounded in the rational, reasoning individual. While independent persons may construct multiple knowledges, understandings, and realities, the individual is in charge. Two of the Enlightenment and modernist cultural sites of both power and subjugation are perpetuated: the focus on the individual and the belief in reason. This emphasis on individuality places teachers in a position in which the self (and/or other individual teachers) is responsible for the functioning and improvement of education. If enough knowledge is obtained and individual thinking is appropriately reflective, right actions will be taken. If not, the teacher is to blame for not being smart enough or reflective enough. A human subject is created who counts on him- or herself to use good-quality thinking, to make the best-informed decisions. There is no dialogue as to how these reflective expectations may disempower a teacher; the assumptions have been empowerment, action, and voice.

The overall message of reflective thinking is that objective, thoughtful rationality, whether based on the positivist truth revealed through research about teaching or the critical analysis of oppression in society, will result in the appropriate detection or identification of problems and alternatives for solutions. Additionally, reflective thinking assumes that the individual is positioned in a manner that will allow for action, that the teacher is not oppressed or dominated in ways that deny reason. What if the individual is physically and/or politically obstructed with every attempt to act? Further, the language of "teacher empowerment," "teacher as researcher," "action research," or "reflective action" constructs an illusion of power. Teachers can remain oppressed within their own notions of reflection and the knowledge that they have accepted as useful for reflection. "An illusion of teacher development is often created that maintains in more subtle ways the subservient position of the teacher in relation to those removed from the classroom" (Zeichner, 1996c, p. 202). Power is actually maintained over teachers as those from outside determine the knowledge for reflection.

Multiple voices and multiple ways of functioning as human beings are absent from the notion of reflective thinking. Enlightenment and modernist myths of truth abound in the dichotomous construction of reflective versus routine (or whatever is nonreflective); in the focus on the independence of the individual; in the superiority of reflection over ambiguity, intuition, and uncertainty; in the privileging of rationality; in the implication of objectivity; and in the denial of the social. These myths serve to legitimate and extend the authority of educators who are part of the system and perpetuate various institutional forms of injustice. Even when teachers have taken or gotten more power, which might be possible with reflective thinking and teaching, the interests of diverse groups of children and their families have not been served (Ayers, 1992). Again, those who have been unjustly treated within the context of educational dominance and regulation are not heard, silenced by the classroom teacher or by various institutionalized educational practices. They are excluded from the conversation. The reflection disqualifies their knowledge(s), does not even acknowledge their existence; they are denied.

RECONCEPTUALIZATION AND POSSIBILITY

As a teacher educator, I believe that study by preservice teachers in university, public school, and especially community environments can foster social justice in education and society. If not, I would not remain in teacher education. However, as critical and feminist theorists have reminded us, everything that we do is value-laden and embedded within historical, political, and social contexts. Whatever the values that we choose to promote, we must recognize that they are human constructions that are complex and always potentially dangerous to ourselves and others. Our beliefs, values, and actions must therefore undergo continuous critique. Postformal thought provides one method, one view of the world, that can foster this critique. There are and will be additional reform efforts in teacher education. Postmodern perspectives combined with the focus on human dignity, social justice, and equity as developed through postformal thinking provide questions through which reform possibilities can be analyzed and from which teacher education can be reconceptualized (see Kincheloe, 1993). The following are sample questions that are my constructions, based on my consideration of the possibilities offered by Joe Kincheloe and Shirley Steinberg and on my attempt at postformal analysis in this time and context. They do not represent a grand narrative for critique, but my personal attempts to use postformal thought to generate new ways of reading and understanding the world of teacher education reform:

What are the historical origins of the reform? What is validated as knowledge in the reform movement? How is knowledge viewed?

What cultural perspectives have produced the reform effort? How is power reproduced within the perspectives?

Are human beings limited in their beliefs about themselves through the conceptualization and/or implementation of the reform? Are disciplinary and regulatory powers constructed that will oppress particular groups of people?

Are questions that have not previously been asked included? Are new problems detected?

What is the overall message of the reform effort? What are the underlying assumptions of the reform? Who benefits from these assumptions?

Is the institution of teacher education, and education in general, critiqued from the perspective of those who may have suffered from its existence?

Are traditional boundaries challenged in ways that join diverse perspectives?

What (knowledges, perspectives, views of the world, ways of functioning and/or being in the world) and who is missing from the reform?

Does the reform inhibit or generate greater possibilities for social justice in education and society?

Are possibilities limited by adherence to the "myths of truth" generated by one perspective on life and education?

Is taken-for-granted authority recognized and challenged? Or is this authority perpetuated?

Are new ways of reading and knowing the world actually physically supported through daily action? What are examples of new possibilities for human beings that are generated?

Are knowledge, content, and meaning always recognized as contextual?

Is knowledge recognized as an autobiographical construction, embedded within culture and individual place?

Does the reform decrease reductionist views of the world that result in oversimplification of our lives and reification of people?

Does the reform generate an analysis of the role of power (and multiple, complex sites of power) in education (and teacher education)? Who is heard? Who is silenced? What is included? What is excluded?

The reader may note that I did not discuss all of these questions related to each reform movement. The major reason is that the answer to many questions is no. Basically, current teacher education reform does not function with the recognition of a postformal, postmodern perspective. Although critique is of utmost importance, perhaps the greater benefit for teacher education reform would be to use the issues and questions generated by postformal thought to reconceptualize our concepts of teacher education and our necessity for reform. What would happen in teacher education if our educational goals were the recognition of multiple and diverse voices, the appreciation of humanity in infinite forms, and the pursuit of social justice?

REFERENCES

Abdal-Haqq, I. (1991). *Professional development school and educational reform: Concepts and concern.* Washington, DC: American Association of Colleges for Teacher Education.

Andrew, M. D. (1997). "What matters most for teacher education?" *Journal of Teacher Education, 48* (3), 167–176.

Andrews, L. O. (1964). *Student teaching.* New York: Center for Applied Research in Education.

Apple, M. W. (1987). Gendered teaching, gendered labor. In T. Popkewitz (Ed.), *Critical studies in teacher education: Its folklore, theory, and practice* (pp. 57–83). New York: Falmer.

Ayers, W. (1992). "Work that is real: Why teachers should be empowered." In G. A. Hess (Ed.), *Empowering teachers and parents: School restructuring through the eyes of anthropologists* (pp. 13–28). Westport, CT: Bergin & Garvey.

Beyer, L. E. (1988). *Knowing and acting: Inquiry, ideology and educational studies.* New York: Falmer.

Charters, W. W., & Waples, D. (1929). *Commonwealth teacher training study.* Chicago: University of Chicago Press.

Corwin, R. (1973). *Reform and organizational survival: The Teacher Corps as an instrument of educational change.* New York: Wiley.

Darling-Hammond, L. (Ed.). (1993). *Professional development schools.* New York: Teachers College Press.

Davis, B., & Sumara, D. J. (1997). "Cognition, complexity, and teacher education." *Harvard Educational Review*, 67 (1), 105–125.

Delpit, L. (1993). "The silenced dialogue: Power and pedagogy in educating other people's children." In L. Weis & M. Fine (Eds.), *Beyond silenced voices: Class, race, and gender in United States schools* (pp. 119–139). Albany: State University of New York Press.

Dewey, J. (1933). *How we think.* Chicago: Henry Regnery.

Duckworth, E. (1987). *The having of wonderful ideas.* New York: Teachers College Press.

Foucault, M. (1980). *Power/knowledge: Selected interviews and other writings, 1972–1977.* New York: Pantheon.

Gillette, M. (1990). *Making them multicultural: A case study of the clinical teacher-supervisor in preservice teacher education.* Unpublished doctoral dissertation, University of Wisconsin—Madison, School of Education.

Ginsburg, M. (1988). *Contradictions in teacher education and society: A critical analysis.* New York: Falmer.

Giroux, H., & McLaren, P. (1986). "Teacher education and the politics of engagement: The case for democratic schooling." *Harvard Educational Review*, 56 (3), 213–238.

Goodlad, J. I. (1994). *Educational renewal: Better teachers, better schools.* San Francisco: Jossey-Bass.

Gore, J. (1993). *The struggle for pedagogies: Critical and feminist discourses as regimes of truth.* New York: Routledge.

Grumet, M. (1988). *Bitter milk: Women and teaching.* Amherst: University of Massachusetts Press.

Heath, S. B. (1983). *Ways with words: Language, life, and work in communities and classrooms.* New York: Cambridge University Press.

Kincheloe, J. (1993). *Toward a critical politics of teacher thinking: Mapping the postmodern.* Westport, CT: Bergin & Garvey.

Kincheloe, J. L., & Steinberg, S. R. (1993). "A tentative description of postformal thinking: The critical confrontation with cognitive theory." *Harvard Educational Review*, 63 (3), 296–320.

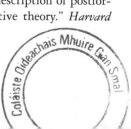

Lather, P. (1991). *Getting smart: Feminist research and pedagogy with/in the postmodern*. New York: Routledge.

Lanier, J., & Little, J. (1986). "Research on teacher education." In M. Wittrock (Ed.), *Third handbook of research on teaching* (pp. 527–569). New York: Macmillan.

Levine, M. (1992). *Professional practice schools: Linking teacher education and school reform*. New York: Teachers College Press.

Lindsey, M. (1969). *Inquiring into teaching behaviors of supervisors in teacher education laboratories*. New York: Teachers College Press.

Lyotard, J. (1993). *The postmodern explained*. Minneapolis: University of Minnesota Press.

McIntyre, D. J. (1983). *Field experiences in teacher education: From student to teacher*. Washington, DC: Foundation for Excellence in Teacher Education and the ERIC Clearinghouse on Teacher Education.

Michell, L. S. (1931). "Cooperative schools for student teachers." *Progressive Education, 8,* 251–255.

Morain, T. (1980). "The departure of males from the teaching profession in nineteenth century Iowa." *Civil War History, 27* (2), 161–70.

National Commission on Teaching and America's Future. (1996) Summary Report. What Matters Most: Teaching for Americas' Future. Washington, D.C.

Ross, D., & Kyle, D. (1987). "Helping preservice teachers learn to use teacher effectiveness research." *Journal of Teacher Education, 38,* 40–44.

Shor, I. (1986). "Equality is excellence: Transforming teacher education and the labor process." *Harvard Educational Review, 56* (4), 406–426.

Shulman, L. (1987). "Knowledge and teaching: Foundations of the new reform." *Harvard Educational Review, 57,* 1–22.

Smith, W. F., Gottesman, B., & Edmundson, P. (1997). *Constructing a language of collaboration*. National Network for Educational Renewal Reflections on Practice Series, No. 2. Seattle, WA: University of Washington.

Tabachnick, B. R., Popkewitz, T. S., & Zeichner, K. M. (1979). "Teacher education and the professional perspectives of student teachers." *Interchange, 10* (4), 12–29.

Tom, A. R. (1996). "External influences on teacher education programs: National accreditation and state certification." In K. Zeichner, S. Melnick, & M. L. Gomez (Eds.), *Currents of reform in preservice teacher education* (pp. 11–29). New York: Teachers College Press.

Zeichner, K. (1991). "Contradictions and tensions in the professionalization of teaching and the democratization of schools." *Teachers College Record, 92,* 363–379.

Zeichner, K. (1993). *Educating teachers for cultural diversity*. East Lansing, MI: National Center for Research on Teacher Learning.

Zeichner, K. (1996a). "The role of community field experiences in preparing teachers for cultural diversity." In K. Zeichner, S. Melnick, & M. L. Gomez

(Eds.), *Currents of reform in preservice teacher education* (pp. 176–196). New York: Teachers College Press.

Zeichner, K. (1996b). "Designing educative practicum experiences for prospective teachers." In K. Zeichner, S. Melnick, & M. L. Gomez (Eds.), *Currents of reform in preservice teacher education* (pp. 215–234). New York: Teachers College Press.

Zeichner, K. (1996c). "Teachers as reflective practitioners and the democratization of school reform." In K. Zeichner, S. Melnick, & M. L. Gomez (Eds.), *Currents of reform in preservice teacher education* (pp. 199–214). New York: Teachers College Press.

Zeichner, K., Melnick, S., & Gomez, M. L. (Eds.). (1996). *Currents of reform in preservice teacher education.* New York: Teachers College Press.

Zeichner, K., & Tabachnick, B. R. (1991). "Reflections on reflective teaching." In B. R. Tabachnick & K. Zeichner (Eds.), *Issues and practices in inquiry-oriented teacher education* (pp. 1–21). New York: Falmer.

Chapter 9

Preparing Postformal Practitioners:
Pitfalls and Promises

Ann Watts Pailliotet and
Thomas A. Callister Jr.

Kincheloe and Steinberg (1993) critique existing theories of cognitive development and propose a postformal framework to guide curricular and pedagogical changes. Their principles support our conceptualizations, restructuring, and teaching in preservice education. In this chapter, we discuss possibilities and pitfalls of postformal thinking in our program, foundations, and literacy methods courses.

> It was clear that Mary Lou, John, and Barbara had constructed the best bulletin boards in the class depicting the theme "The Joy of Reading." Happy images were carefully cut from the pages of *Time, Life,* and *Seventeen* and pasted onto large yellow or blue sheets of construction paper: Dick and Jane parents reading to *Father Knows Best* children; cutouts of cute Disney characters, pictures of pristine wildlife and contented domesticated pets, and images of modern technology—the space shuttle, a computer, an oil refinery. All were captioned with slogans like "I Love to read" and "Learn About the World—Read the Book." No one in the class of fifteen received less that a B+ on their week-long project. John and Barbara each received an A, but because she laminated her bulletin board, Mary Lou received an A+. Her literacy methods instructor praised her "extra effort."

In their book *Human Interests in the Curriculum,* Bullough, Goldstein, and Holt (1984) discuss the notion of technocratic-mindedness. They use this term to define a belief that the methods of positivistic empirical science serve as universal strategies for the acquisition of knowledge and tools for solving problems—problems that are not just scientific and technical, but exist across all realms of human endeavor. This belief in what Jürgen Habermas (1979) called "instrumental rationality" manifests itself as a "preunderstanding," and as a result causes us to view all problems as technical problems.

It is with such a preunderstanding, an unreflective belief in the naturalness and adequacy of the technical, that we operate our schools and create our curricula, conceptualizing the process of teaching and learning from a technocratic-minded perspective. By making the educational process technical, we pattern the curriculum after a stair-step model of linear fact-by-fact learning, trivialize teaching as a series of generic "how-to's" or formulaic "hints and tips," and too often reduce the act of learning to simple models of behavioral stimulus-response mechanisms.

Such positivistic thinking not only informs teachers' understandings of their proper role and work in schools, but creates a general and pervasive conception of what it is to teach and be a teacher. In this conception, a teacher's work is technological in nature and concerns matters of efficiency—time efficiency, managerial efficiency, and learning efficiency. Teachers are little more than administrators of tests and managers of records—appendages of the educational machine. As one classroom teacher we know said of her work: "I spend a lot of time testing and identifying problems." Not personal human problems, but the kinds of problems we believe tests ferret out—technical problems.

Of great concern to us is that many of our students, like other preservice teachers, arrive preinformed about what it is to be a good teacher (Calderhead & Robson, 1991; Cole, 1990; Perry & Rog, 1992) . After all, they've observed teaching nearly all their lives (Lortie, 1975). So with good hearts and willing minds, they are ready to become, to pervert a perverted phrase, the best technical teachers they can be.

Elsewhere we have used this notion of technocratic reductionism as a framework to critique computer use in classrooms (Callister, 1994) as well as to question essentialist assumptions in preservice education (Watts Pailliotet, 1995a) and literacy instruction (Watts Pailliotet, 1996). But certainly technocratic thinking has far broader effects on the whole of teaching and the curriculum. We believe that this kind of positivist mind-set, which retains a tenacious grip on both the intellect and the imagination of the public, the schools, and many programs for the preparation of teachers, is antithetical to the preparation of what Joe Kincheloe and Shirley Steinberg (1993) call postformal teachers. Not only does such a perspective fail to prepare future educators for the students, issues, and realities they will face in contemporary schools and society, but it often stands as a formidable obstacle in establishing the kind of program we have attempted to create and which we describe below—one that tries to fashion reflective, compassionate, politically and socially sensitive teachers.

PROGRAM CONTEXT: "THE TOWN SO NICE, THEY NAMED IT TWICE"

We teach in a small college in Walla Walla, Washington, that has a strong and proud tradition of liberal arts teaching. First-year students complete a year-long study of the "great books"; about a third of them travel abroad at some point in their college career; all are required to complete courses in fine arts, humanities, and the social and "hard" sciences. The isolated, parklike setting and low faculty-to-student ratio encourage campus interaction and intimacy. There also exist interesting philosophical, but usually not political, tensions—we have been commended by William F. Buckley for our traditional curriculum and by *Mother Jones* magazine for our social activism.

Our preservice teachers, like most across the country, are overwhelmingly young, white, and middle class (Su, 1993). Unlike in many programs, however, our education students major in a liberal arts discipline and minor in education. We have no graduate program. Because of the flexibility afforded our small size and homogeneous student population, our program is grounded more on the notion of a community and less on the strictures of a bureaucracy. We require more foundations courses than methods; we stress writing as a major component throughout our curriculum; we employ school practica and ethnographic observations in nearly all our classes, including foundations; we emphasize qualitative research methods and critiques of print, electronic, and situational texts as ways for our students to read and reflect on the world; and we incorporate mindful analysis and uses of technology and mass media throughout our courses.

In many ways we have the best of all worlds. We have a cohort of students who are mostly politically liberal, altruistic, bright, and highly motivated. We enjoy a high degree of autonomy, a generous allocation of resources, and support from colleagues across campus. As this is a small program, we know all our students well. Our methods courses, for example, rarely enroll over ten individuals, enabling us to shape curricula in creative, flexible, and personal ways. Our required teaching loads are light enough to afford us ample time for planning, research, and student interaction. We are aware that this context affords us unique freedoms and near-perfect opportunities to implement our educational beliefs—freedoms and opportunities that participants in larger or more established programs may lack. It is in this setting, then, that we set about to educate future teachers.

PROGRAM GOALS: "YOU CAN GET THERE FROM HERE"

As teachers of foundations and literacy, our educational goals reflect many of the postformal principles explicated by Kincheloe and Steinberg (1993). We too are concerned with reconceptualizing the way thinking is defined subverting a technicist view of teaching, and grounding our program in notions of "social justice and the way unequal power relations in school and society destroy the promise of democratic life" (p. 301). Like Kincheloe and Steinberg, we too endeavor to develop teachers who are committed to issues of "human dignity, freedom, authority and social responsibility" (p. 301). Above all else, our goal is to teach teachers, not to offer technical training. We want our students to evolve into critical, compassionate thinkers who are guided by ethical, egalitarian, empowering, and reflective purposes. And if that is not enough, we also expect them to become knowledgeable and capable practitioners well versed in their subject matter.

Kincheloe and Steinberg reject "formalist partiality" (p. 314), artificial boundaries among academic disciplines, private and public contexts, actions and outcomes, emotions and cognition. Rather, they employ the notion of sychronicity and the metaphor of a "dance between students' experiences and knowledge" (p. 308) to describe the complex relationships implied in postformal ways of thinking. We heartily agree with this perspective of interconnectedness, realizing that components of this theory intersect at multiple junctions. However, as a way of describing in some detail our attempts at creating a program that mirrors postformal thinking, we found it necessary to temporarily categorize some of these elements. Thus we will examine our program in light of Kincheloe and Steinberg's principles by discussing our attempts for students to politicize education, search for identity, make the familiar strange, value the ethical and emotional, ask the right questions, and reconceptualize responsibility and power. With the caveat that many of the ideas and experiences we explore here are highly interdependent, what follows are personal anecdotes, quotes, and practical examples that illustrate the possibilities and pitfalls of practicing postformal thinking in a preservice teacher education program.

POLITICIZING EDUCATION: HARD TRUTHS AND SELF-DISCOVERY

"But we have to have inequality," cried one exasperated student. "It's what makes the American system work!"

"No, class. Leibniz was wrong."

Kincheloe and Steinberg (1993) assert that "critical educators politicize cognition," "examine ideological expectations" (p. 297), and do not distinguish "the political from the cognitive" (p. 314). We agree. One of our primary purposes is to disabuse our students of the notion that somehow teaching is some sort of technical, neutral activity that exists in a political and ethical vacuum. Postformal practitioners are aware of "the process by which social forces shape our subjectivities, or, less subtly, our identities" (p. 303), but arriving there presents challenges. One is just getting students to believe that not all is right with the world. The other is showing them that their identities come from the environments in which they were raised.

Our students are good and caring people. Like all preservice teachers, they are also products of their environment (Britzman, 1991; Zeichner & Gore, 1990). We try to point out to them that when they go home over a break, stand in front of their parents' house, and look around the neighborhood, they are most likely not looking at America. They are most likely not seeing the people or communities from which their first students will come. And they are not experiencing the kinds of abysmal living conditions and neighborhoods about which they have no understanding except for the lies and stereotypes they see on television.

In our foundations courses, we purposely try to disassemble their preconceptions about issues of race, class, gender, and ability—while throwing into doubt any understanding about what they believed teaching and learning to be. Then, in a political context, against a stark background of political and social reality, we work with them to construct new concep-

tions of the educational process. Through case studies, debates, simulations, discussions, school observations, written reflections, and role playing, we ask them to examine their taken-for-granted beliefs and begin to
build new ones. We believe students actually should reinvent the wheel
when it comes to developing a political identity.

When our students begin taking methods courses, they mistakenly
breathe a collective sigh of relief, believing that their "theoretical" course-
work is over and that they can finally get down to the "real business" of
teaching. In literacy methods, for example, individuals expect to learn a
host of quick and surefire techniques for instruction in reading and writing. Often to their surprise, however, they see that we understand literacy as profoundly political.

Our methods courses are grounded in emancipatory goals of justice,
critical action, individual empowerment, and social constructivism.
Through readings, discussion, and a great deal of writing, students discover that many of the views they initially voice regarding instruction
mirror traditional idealogies that are based on the idea of deficit, perpetuate inequities, and prevent meaningful learning (McCaleb, 1994; Nieto,
1996). We teach them to question agendas of competing literacy paradigms (Mosenthal, 1993) by asking, "Who defines the problem or goal?"
"Who is excluded?" and "Who benefits?" Throughout their courses, our
students compare the political and pragmatic implications of their beliefs
with those conveyed in teacher interviews, textbooks, national standards,
and classroom practices. We ask students to examine varied curricula,
strategies, texts, and practical experiences for ideologies; to make
informed judgments about winners and losers; and to identify political
and ethical outcomes involved with different materials and instructional
strategies.

Our goal, of course, is to bring our students to an appreciation of education's political dimensions. They experience these firsthand when, for
example, they observe marginalized students sitting in the back of the
classroom, read texts that present biased perspectives or stereotypical
characterizations, discover who actually is involved in decision making
(and who is not), and see practices or assessment that favor the few over
the many.

The downside is that this political emphasis can be a disturbing and
very painful experience. Armed with eighteen or more years of dinner-
table political and social indoctrination, our students usually find that a
reexamination of one's beliefs does not come easy. Worse yet is their ini-

tial general inability to articulate, beyond the superficial "party line," why they believe what they do. Too often, to their surprise and disappointment, we must inform them that entreaties to "human nature" or "it just is" are less than compelling.

A second pitfall is that confronting students with their own biases is not always the best way to earn those coveted "superior" teaching evaluations. Very often have we heard something like "The instructor was too one-sided and didn't present the other side of the issue." What other side? That racism is okay? That the point of education isn't equality? We obviously didn't get our broader point across to these individuals, but their remarks (and low evaluations of our teaching) illustrate something we do worry about—that in pursuit of good evaluations, less cognitive dissonance in the classroom, or a greater sense of community, the "hard" lessons our students need to learn are too often watered down and made unproblematic by their instructors. (We will discuss an additional pitfall —the problem of the reluctant colleague—later.)

Still, we persevere on our present course because, as Britzman (1991) points out, it is only through an examination of ideologies and discourses that we can create more a relevant and equitable education. Still, from a political standpoint, the road to reflection and critical action is a bumpy one.

SEARCHING FOR IDENTITY: ETYMOLOGY, EMOTION, AND SPIRITUALITY

> "I don't see how what I did in second grade or where I went to school has anything to do with what we're doing now."

The preparation of postformal teachers requires more than the ability to place education in a political context. Students must examine the etymology of their own belief systems. As Kincheloe and Steinberg (1993) explain, postformal teachers "analyze what [they] know, how [they] come to know it, why [they] believe or reject it, and how [they] evaluate the credibility of the evidence" (p. 302). Part of this process involves examining notions of "objectivity," "ideological passivity," and their "acceptance of privileged socioeconomic position" (p. 312). The authors cite Foucault's notion of genealogy: "As post-formal teachers grow to understand the etymology of the race, class and gender locations of students and others...they come to appreciate their own etymology, their location, and the social relationships such locations produce" (pp. 303–304). The goal is for teachers to "repudiate the intimacy of our own autobiographies" (p. 316).

Although our goal for our students—creating new and emancipated identities—echoes the politicization we have already discussed and foreshadows notions of values that lie ahead, we see a particularly emotional and even spiritual element in the formation of a new identity. Therefore we "design lessons that illustrate the physical and spiritual connections between self and ecosystem" (p. 310). For example, like all preservice teachers, our students enter our program with institutional biographies (Britzman, 1991) and strong beliefs about schooling, formed through years of observation (Lortie, 1975). But students in school see and experience only one small part of schooling, and as a result they do not see well or completely. As the old saying goes, fish are the last to discover water. We employ peer interviews, educational autobiographies, and ongoing reflection papers to help students articulate past experiences and connect them to present beliefs. We favor cooperative activities to create communities of learners where they can share, question, and sometimes even challenge each other in safe and supportive environments.

The activity of teaching is comprised of human acts that assist students in forming ethical frameworks, emotional balance, and spiritualism to guide their lives. Like Lickona (1991), we perceive that all teachers, in addition to their instructional responsibilities, are caregivers, role models, and ethical mentors. We strongly feel that our task is to aid students in this growth as they begin to work with children and young people and reflect upon this work. We promote positive identity formation and help students "uncover new talents" (Kincheloe & Steinberg, 1993, p. 301) through ongoing praise, frequent interaction, constructive comments, and individual assignment choices. We attempt to embody core values of truth, caring, appreciation of others, the merits of work, happiness, and living well through our behaviors in and (sometimes) out of the classroom (Jarrett, 1991).

But these endeavors are also filled with pitfalls. Postformal teachers are concerned with "developing a teaching disposition and constructing identities in a way that parodies the rigid conceptions of modernism, thus assuming the role of postmodern stand up comics and social satirists" (Kincheloe & Steinberg, 1993, p. 304). Our classes generally are filled with a great deal of laughter, "playful parody" (p. 304), and satire. On one hand, critical humor allows our students to examine issues that might be too painful in more sober settings. But we do worry that it may also prevent them from engaging meaningfully. Some fail to distinguish between satire and sophomoric sarcasm; others see our humor as an invitation to frivolity or less than complete commitment to our principles.

Support and open exploration can also degenerate into an "anything goes" relativism. There's no easy solution when students interpret free expression of emotion as a justification for cutting class because they "felt like it." We tell them, "Just because you see us as liberal (radical, we hope) doesn't mean you can blow us off or do less than your best work," but it's a message that is sometimes lost.

We walk another thin line, too—the one between student validation and our own values. It's hard to be affirming and positive when an individual refuses to move beyond bigotry or sexism, or asserts that teachers should not be concerned with values. Emotional balance and ethics are also tough to model. Just like students, we have bad moods, and frankly, there may be some individuals we just don't like very much. Yet if they are to become ethical people, we must show them what sound values look like on a daily basis—monitoring what we say and do. It is hard for our students to grapple with how they feel, who they are, and what they believe. It is a risk for us as well, in terms of our identities, authority, and credibility, when we ask ourselves the same hard questions.

Finally, like many preservice teachers, our students often enter the program with unrealistic expectations or simplistic altruistic motivations that center on caring for children (Demetrulias, 1994; Weinstein, 1989, 1990). Our task is to help our students articulate their feelings, judge if they are realistic, and build on those that provide positive motivation. Occasionally, however, we must offer unpopular alternatives and advice. Misguided souls are often the most earnest, and though it is far beyond us to judge motives or intent, some of the people who enter our program seem to have wandered in through the wrong door. Teaching, for better or worse, may at times look similar to baby-sitting or simply playing with little children, drilling army recruits, being a cop, or even performing as Mr. Science or Ms. Comedy before an enthusiastic audience. But teaching is really none of those things, and we have a responsibility to nurture those who we believe can grow to become reflective teachers—ones who teach from their head through their heart. To the others, we recommend the army, the police academy, or majors in behaviorism.

MAKING THE FAMILIAR STRANGE:
AMBIGUITY AND COMPLEXITY

"Why do we have to do all this theory junk? Why can't you just tell us how to teach social studies?... Just tell us the answer.... Tell us what to do."

From a test given by a former colleague:
"List the seven models of teaching and identify the positive and negative aspect of each."

Identity formation has another component: the development of new ways of knowing, and the development of a strong voice through which to articulate that knowing. Too often, "knowing the world" for our students is through linear, Cartesian terms—a technocratic rationality so completely embedded in their worldview that many assume that it is the only possible perspective. In contrast, Kincheloe and Steinberg (1993) call for a "nonlinear holism," a way of thinking that "transcend[s] simplistic notions of the cause effect process" (p. 313).

How individuals will teach depends on great part how they conceptualize teaching and learning (Hollingsworth, 1989). One of our first tasks, then, is to complicate students' usually inadequate, but certainly predictable, understandings of education: that teaching is telling, and that learning is recall. We agree that "a post-formal analysis of curriculum is grounded in the recognition that there are complimentary, contradictory, emancipatory, repressive social forces" (Kincheloe & Steinberg, 1993, p. 307). It is important that we guide students around this thing we call education and allow them to look at it from different perspectives. In doing so, students begin to realize, that, as in the tale of the blind men and the elephant, education is neither as simple nor as complex as they once had imagined. We set out to make the familiar strange, the simple complex, the seemingly complex simple, the concrete ambiguous, and the isolated contexualized. If we have any sort of quick solution for our students when they so desperately want to know *the* answer, it is that the answer to most questions is "It depends."

For example, we spend a great deal of time involving our students in case studies. We find that these introduce complexity and ambiguities, necessitating assessments and reassessments of their views. Case studies and moral dilemmas also provide the opportunity for students to "walk in another's shoes," an important consideration given the homogeneous nature of our college population. Having students work out the educational and personal implications of consequentialist versus nonconsequentialist courses of action, then suggesting what teachers might do in complex situations, sets about purposely to demonstrate that there are no simple answers. They find that answer to most questions really is "It depends."

By standing some traditional notions of teaching on their head, we maintain that the technical aspect of teaching, the aspect that we believe receives too much attention, is actually fairly simple and straightforward. We demonstrate alternatives to methods they have grown up with. We are guided by principles that promote complex thinking: reflection (Schön, 1987), clear rationales (O'Brien, 1988; O'Brien & Stewart, 1990), modeling (Mosenthal, Schwartz, & MacIsaac, 1992), and guided practice (Hollingsworth & Teel, 1991). We attempt to show our students, through an emphasis on education's emotional, spiritual, and moral aspects, that complexity does not mean that teaching is exactly "rocket science." It is the human interaction of teaching, an aspect too long ignored, that is complex.

Our point is this: a nonreflective, technically oriented mind-set clearly focuses on the how rather than the why of teaching. By turning this around—conceptualizing teaching and learning as a human (rather than technical) activity that respects all participants, as ends rather than means—our primary concentration must then be on the why and not the how of our enterprise.

Pitfalls? Of course. When the going gets tough, students want to fall back on the tired myth of the tried and the true—a bag of easy answers applicable to all situations. But if we are successful, we have taken those simplistic answers away. That leaves some of our students, we imagine, feeling as if they're hanging in midair—not something they enjoy much. Another, more problematic obstacle is that, not surprisingly, not everyone agrees with us. This is certainly not the arena to demonstrate the adequacy of our methods, but suffice it to say that there is clearly a tension between a technical conception of teaching and one that is more based in notions of reflectiveness. Postformal teachers "examine their teaching from many vantage points" (Kincheloe & Steinberg, 1993, p. 309), and certainly we try to model this behavior. But we do not work in isolation. Consider this composite:

> Professor Smith stood safely behind the overhead projector at the front of the room, where she delivered a fifty-minute lecture taken from the instructor's manual of the textbook. She imparted information such as "the five discipline strategies" while her students sat in neat rows and dutifully took notes to prepare for the upcoming multiple-choice test. In her methods

class, students mimicked instructional models by microteaching in front of their friends (who wisely and strategically demonstrated just the right response behaviors, knowing their turn would soon come). Students were graded (as opposed to assessed or critiqued) on how well they followed the sequences detailed in the textbook. One day Professor Smith remarked, "The [high] school only wants two students watching the class at a time. So I'm going to rotate the [three] students. While two are observing, I'll teach the textbook chapter to the other one." Reading from an outline, she delivered the same lesson to each individual. Another day, she let her students go early "because the chapter ended."

Professor Smith illustrates some of the institutional barriers we encounter. First, our goals and methods can be contradictory to those of other college faculty (Bartel & Young, 1993). Second, Kincheloe and Steinberg note that "postformal teachers become 'ungrounded' and 'unrigorous' from the perspective of the technicists who wag their fingers at their lack of formal procedure and formal systemization" (1993, p. 303). Many senior colleagues, like Professor Smith, are grounded in technicist philosophy and pedagogy, and they will judge the merits of our teaching or promotion.

Kincheloe and Steinberg also point out that "it is not easy to teach products of Cartesian-Newtonian consciousness construction to think in terms of this simultaneous cognitive process and the holism it implies" (p. 314). Our students are successful in the traditional educational paradigm. They know, in Dyson's (1984) words, "how to do school." Additionally, preservice teachers often resist complex concepts, methods, and materials when they experience heavy workloads or lack of time in an intensive program like ours (O'Connor & Taylor, 1992; Stover & Vocke, 1992). For our part, a curriculum that stresses ambiguity and complexity is time-intensive and hard to construct. Individuals like Professor Smith undermine reflection and foster resistance to complexity through reductionist pedagogy, simplistic assessment, positivist mind-sets, and easy, less labor-intensive experiences. Furthermore, complex thinking requires more time to teach and assess than "objective" content. Long after Professor Smith has developed her syllabi, scored her multiple-choice exams, and left for break, we remain in our offices planning future lessons or responding to student projects.

Despite these pitfalls, we resist simplicity or easy answers in our pedagogy and program. In fact, we introduce further complexity as we teach students to value education's many ethical and moral aspects.

VALUING THE ETHICAL AND MORAL

"Education is about efficiency in delivering facts and information. Teachers have no right to impose any values on students. I argue teachers should not teach values in any way."

—*Student paper*

"All this touchy-feely PC crap is well and good, but I'm here to teach kids content. Can't we just focus on how to teach the subject and forget all this moral stuff?"

—*Student comment during class discussion*

We have made the argument that education is an inherently political activity. It is our strong belief that it is no less moral and ethical as well. One of us taught for a number of years in a low-SES elementary school where the running joke was that although many of our young charges would probably grow up to be criminals, at least they'd be smart criminals if we had anything to say about it. This is a sentiment that is clearly antithetical to what we believe education should be about. John Dewey distinguished between growth and positive growth, and we think this is a useful contrast. To twist a cliché, we believe all teachers should teach children and young people, not just subjects.

Kincheloe and Steinberg (1993) assert that human morality cannot be divorced from educational contexts when they write, "In settings such as schools, student and teacher behavior cannot be understood without careful attention to the setting and individuals' relationships to the norms, roles, and values that are inseparable from the lived world of institutions" (p. 315). Postformalism embraces a "unified process of thinking" that connects realms of human experience (p. 311). Postformal teachers "see their role as creators of situations where student experiences could intersect with information gleaned from the academic disciplines" (p. 301). They develop "new levels of activity" (p. 303) that assist students to examine "explicate" orders of knowledge as well as to explore deeper, "implicate" orders of personal and social realities (p. 306).

Attention to these ethical and moral realities of teaching has two parts: first, convincing our students that there is a moral component in what they are setting out to do, and second, helping them understand their own ethical constructions.

If education were simply the technical skill of transferring information from one person to another, then we really could use computers as teachers. But, as we have talked about before, education is much more complicated. Yes, we teach skills, information, and (shudder) even a "fact" now and again. However, unlike stereotypical mad scientists in 1950s science fiction movies we watched as kids ("We just invent the weapons of mass destruction, how they are used is not up to us"), we are acutely aware that what we teach is not neutral. Through posing moral dilemmas, role playing, and making constructs such as intelligence problematic, we encourage students to make thorough examinations of their own schooling. We persist in demonstrating to them that what people do with the knowledge they learn is as important as the knowledge itself. The decisions they make about and for their students—how they interpret tests, group pupils, or choose instructional materials, for example—will have profound effects on their students' lives. And as such, pedagogical choices are also moral and ethical decisions, not simply instructional ones.

These are only the conscious choices. Schooling is replete with the effects of the hidden curriculum—the tacit communications that serve powerfully to shape students' opinions and values about everything from strictures against cheating to the importance of punctuality (which varies depending on the SES of the school's students, of course), to their attitudes about women, minorities, and their own successes and failures. By a teacher's example, by the school's structure, by the curriculum's inclusions and omissions, children learn a lifetime of moral and ethical lessons.

But these are external factors. Values come from within as well. Kincheloe and Steinberg (1993) assert that "sciencemaking," for example, is "expressive of our values" (p. 312), and we too believe knowledge is socially constructed. If this is the case, then knowledge must be infused with personal values. Our task is to get our preservice teachers to look at their value structures, because only after making them visible and explicit can they then analyze and possibly change them (Ross, 1992). For example, analysis of literature enables students to access and evaluate their own and others' cultural values (Lickona, 1991). One exercise in the literacy methods class includes reading Disney, Grimm, and multicultural variants of Cinderella. Using Campbell's (1968) notion of the monomyth as a reflection of values, we identify heroes' and villains' traits, which actions or characteristics are rewarded or punished, and how taken-for-granted texts convey diverse and often contradictory constructions of proper ethical behavior, gender, and power.

Finally, "morality deals in large part with relationships—with the way people treat each other" (Lickona, 1991, p. 71). Like Lickona, we teach procedures for constructive communication and collaboration. We set high standards for ethical behaviors, offering corrective feedback and (what we hope are) just consequences when students fall short of our ideals. We explain how our procedures and actions reflect our own values and the ones we are trying to instill. We spend much time with students outside classrooms, since we believe these interactions help us establish ethical and emotional common ground with them.

But instruction like this is difficult within the typical institutional constraints of colleges and state bureaucracies. Accreditation boards and state certification personnel want to see "academic" outcomes. It is hard to measure and quantify morality, positive identity, emotional maturity, or caring. We face further pitfalls similar to those involved with introducing complexity and fostering positive identity. We sometimes find ourselves in situations where a little knowledge is dangerous. It takes a mature thinker to understand that an examination of the ethical is not simply an exercise in relativism—that concession to a situation is not the same as "doing what you feel at the time." Additionally, we have no easy answers to moral dilemmas, and if we want our students to become ethical, thinking people, we must serve as models for them. Making sound moral judgments and maintaining the highest possible ethical standards in our classrooms are challenging.

In our case, we have the luxury of requiring a course about the hidden curriculum and another dealing in large part with the ethics of teaching. These courses, and our emphasis on values throughout our program, demonstrate to the students our commitment to these aspects of teaching. But to deal with the ethical, to see well enough to understand the moral complexity of situations, requires that students learn to become critical—to become inquisitive and skeptical.

RECONCEPTUALIZING RESPONSIBILITY AND POWER

On the first day of class I ask a student to open the door, then to close it, then to reopen it. She or he always complies with my request. When I ask why, we always have the same exchange:

"You're the professor."
"So?"
"You asked me to."
"So?"
"You do what the professor says."
"Why?"

> There is usually an awkward pause at this point.
> "Because that's the way it is! That's how it works."

Politicizing education, searching for identity, making the familiar strange, valuing the ethical and emotional, and asking the right questions are, in great part, resultant on our students' and our own understandings of responsibility and power. We agree with Kincheloe and Steinberg (1993) that "the way we make sense of the world...is not as much a product of our own ability to assimilate information as it is the result of dominant ideologies and forces of power in the larger society " (p. 316). We are constantly "uncovering the role of power in shaping the way the world is represented" (p. 316) and assisting our students "to understand the way power shapes their lives" (p. 317).

Kincheloe and Steinberg also identify "the great paradox of contemporary schooling and teacher education: educators speak of empowerment as a central goal but often ignore the way power operates to subvert the empowerment of teachers and students" (p. 317). They explain that "teachers internalize norms and conventions, [and] they allow power to create a context that dictates their views of 'appropriate ways of being'" (pp. 317–318). When preservice teachers fail to examine internalized views of power, negative outcomes may occur, such as focusing on others' assessment rather than personal growth (Duffy, 1991), poor communication (Bean & Zulich, 1993), passive behaviors (Zeichner, 1980), resistance (Watts Pailliotet, 1995b), or replication of irrelevant, inequitable practices (Britzman, 1991).

For us, responsibility and power are interdependent. We believe students must examine and redefine normative discourses in larger social contexts, as well as construct new roles for power and responsibility in their own lives. On one level, our task involves helping them question power relations across broad levels of educational and social experience. For example, we agree that when "educational leaders use particular words, metaphors and models to design programs and policies, they reflect the effects of the influence of power" (Kincheloe & Steinberg, 1993, p. 316). Our students learn to examine overt and covert power through deconstructing dominant imagery in educational documents, observing in classrooms, and analyzing how textbooks or technology deskill teachers. We also teach through our own modeling that educational jargon may perpetuate or change power and we require accessible language in student papers and conversations.

Our second goal is an emancipatory one—to shift responsibility and power to students. Britzman (1991) asserts that acceptance of normative power relations perpetuates cultural myths about proper educational roles, leading preservice teachers to believe "everything depends on the teacher" and view students as being acted upon without responsibility for learning (pp. 221–232). We too reject these mythic educational roles and responsibilities; we strongly believe they perpetuate technocratic schooling and are antithetical to the postformal principles we espouse. Because "power serves to reward particular ways of seeing and acting" (Kincheloe & Steinberg, 1993, p. 316), we see further dangers in traditional power roles—students may simply mimic our actions with little personal understandings (Herrmann & Sarracino, 1993), and our educational vision may degenerate into yet another form of dogmatic indoctrination. Therefore, we believe we have the power not to exercise power. We model actions that enable our students to see how they might act in order to empower their own students.

We attend to many small but important elements that aid in redefining roles and responsibilities. We purposely ask students to call us by our first names rather than by formal titles that reinforce our authority. We are easily accessible, interacting frequently and informally with them. In classes, we purposely move desks into circles or sit at tables or on the floor; we avoid standing only in the "front" of the classroom. We ask students to write information on the board and to lead discussions; we move about as we teach. We monitor our ratios of talk so that students are saying more than we are; we sometimes endure long periods of silence waiting for them to initiate questions. We offer choices for most assignments. Students formulate new roles as they develop personal teaching metaphors (Bullough & Stokes, 1994), lead discussions, present group projects, and microteach. They increasingly assume responsibility by setting course objectives, developing assignments and grading criteria, engaging in ongoing self-reflection, and completing peer assessment.

We know we have accomplished our goals when we read comments like "You have empowered me to learn" or watch as individuals confidently assume new educational roles. But redistributing responsibility and power is also one of the most precarious paths we take. First, students may resist. As we've noted, many are socialized into ways of thinking and behaving that contradict our aims. Some see education as a product they buy and then expect us to deliver—without further effort on their part. Others are resentful of the time and effort increased responsibility involves. It's hard to counter assertions like "I've paid thousands of dollars for this course, so just tell us what to do" or grumbled complaints like "I wish I'd taken this class when it was easy." Above all else, students may be reluctant to assume power and responsibility, because that process involves self-disclosure, accountability, and risks—risks that challenge their established identities. It's one thing for them to blame faceless powers outside themselves for inequities in large social institutions. It's quite another to accept their own roles as oppressors or to take responsibility for personal failures and educational outcomes.

Kincheloe and Steinberg believe that teachers "fight such tendencies by drawing on student autobiography, theater and literature to connect public knowledge to our private lives" (1993, p. 316). We employ these activities throughout our courses. We also disclose a great deal about our private lives to students. Sharing our own dilemmas and doubts with them demystifies teaching, helps them see their own responsibilities as future educators, and lessens distances among us. But when you empower critical learners and share personal experiences with them, they sometimes turn their critiques on you. On one hand, this leads us to reflection, personal, and professional growth—knowing that students may challenge us creates an exciting teaching context. By modeling positive comments, we show them that negative assaults on problems are not the same as solution, analysis, or informed critique. Learning to communicate in these ways makes them more articulate, empowered people. However, many fail to distinguish between constructive and destructive feedback.

Student empowerment and personal disclosure threaten our own status and identities. Like those spiders in South America who eat their parents, students can be downright vicious in their attacks on who we are and what they do. It's painful to read evaluations like "I can honestly say there was nothing I liked about this class or the teacher." Furthermore, "teachers who let themselves be known too well by students are immediately under suspicion" (Kincheloe & Steinberg, 1993, p. 316). Our redefining of relationships and responsibilities is not always embraced by colleagues, who may see our actions as undermining their own authority. As with the politicization of education, outspoken and empowered students are not always popular. Not all professors or schoolteachers want frank appraisals about how they're doing.

Students may also perceive shared power as a personal weakness that invites excuses. We regularly hear requests such as, "Can I have an extension? I have two other papers due the same day and I can't go to those other profs. They wouldn't understand like you do." Others may take advantage of their newfound freedom, reverting to irresponsible acts. For instance, our syllabi suggest assignment deadlines and we offer frequent reminders, but we believe empowerment involves student accountability for time management. However, when we face a deluge of projects turned in at the last minute or read the consistently low rating for "clarification of student responsibilities" on our evaluations, we sometimes have doubts. Frankly, as one colleague remarked, "We get damned tired of being moms and dads!"

Furthermore, although we seek to guide students toward emancipation, there are times when we have to take back authority, such as when testy individuals argue for higher grades on substandard work or classroom disagreement turns destructive. Empowerment also implies personal choices about failure and success. It's tough for us to judge when we should give a gentle (or not so gentle) push and when to let students find their own way. It's heartbreaking when individuals filled with potential make bad choices and we have to impose consequences. Perhaps we wrestle most with how to provide guidance without becoming dogmatic. We constantly worry that despite our efforts, students may merely mimic what we say and do rather than find their own voices.

We negotiate profound tensions as we work to redefine responsibility and power. Throughout this text, we have identified many other tensions inherent in postformal processes. We conclude by discussing the role of conflict in caring communities.

CONCLUSION: POSTFORMALISM AS HUMANE CONFLICT IN HUMAN COMMUNITIES

> As we walked to lunch, Callister chuckled sardonically. "I'm systematically pulling the rug out from under everything they ever believed or did. Our students are not happy campers right now."

Politicizing education, forming new identities, exploring emotions and spirituality, making the familiar strange, valuing the ethical, and reconceptualizing existing power relations reflect many postformal principles and actions. We believe the integral thread that connects each of these processes is the conflict that resides within human communities.

Kincheloe and Steinberg (1993) evoke a dance metaphor to describe postformalism (p. 308). They also note that "disorganization is a positive step," because it enables teachers and learners "to critically accommodate our perceptions of ourselves and the world around us" (p. 313). Paradoxically, postformal teachers must introduce conflict into their students' lives to help them "look for connections" (p. 309) and create deeper meanings.

We assert that the postformal dance does not follow singular techniques or established, static patterns. It cannot be taught using an instructor's manual or learned through repetition and replication. Instead, it proceeds and unfolds in "the uncertain play" of possibilities, each inducing complex tensions among educational partners who constantly shape and reshape its directions and actions. Moving toward postformalism requires that students and teachers embrace conflict as a positive developmental step—a factor inherent in the advancement of new understandings.

Preservice teachers must experience cognitive dissonance to become complex, critical thinkers (Hollingsworth, 1989). They must also grapple with contradictory educational and social forces to achieve just, equitable outcomes (Britzman, 1991). Kincheloe and Steinberg assert that "the development of a context in which an observation can assume its full meaning is a key element in the construction of a post-formal mode of thinking" (p. 314). For us, this context occurs where conflict and community dance in harmony and dissonance. Like Palmer (1995), we believe that:

> community is not opposed to conflict. On the contrary, community is precisely that place where an arena for creative conflict is protected by the compassionate fabric of human caring.... [It] includes conflict at its very heart, checking and correcting and enlarging the knowledge of individuals by drawing on the knowledge of the group. (p. 25)

Much of what we think and do is designed to create caring communities where students may collectively experience and work through conflict. By purposely and compassionately pulling that rug out from under them, we make them aware of, then uncomfortable with, their preexisting ideas and behaviors. Only after experiencing the genuine need for learning and change that arises out of conflict are they able forge new knowledge and connections.

But, as always, there are pitfalls. As we have pointed out, postformal processes require students—and us—to grapple with complex, often unpleasant tensions. Like other white middle-class preservice teachers (Florio-Ruane & de Tar, 1995), our students often associate conflict with negative feelings or impolite confrontation. They tend to avoid the interpersonal, emotional, or intellectual experiences that might initially induce dissonance but will eventually bring them to deeper understandings. Although we teach strategies for communication and reaching consensus through modeling, discussion, role playing, problem solving, and writing, we constantly struggle with their polite reluctance and distancing. Second, change implies conflict between the safety of what is and the unknown possibilities of what could be—or should be. Change is destabilizing and frightening for many of our students. There are times when they definitely aren't happy campers. Change requires them to confront acutely personal conflicts in their own identities and lives—conflicts involving their whiteness, gender, socioeconomic status, and educational privilege—as well as dissonances among their beliefs and behaviors.

We too experience tensions. We must confront our own middle-class whiteness—our own preunderstandings. We feel compassion for the students' immediate discomfort and know the hard lessons they must learn—we have been there and still wrestle with our own personal and professional dissonances. As Palmer points out, balancing healthy conflict within caring communities is "terribly difficult work for which we are not well prepared" (1995, p. 20). Throughout our own educational experiences, we have seen too few postformal practices or practitioners from which to draw on how this is done. As a result, our courses involve a great deal of improvisation and mutability. To some, this may look like disorganization and poor planning, but we're making our way through a jungle while they commute from point A to point B year after year.

It is also occasionally difficult to judge when we have stepped over the line from healthy dissonance into resistance or undue stress. We carefully monitor students, class discussions, and assignments for negative signs. We talk with student "moles" who give us honest feedback about the current state of their peers, but balancing compassion with conflict, change with comfort, and the descriptive with the normative can be difficult endeavors. Sometimes we get it right, sometimes we don't.

We began this chapter by identifying conflicts among the realities of technical teaching and the postformal possibilities we envision. We experience these same dissonances in our own communities. Colleagues in our college may counter our ideals, methods, or materials. Like educators in many teacher preparation programs, we also find that people, practices, and conditions in schools may contradict many of the values, knowledge, and practices we teach (Britzman, 1991; Clift & Say, 1988; Goodman, 1988). Because we know unresolved differences may lead to negative outcomes, we seek to forge a greater sense of connection and community among educational participants. But often conflicts of time, geography, philosophy, power, or history keep us apart.

All human endeavor and meaning-making involves conflict within social arenas (Blumer, 1969). Postformalism sets the stage where the communal dance of meaning, caring, and conflict can arise and unfold. Above all else, postformal principles offer possibilities for humane ways of acting and thinking that better us, our students, and the greater human condition. After all, teaching and learning, like dancing, aren't about techniques or steps. Postformalism, like dancing, is about people—people moving, exploring, jostling, positioning, learning, experiencing, innovating, touching, and feeling. It is our hope that postformal practitioners may help choreograph and lead the dance.

REFERENCES

Bartel, V., & Young, B. J. (1993). "Redesigning teacher education: Lessons from a school-university collaboration." *Education, 114* (1), 85–91.

Bean, T. W., & Zulich, J. L. (1993). The other half: A case study of asymmetrical communication in content-area reading student-professor dialogue journals. In D. J. Leu & C. K. Kinzer (Eds.), *Examining central issues in literacy research, theory and practice* (pp. 289–296). Chicago: National Reading Conference.

Blumer, H. (1969). *Symbolic interactionism.* Englewood Cliffs, NJ: Prentice Hall.

Britzman, D. P. (1991). *Practice makes practice: A critical study of learning to teach.* Albany: State University of New York Press.

Bullough Jr., R. V., & Stokes, D. K. (1994). "Analyzing personal teaching metaphors in preservice teacher education as a means for encouraging professional development." *American Educational Research Journal, 31* (1), 197–224.

Bullough, R. V., Goldstein, S. L., & Holt, L. (1984). *Human interests in the curriculum.* New York: Teachers College Press.

Calderhead, J., & Robson, M. (1991). "Images of teaching: Student teachers' early conceptions of classroom practice." *Teaching and Teacher Education, 7* (1), 1–8.

Callister, T. A. (1994). "Educational computing's new direction: Cautiously approaching an unpredictable future." *Educational Theory, 44* (2), 239–255.

Campbell, J. (1968). *The hero with a thousand faces.* Princeton, NJ: Princeton University Press.

Clift, R. T., & Say, M. (1988). "Teacher education: Collaboration or conflict?" *Journal of Teacher Education, 39* (3), 2–7.

Cole, A. L. (1990). "Personal theories of teaching: Development in the formal years." *The Alberta Journal of Educational Research, 36* (3), 203–222.

Demetrulias, D. M. (1994). "Caring: Its centrality to teachers and teacher education." *Teacher Education Quarterly, 21* (2), 91–100.

Duffy, G. (1991). "What counts in teacher education? Dilemmas in educating empowered teachers." In J. Zutell & S. McCormick (Eds.), *Learner factors/teacher factors: Issues in literacy research and instruction* (pp. 1–17). Chicago: National Reading Conference.

Dyson, A. H. (1984). "Learning to write/learning to do school." *Research in the Teaching of English, 18,* 233–264.

Florio-Ruane, S., & de Tar, J. (1995). "Conflict and consensus in teacher candidates' discussions of ethnic autobiography." *English Education, 27* (1), 11–39.

Goodman, J. (1988). "The political tactics and teaching strategies of reflective, active preservice teachers." *The Elementary School Journal, 89* (1), 23–41.

Habermas, J. (1979). *Communication and the evolution of society.* Boston: Beacon.

Herrmann, B. A., & Sarracino, J. (1993). "Restructuring a preservice literacy methods course: Dilemmas and lessons learned." *Journal of Teacher Education, 44* (2), 96–106.

Hollingsworth, S. (1989). "Prior beliefs and cognitive change in learning to teach." *American Educational Research Journal, 26* (2), 160–189.

Hollingsworth, S., & Teel, K. (1991). "Learning to teach reading in secondary math and science." *Journal of Reading, 35* (3), 190–194.

Jarrett, J. I. (1991). *The teaching of values: Caring and appreciation.* London and New York: Routledge.

Kincheloe, J. L., & Steinberg, S. R. (1993). "A tentative description of postformal thinking: The critical confrontation with cognitive theory." *Harvard Educational Review, 63* (3), 296–320.

Lickona, T. (1991). *Educating for character: How our schools can teach respect and responsibility.* New York: Bantam.

Lortie, D. C. (1975). *Schoolteacher: A sociological study.* Chicago: University of Chicago Press.

McCaleb, S. P. (1994). *Building communities of learners: A collaboration among teachers, students, families, and community.* New York: St. Martin's.

Mosenthal, J. H., Schwartz, R. M., & MacIsaac, D. (1992). "Comprehension instruction and teacher training: More than mentioning." *Journal of Reading, 36* (3), 198–207.

Mosenthal, P. B. (1993). "Understanding agenda setting in reading research." In A. P. Sweet & J. I. Anderson (Eds.), *Reading research into the year 2000* (pp. 115–128).

Nieto, S. (1996). *Affirming diversity: The sociopolitical context of multicultural education* (2nd ed.). White Plains, NY: Longman.

O'Brien, D. G. (1988). "Secondary preservice teachers' resistance to content area reading instruction: A proposal for a broader rationale." In J. E. Readence & R. S. Baldwin (Eds.), *Dialogues in Literacy Research* (pp. 237–243). Chicago: National Reading Conference.

O'Brien, D. G., & Stewart, R. A. (1990). "Preservice teachers' perspectives on why every teacher is not a teacher of reading: A qualitative analysis." *Journal of Reading Behavior, 22* (2), 101–129.

O'Connor, J., & Taylor, H. P. (1992). "Understanding preservice and novice teachers' concerns to improve teacher recruitment and instruction." *Teacher Education Quarterly, 19* (3), 19–28.

Palmer, P. J. (1995, September-October). "Community, conflict, and ways of knowing." *Change,* 20–25.

Perry, C. M., & Rog, J. A. (1992). "Preservice and inservice teachers' beliefs about effective teaching and the sources of those beliefs." *Teacher Education Quarterly, 19* (2), 49–59.

Ross, E. W. (1992). "Critical constructivism and the use of knowledge about teaching." *Teacher Education Quarterly, 19* (2), 19–31.

Schön, D. (1987). *Educating the reflective practitioner.* San Francisco: Jossey-Bass.

Stover, L., & Vocke, D. E. (1992). "Developing a disposition to reflect in preservice teachers." *The Teacher Educator, 7* (3), 15–25.

Su, J. Z. X. (1993). "The study of the education of educators: A profile of teacher education students." *Journal of Research and Development in Education, 26* (3), 125–132.

Watts Pailliotet, A. (1995a). "Extending inquiries initiated in the future teachers' autobiography club." *English Education, 27* (1), 6–10.

Watts Pailliotet, A. (1995b). "Seven elementary preservice teachers' perspectives of literacy: A longitudinal study." In K. A. Hinchman, D. J. Leu, & C. K. Kinzer (Eds.), *Perspectives on literacy research and practice* (pp. 66–84). Chicago: National Reading Conference.

Watts Pailliotet, A. (1996). "Bridging distances: Building communities." *English Education, 28* (2), 161–165.

Weinstein, C. S. (1989). "Teacher education students' preconceptions of teaching." *Journal of Teacher Education, 40* (2), 44–51.

Weinstein, C. S. (1990). "Prospective elementary teachers' beliefs about teaching: Implications for teacher education." *Teaching & Teacher Education, 6* (3), 279–290.

Zeichner, K. M. (1980). "Myths and realities: Field-based experiences in preservice teacher education." *Journal of Teacher Education, 31* (6), 45–50.

Zeichner, K. M., & Gore, J. M. (1990). "Teacher socialization." In R. W. Houston, M. Haberman, & J. Sikula (Eds.), *Handbook of research on teacher education* (pp. 329–48). New York: Macmillan.

Chapter 10

The Power of Classroom Hegemony:
An Examination of the Impact of Formal
and Postformal Teacher Thinking in an
Inner-City Latina/o School

Marc Pruyn

This chapter attempts to examine in pedagogical situ and further elaborate the notion of postformal thinking advanced by Joe Kincheloe and Shirley Steinberg (Kincheloe, 1993; Kincheloe & Steinberg, 1993)—and, by way of contrast, the more static and positivistic ways of thinking embodied in formalist views of education. That is, this chapter's main goal will be to hold the theories of formalism and postformalism up to the harsh light of classroom-gathered ethnographic data in order to more fully understand what kinds of environments teachers guided by these divergent knowledges might help to foster (intentionally or otherwise).[1]

Specifically, this study examines the discursive classroom interactions of students and their teachers in two classroom settings—in a predominantly Latina/o inner-city school in Los Angeles—for the purpose of understanding how the forms of thinking employed by two very different teachers influenced classroom discourse and the formation of specific classroom cultures and hegemonies. The study presented here scrutinizes how students were socially constructed through different classroom discourses by two teachers—one guided by formalist and the other by postformalist ways of thinking. The first group of students consisted of a teacher-formed and -labeled "remedial" Spanish reading group in a bilingual second-grade classroom. This teacher tended to be guided by formalist views of education and presided over a classroom where hegemonic pedagogical structures *maintained* her learners as "remedial." The second group of students consisted of a set of youngsters from the same school who were placed in a

Spanish reading enrichment "pull-out" program. Several members of the second-grade "low" reading group described previously also participated in this program, as did other students who were identified as "reading below grade level" by their classroom teachers.[2] The teacher in this second context tended to be guided by liberal (not radical) and what I will call *pre-postformalist*" notions of education. The data indicate that this teacher facilitated a learning environment where formalist structures were challenged on several levels, as students were redefined as capable instead of below grade level, low, or remedial.

In the following section I will elaborate the key elements of the postformal, sociocultural, and sociolinguistic theories that support and help to guide this study.

POSTFORMAL, SOCIOCULTURAL, AND SOCIOLINGUISTIC THEORIES

Postformalism is a critical postmodern heuristic whose goal is to develop, among other things, forms of critical consciousness ("connected consciousness," to use Kincheloe's term), analysis, and knowledges in students, teachers, and teacher educators that go far beyond Piaget's stage theories of formal-knowledge development.[3] Kincheloe (1993) defines postformalism (and postformal thinking) in the following way:

> Post-formal thinking is not disinterested, it is committed to the critical system of meaning and the notion of social justice it assumes; post-formal thinking is not objective, it is unabashedly subjective with its celebration of intimacy between the knower and the known; post-formal thinking is not simply an adult stage of cognition, it recognizes expressions of post-formality in adolescents; post-formal thinking does not seek simply to solve defined and structured problems. Post-formal thinking is interested in the ability to see problems where others see tranquillity. (p. 143)

To more fully understand postformalism, it is important to review what we know about formalism. Formalist thinking grows out of Jean Piaget's stage theory of infant to adult cognitive development. The stages of this theory include the sensorimotor stage, the preoperational stage, the concrete-operational stage, and the formal-operational stage.[4] More specifically, the formal-operational stage, which begins at approximately age twelve and carries the adolescent into adulthood, is marked by the emergence of (positivistic) "scientific thinking" and the beginning of abstract and formal reasoning. This stage ushers in the beginning of the end of one's intellectual development.[5] From this "child-centered" individualistic approach—very helpful in maintaining hierarchical structures of power in our hypercommodified, noncommunal late capitalist society—the child is seen as an active, if socially solitary, creature who interacts with his or her environment in order to make sense of it. Yet the trajectory of one's cognitive development (and also, therefore, one's potential for "intelligence") is genetically prewired. This hegemonic theory of child development would have us move youngsters away from emotion, social interaction, and socially contextualized ways of understanding our worlds and each other, toward cold scientific rationality (Kincheloe, 1993; Kincheloe & Steinberg, 1993; Piaget, 1928, 1965, 1970; Scarr, Weinberg, & Levine, 1986).[6]

Conversely, the paradigm of postformalism would have us view cognitive development and thinking as "an act of emotional commitment which leads to political transformation" (Kincheloe, 1993, p. 156). Further, understood from a perspective of postformalism, Piaget's stage theory of sequential cognitive development itself was a social construct, no more "objective" or "true" than a moving poem by Langston Hughes[7] or a novel by Ursula K. LeGuin.[8] Kincheloe (1993) further delineates the differences between formalism and postformalism:

> In formal thinking and teaching it does not matter what constitutes student or teacher perceptions. Student or teacher meta-awareness of discursive practices, consciousness construction, or knowledge legitimation has little to do with traditional developmentalism and its attempt to move thinkers through a regulated progression of discrete cognitive stages eventuating in formal thinking. (p. 139)

On the other hand, a postformal pedagogy has as its central goal the facilitation by teachers of "connected consciousness" among their students and themselves. That is, postformally informed teachers attempt to foster within themselves and their students the skills of critical analysis and action, and further, to develop "critical consciousness" so that students and teachers alike can go from whole to part and back again as they make connections to larger social worlds and work in solidarity and for social justice with the people they come to meet in those worlds (Freire, 1970; Kincheloe, 1993; Kincheloe & Steinberg, 1993; McLaren, 1989; Pruyn, 1996).

Postformal teachers encourage their students to look for hidden and unintended meanings in society's texts and to see words (and worlds, and schools) as places of power contestation. These teachers are driven by a "critical constructivism" versus an acritical positivism and believe we should embrace the uncertain and tentative nature of knowledge and "intelligence" while at the same time working in solidarity with others (Freire & Macedo, 1987). Instead of lauding the forms of microawareness advanced by limited (and limiting) tautologies such as the Enlightenment's (and Piaget's) positivistic and so-called pure scientific thinking, postformal pedagogues encourage their students to develop a meta-awareness of different social contexts and structures of power as they develop empathy for others. Instead of patiently waiting for students to progress to the next allowable cognitive stage, postformalist-inspired teachers advise their students to question everything and to recognize that human beings are capable of developing forms of cognition and intelligence in divergent and simultaneous ways throughout their lifetimes—and that the *mind itself* is socially constructed (Kincheloe, 1993; Kincheloe & Steinberg, 1993; Pruyn, 1994, 1996).

Postformal thinking has the potential to help teachers (novice to senior K-12 teachers as well as those of us who work with adults) to more fully understand and then begin to deconstruct the subtle, limiting (and, at the same time, commonsense) and oppressive "truths" of myopic Enlightenment modernism. In drawing on the work of Russel, Cherryholmes, and Foucault, Kincheloe (1993) describes the terrain of struggle postformalist educators must learn to navigate:

> The habitual beliefs of an individual's age become tyrants to a mind unable to reflect upon their genesis.... When teachers internalize these norms and conventions, they allow power to dictate their views of appropriate "ways of being." (pp. 139, 169)

In making more concrete the philosophical notions forwarded by postformalism and critical theory, it would be helpful to review work done in the area of sociocultural and sociolinguistic theory (noncritical and critical traditions alike).[9]

As with postformalism, sociocultural and sociolinguistic theorists hold that knowledges and "intelligence" are socially constructed (Cole & Griffin, 1983; Gutierrez, 1992b, 1994; Vygotsky, 1962, 1978). Civilizations develop cultural tools, such as literacy and numeracy, to help them mediate and understand their environments. These tools are developed and refined over long periods of time within societies and groups

(Gutierrez, 1992b, 1993a; Vygotsky, 1962, 1978). New members of a society are given access to these tools in daily, meaningful social activities with more proficient and expert others until they themselves become experts in the use of the set of tools that their society has deemed important (Cole, 1991, 1996; Rogoff, 1990, 1991; Vygotsky, 1978). As Kris Gutierrez (1992a) notes, "Central to children's development of competence is the opportunity to participate in contexts with other competent members of their social group" (p. 251).

Socioculturalists and sociolinguists would argue, then, that through analyzing schooling from this perspective, we might be able to gain insight into how traditional pedagogical sites function on an interpersonal basis and what the relationships and activities established through these interactions portend for the cognitive and social development of students. Investigations undertaken from this perspective attempt to illuminate how, through linguistic and other forms of social and cultural interaction, novices are given access to new skills and ways of knowing and behaving—or, conversely, *not* given access to them.

Sociocultural and sociolinguistic theorists view language development, in particular, as a process of language socialization in which people are socialized both *through* language and *to use* language in different ways (Ochs, 1988; Ochs & Schieffelin, 1984). Elinor Ochs contends that we are socialized through language when we learn cultural norms and ways of being through language. We learn sociocultural knowledge, what is acceptable and unacceptable. She notes, "Children develop concepts of a socioculturally structured universe through their participation in language activities" (1988, p. 14). We are socialized to use language when we learn how to manipulate the language through words and gestures. Through this process, we acquire linguistic knowledge, rules, and norms (as they are defined within specific contexts).

While analytically helpful, and even largely agreeable to poststructuralist thinkers, these guiding tenets of noncritical sociocultural and sociolinguistic theory do not go far enough in making connections between language/discourse and oppression/liberation. A distinguishing factor between noncritical and critical sociocultural and sociolinguistic theories is how the connection between discourse—the written, oral, and gestural languages we use with one another as human beings—and power is viewed. Sociolinguist James Paul Gee (1990) believes it is of utmost importance to understand that the "Discourses" we (co- or re-) produce together as human beings can serve to either confine or liberate us.

Discourses are not power-free or neutral.[10] Noted critical discourse theorist Norman Fairclough (1992) has pointed out that "discourse as a political practice establishes, sustains and changes power relations, and the collective entities...between which power relations obtain" (p. 67). Building on Foucauldian and Gramscian notions of power, Fairclough asserts that these power relations, far from being overt and outwardly coercive—although they *can* be—are more often than not invisible. Further, those individuals who produce and/or suffer under various oppressive relations of power are not always aware of their existence, for they tend to become "regularized" in ongoing social practices (Fairclough, 1992, pp. 3, 6).

Gutierrez and her colleagues (Gutierrez, 1992b, 1994; Gutierrez, Larson & Kreuter, 1995) take *critical* sociocultural positions in their discourse analyses of the social contexts for success or failure for Latina/o youth in southern California classrooms. Their work, unlike that of their noncritical counterparts, demonstrates an understanding of the intimate connections between culture, power, discourse, and hegemony. Building on the work of Jean Lave and Etienne Wenger (1991), Gutierrez's work has consistently shown how students and teachers naturally develop identities and take up subject positions as they participate in learning activities in the social world that have specific and identifiable power outcomes. According to Gutierrez, Rymes, and Larson (1995), relations of power *between* people shape the identities of those people through their ongoing and regular discursive and linguistic interactions—whether those identities be of "high group" (so-called intelligent) students, or "low" group (so-called remedial) students.

Also working in the critical socioculturalist tradition, Wenger (1991) has put forth the idea that we acquire knowledges, sociocultural ways of being, through what they call "communities of practice." It is through participation in such communities that students, over time, gain the sociocultural and technical skills necessary to be productive, full members of various learning communities—or, conversely, to "learn" how to be unsuccessful in mainstream learning communities. Critical sociocultural and sociolinguistic theorists suggest that skills and behaviors that provide students with greater levels of success are more easily learned if favorable power arrangements exist in classrooms and learning settings (Lave, 1988, 1991; Lave & Wenger, 1991; Wenger, 1997). Restrictive and asymmetrical power distributions, discourse patterns, and physical arrangements tend to (re)produce dominant, and often repressive, hegemonic practices (Gutierrez & Larson, 1994; Pruyn & Fischman, 1994).

Gee (1990) suggests that as researchers and teachers (especially the latter), we must go beyond a mere recognition of discourse's role in producing or potentially challenging hierarchies of power; we must take theoretical and pedagogical stands against oppressive forms of discursively produced power hierarchies and "out" our own tacit theories about students and their abilities to learn that help inform and construct these hierarchies and specific classroom learning environments in the first place. He notes (pp. xviii, xx) that teachers must have a "full commitment to social justice, if they have a commitment to allowing every child to acquire [and to critique] the school's and society's Discourses" (p. xviii). He adds that it is a teacher's moral obligation to "render one's tacit theories overt when they have the potential to hurt people" (p. xx).

Critical sociocultural and sociolinguistic theorists such as Gutierrez (Gutierrez, Larson & Kreuter, 1995), Gee (1990) and Lave and Wenger (1991) hold not only that pedagogic identities are formed in social interactions with others, but that these interactions are intimately tied up with power relations between individuals and between individuals and groups. Put another way, power relations, discourse, and social identities (of "success" or "failure") are mutually informative.

As this chapter draws from postformalist approaches to teacher thinking and critical philosophy, it will also mine critical sociocultural and sociolinguistic theories as it analyzes and critiques the classroom discourse in two specific educational sites. As with all social theory, we need to examine and deconstruct the theory of postformalism—especially within specifically situated discursive pedagogic settings (i.e., classrooms)—in order to move this potentially very useful critical postmodern heuristic forward to a larger audience of practitioners and teacher educators. This present study hopes to be part of that project.

THE SITE AND THE DATA

Maple Street Elementary is part of Los Angeles's inner city.[11] It is a pre-K through fifth-grade school where 97 percent of the students are Latina/o and Spanish is the predominant language. Of the Latina/o student population, the majority are Salvadoran and Guatemalan—many of whose families fled their countries as political and/or economic refugees. Most residents live near or below the poverty line, with both parents usually working—in sweatshops, as day laborers, doing piecework at home, or as street vendors. The school itself has approximately 1,900 students and 80 teachers; it operates on a year-round schedule and has a very well staffed and administratively supported bilingual education program.

An ethnographic case study methodology was chosen for this study because what was encountered at this site was a naturally occurring, ongoing case (Walcott, 1988). Initially it was my intention to examine classroom discourse patterns during reading time in the second-grade classroom exclusively. The teacher, Susana Rivera, was a professional acquaintance, and I knew from our interactions that she considered herself a "traditional" and "skills-based" teacher. Based on our conversations and how she described her classroom practices, I hypothesized that she was informed by formalist ways of thinking and teaching. A discursive examination of the practices of her "low" reading group, I believed, would shed light on this question.[12] When I learned that three of the students in Susana's "low" reading group also attended Pedro García's pull-out Spanish reading enrichment program, a naturally occurring, ongoing comparative case study presented itself.[13] These types of qualitative methods also allow us to contextualize the social interactions we observe at research sites (Walcott, 1988), which was one of my primary concerns in this study. Qualitative research generally, and case study methods in particular, can help us as researchers to access simultaneously the micro and macro processes within the social interactions that comprise phenomena within educational and other settings (Miles & Huberman, 1984; Oakes, Gamoran, & Page, 1992). This is especially important in a study such as this, informed by postformalism and critical socioculturalism and sociolinguistics. Further, qualitative case study methods can help us see how participants construct understandings for themselves as they participate in their everyday experiences at a site. Additionally, case study methods allow researchers to look at real-life change as it occurs naturally over time (Yin, 1994). For the purposes of this study, which attempts to unpackage both micro and macro social phenomena within one educational setting, there was no other choice, for practical or theoretical reasons, than to use case study research methods.

Over the span of one semester, site observations were conducted of Susana Rivera's second-grade "low" Spanish reading group and of Pedro García's pull-out Spanish reading enrichment group. Within the ethnographic, qualitative research tradition, language arts lessons, which ranged from twenty to thirty minutes in length, were observed in each setting, and field notes, videotapes of activities, and lengthy interviews with both teachers and the three crossover students were collected. The activities observed were first summarized, and then key representative segments of classroom discourse were transcribed from the videotapes and field notes; the interviews with the teachers and the students were also transcribed. These data were then analyzed from a critical perspective using discourse analysis.

INFORMED BY FORMALISM: THE HEGEMONY OF SUSANA'S "LOW" READING GROUP

The Teachers and the Students

Susana Rivera is a fully bilingual teacher in her late twenties from Mexico. She is dedicated and hardworking—often spending hours before and after school preparing—and seems to care very much for her students. Methodologically, Susana believes in the "skills" and "phonics" approaches to literacy instruction. Susana's teaching assistant, Ernesto Ortega, an older Salvadoran, is also favorably disposed to the traditional pedagogical approaches used by Susana.

One day Ernesto was leading the "low" reading group. Seven children made up this group: two girls (Gloria and Hilda) and five boys (Gregorio, Sylvestre, Jacobo, Freddy, and Joshua). These students were generally discouraged from reading along as their classmates read (or from assisting their classmates at all), unless requested to do so by the teacher. Several times the students were asked to "cover your work" so that those sitting next to them wouldn't be tempted to "copy." The students in this group are all Latina/o, and Spanish is their primary language.

One of the children in the group was having difficulty decoding a word off the board. Ernesto, in an aside to me that could be heard by half the class, commented, "We should send him back to kindergarten. He's confusing letters." Another boy in the same group concurred with Ernesto's assessment of the struggling reader and added—also in a loud voice—"He can't read."

Susana, the pedagogue proper, elaborated during one of many interviews that she saw the teacher's role as one of providing behavioral "reinforcement" and of being very "demanding" of the students. Literacy, she said, involves being able to "read and write" and to acquire a number of discrete skills, such as learning how to decode letters, then syllables, then words, then sentences, and then stories. This is a "very structured" process that requires a lot of hard work on the part of all those involved. She said learning to read and write entailed "a lot of repetition and practice...mainly it's having them work.... You have to keep pounding and pounding and pounding until they finally get it." For Susana, literacy is not something that was easily acquired, especially for children. In emphasizing the cumulative nature of skill and vocabulary development in the literacy acquisition process as she saw it, she noted, "I think kids get literate at about maybe the fifth or sixth grade. In these grades they can just pull some things together and become literate." Following from these understandings of learning processes as well as her criteria for students being "literate" and being able to demonstrate "preliterate acts," she labeled the group of students observed for this study in her classroom as "low" in ability. For these students, their teacher, and the teaching assistant who occasionally worked with them, being "able to read"—that is, being able to decode and encode syllables—and "not being able to read" had become a constant preoccupation.

This curriculum of syllable decoding left little room for student-initiated text production or student reading of self-produced or original texts. Reading time that was not dedicated to the type of syllabic decoding described above was devoted to copying words off the board that students would later have to recopy and practice at home. Few examples of students having the opportunity to experiment on their own with reading (silent reading time) or writing (journaling) were evidenced. The children appeared bored and frustrated, and this was recognized by Susana. She commented, "They get bored and I get bored. It's not that exciting.... It gets kind of boring." But this, according to the teacher's pedagogy, was unavoidable. That was the nature of literacy instruction as she both understood it and implemented it in her classroom.

Examining Situational Literacy Practice through Discourse

Susana's "low" reading group had been socialized to use and understand literacy, that is, reading and writing, in very specific ways. For these students and their teacher, being socialized to read and write meant being socialized to phonetically manipulate letters and syllables in a very traditional, formalist manner whose goal was discrete mastery. This pedagogical approach is visible in discourse sample #1, below, where Jacobo and Gloria—who regularly struggled with the decoding tasks given them by Susana and Ernesto—are trying to read the word *rasca* ("scratch") from the board.[14]

Discourse Sample #1: *Rasca*

1	Susana:	**a ver**
2		*let's see*
3		((Teacher nods her head at Jacobo to read, but Gloria begins to read instead))
4	Gloria:	**la**
5	Susana:	**r::r qué letra es ésta qué letra estamos vie[ndo**
6		*r::r what letter is this what letter are we [seeing*
7	Gloria:	**[r::r r:re**
8		((Gloria is trying to read the
9		syllable "ra"))
10	Susana:	**r::r**
11	Jacobo:	**r::r r:ro r:ra**
12	Susana:	**ra está bien ra**
13		*ra that's good ra*
14		((Teacher shakes her finger and arm in the air mimicking the movement of rattle
15		snake's tail to help Jacobo with the "S" sound))
16	Jacobo / Gloria:	**s:sa**
17	Susana:	**ras:s ras:s**
18		((The teacher underlines the remaining syllable of the word, "ca," with her finger
19		on the black board))
20	Jacobo:	**ce**
21	Susana:	**rra[ss**
22	Gloria:	**[rrass**
23	Susana:	**ya la tienes casi rrass**
24		*you already have it almost rrass*
25	Gloria:	**rrass**
26		((long pause))
27	Susana:	**hasta aquí van bien**
28		*until here you're doing well rass*
29		((She underlines "ras" with her finger))
30		**rrass**
31	Gloria:	**rrass**
32	Susana:	**qué dice acá ahora**
33		*what does it say here now*

34		((She underlines "ca" with her finger))
35		**rrass**
36	Gloria /	
	Jacobo:	((No response))
37	Susana:	**qué letra es ésta rrass**
38		*what letter is this rrass*
39	Gloria:	**C**
40	Susana:	**entonces cómo suena**
41		*therefore what sound does it make*
42		((The teacher makes the hard Spanish sound for "C"))
43		**rrass**
44	Gloria:	**rrass**
45	Susana:	**rrass**
46	Jacobo:	**rrass**
47		((Long pause))
48	Susana:	**rrass…les puedo decir yo está difícil rras:sca**
49		*rrass…can I tell you it's a little difficult scr:ratch*
50		**él siempre se rasca la mano rasca**
51		*he always scratches his hand scratch*

From the very beginning of this interaction, students are being socialized to use language in ways modeled by the teacher. In line 4, as Gloria first attempts to read "*ra,*" the first syllable of *rasca,* she says, "*la.*" Susana comes in immediately and models (in lines 5–6: "*R::r* what letter is this? What letter are we seeing?") the "*rr*" sound that "*ra*" begins with—as opposed to the "*lll*" sound Gloria read. Gloria then responds with the rolling "*rr*" sound in line 7 ("*r::r r::e*") as she gets closer to reading the syllable "*ra*" correctly. Yet she is still unable to perform the task, so Susana further prompts her with "*r::r*" (line 10).

Jacobo (in line 11) then takes up the task of trying to decode "*ra*" and goes fishing in the syllabic family of "*r*" (*ra, re, ri, ro,* and *ru*) in an attempt to find the syllable the teacher is looking for. As he says "*r::r, r:ro, r:ra,*" the teacher seizes upon his production of "*r:ra*" and praises him: "*Ra.* That's good. *Ra*" (lines 12–13).

Later (in lines 17–19), as both Gloria and Jacobo find themselves unable to decode "*sca,*" the rest of *rasca,* the teacher offers a verbal and gestural prompt to help them along. As she is underlining the syllable "*ca*"—as it appears in the word *rasca*—on the board with her hand, she verbally prompts: "*Ras:s, ras:s*" (line 17). Although Jacobo is unsuccessful in his attempt to decode "*ca,*" he come close with "*ce*" (line 20)—maybe in another attempt to "fish" for the appropriate ending letter to the consonant-vowel combination the teacher is seeking from them.

At other times in the interaction Susana offers praise and encouragement ("You already almost have it," lines 23–24, and "Until here you're doing well," lines 27–28), but ultimately this is an ineffectual exercise. In the specific contextualized setting of this activity, the students are unable to "correctly" decode the word *rasca,* and the teacher ultimately gives them the "answer" (lines 48–49: "*Rrass*...can I tell you? It's a little difficult. *Rras:sca.*"). In the end, these students seem to lack a view of themselves as competent readers and writers, and they also lack the specific reading and writing skills that have been the object of the teacher's instruction—even given her very specific and acontextual definition of those skills.

Within this setting, Susana was apprenticing her students, but not in behaviors and practices that would ultimately give them concrete success in reading and writing. This reading community, far from being empowering, appeared to disempower its novice members. Much like the apprentice butchers studied and described by Wenger (1991)—who, although located within the context of a butcher's professional work site and in the company of more expert others, often failed to gain the expertise that would make this apprenticeship experience effective, because of the ways activities and learning experiences were arranged and constructed around them—these bilingual students gained competence in a group of skills, but skills that served only to redefine and "produce" them as "low" students.

Although the teacher may have been unaware of the consequences of her instruction and interactions with this group, she further entrenched their state of "remedialness." These students *were* legitimate peripheral participants within these activities (Lave, 1991; Lave & Wenger, 1991; Wenger, 1997), but they were legitimate peripheral participants to a community of practice that was defined by being a "remedial student." That is, within this setting, being a good reader meant seeing written language as a connected string of syllables, being able to decode syllabically, and being able to combine syllabic utterances into words—not sentences or paragraphs, or stories, or larger ideas, but words.

Understanding the Culture of This Classroom: (Re)producing Dominant Pedagogical Hegemony

The nature of reading and writing, of literacy, and of classroom discourse for this group of learners seemed to be one of repetition, drudgery, and boredom. Any potential sense of linguistic wholeness on the part of the students was broken down into small parts and never fully reassembled into meaningful and relevant discourse. Susana's pedagogy exalted formalism's belief in youngsters' slow, cautious, and deliberate mastery of formal "logical" categories and incremental cognitive development. This literacy environment was characterized by labored oral reading, where students worked as discrete individuals, without collaborating or helping one another. It was more important to read a little correctly than it was to read a lot imperfectly and with joy. According to Susana, students first had to pass through several normalized and progressive reading and writing "stages": consonant and vowel memorization, written and oral syllabic formation from those consonants and vowels, a further combination of these vowels into words, eventual aggregation of these words into sentences, paragraphs, stories, and ideas (although this was, by Susana's own admission, beyond the scope of her second-grade curriculum), and eventual developing "literacy" by approximately the "fifth or sixth grade."

Despite this teacher's hours of hard work, preparation, and apparent dedication to her students, they were nonetheless socialized through, and to use, language in ways that made them see themselves as less than competent language users, at least in Susana's classroom. This was the case despite her stated objective of just the opposite—that is, to encourage her students to become proficient readers and writers. Not only did her students lack proficiency in reading and writing (as contextually defined), but they came to believe they did not have the *ability* to become proficient. Students were being socialized, as can and often happens (Lave & Wenger, 1991), into a language community that was ultimately *disempowering*.

The instantiated community of practice in this "low" reading group was not one that allowed participants to develop the kinds of literacy behaviors and attitudes that would gain them long-term success as readers and writers. And because of the way they were socialized to use language (they were "illiterates," and reading and writing was "hard" and "boring"), they did not enjoy reading or come to see literacy as something that could be employed as a useful, or even enjoyable, cultural tool in their lives. Rather, they were hegemonized to see literacy as a painful series of skills one must learn in school. Additionally, these students were hegemonically guided to understand the development of literacy as a solitary act. They were not encouraged to help or assist one another, but rather to understand literacy egocentrically, to see it only in terms of the self ("How can *I* decode and make sense of this word myself, for only my own purposes?").

This approach did not allow students to get outside themselves and understand our and our words' social, political, and cultural formation and contextual situatedness. Because of Susana's instantiations of these formalist notions of education, it appeared that, for these students, hegemonic pedagogical structures were maintained, and this group of learners continued to be defined, and to self-define, as "remedial."

Susana, however, is not alone. Her discursive classroom practice, and the formalist or normative teacher thinking that guides it, is in harmony with the dominant formalist pedagogical hegemony of society. Most teachers teach this way. In reporting on the work of Young, Kincheloe (1993, p. 138) notes that over 80 percent of U.S. teachers base their classroom practices on the well-trodden assumptions of formalism.

INFORMED BY *PRE*-POSTFORMALISM:
THE COUNTERHEGEMONY OF PEDRO'S
"PULL-OUT" READING PROGRAM

The Teacher and the Students

Pedro García's Spanish reading enrichment "pull-out" program is the second context for this study. (In referring to Pedro's program, Susana said, "I don't like it. It was good when Mrs. Córdova ran it.[15] But now I don't know....I don't know how they can read *Fiestas* there and then come back here...and they're not doing so well.")[16] Pedro himself defined this program as one designed for "regular" kids who have been "messed up" by the literacy instruction offered in their primary classrooms. Gloria, Sylvestre, and Hilda, in addition to their work with Susana, went to Pedro's classroom once a day to receive, as they put it, "extra help" in reading. During interviews, Pedro stated that he approaches literacy instruction from a "whole-language" and "literature-based" perspective. He is a fully bilingual Chicano teacher whose family emigrated from Mexico when he was very young. He is in his late thirties, is also a dedicated and hardworking teacher, and is well known and liked by many in the Maple Elementary community—although not by a strong and vocal minority of teachers, including Susana, who disagree with his pedagogical approach.

This teacher's conception of literacy is markedly different from that of Susana. For Pedro, literacy (and reading) must start with assisting students in making connections to things with which they are already familiar. He said, "I make sure everything is related to what they understand already." This is important to him because he believes that the learner must be "in control" of the reading and writing process. This, for Pedro, is linked to academic success: "If you're controlling something, there's no way in the world you can fail. Maybe you do something differently than the other person, but there's no way in the world that you are going to fail when you are controlling the whole thing." Pedro believes that when the cycle of literate and academic failure has already been set in motion, a student's chances for full literacy become difficult. He elaborated:

> A lot of times you'll find, in the traditional classrooms, [students] learn[ing] vocabulary words and spelling. [The unsuccessful student] is going to "fail" the test. So the word doesn't mean much to them anyway. So they're failing in their reading, and on their tests, so they're learning [that they can't read]. And a lot of times, instead of the teacher saying, "Well, forget that method, it's not working," they'll make the kid sit down and write the word five times...you know, *every* word.... So they are failing more than once, over, like, *five silly words!* The kids that I get, someone convinced them that they couldn't read. Or somebody showed them that they're "not as good as..." I would say 70 percent of the kids I get in here, all I have to do is convince them they can read.

Pedro's physical classroom and building appear warm and homelike. On the exterior of the portable bungalow where his classes are held, he and his students have painted a mural of a Latin American street scene. This is in sharp contrast to the industrial off-beige and orange colors that cover the rest of the buildings at the school. Further, the finishing trim on the bungalow's doors and windows are in bright, contrasting pastel colors, and plants line the two short staircases that lead up to the room's two doors. Inside, besides the large rectangular grouping of tables where all the students and Pedro sit facing each other for their regular group lessons, we see two small sofas, several house lamps, some throw rugs and a number of open bookshelves well stocked with children's literature. In the bottom and toward the back of a less accessible bookshelf are a number of basal readers that Pedro said he only occasionally used in order to familiarize students with what they are or will shortly be using in their regular classrooms.

Over time, as I watched the students and Pedro sitting and working around the table, I got the impression that they were engaged in working together on a joint task, that they were all on the same "side" in this endeavor to develop student literacy. More empirically, words, sentences, and stories were the focus of instruction here, rather than decontextualized letters and syllables. Student-generated texts competed for wall space with colorful posters of children engaged in reading. In general, students were encouraged and assisted in quickly moving through the literature- and student-based texts that were at the center of their reading program with Pedro, with the primary goal being student comprehension and understanding of the texts as opposed to exact and "correct" decoding and pronunciation of each word that comprises these texts.

In this setting, students frequently read individually and quietly on their own, or out loud as a group or "round robin" style. Students were encouraged to read aloud as their classmates read and to help each other. Students were discouraged, however, from breaking up words into syllables and reading haltingly. Pedro used correction very selectively, not correcting every mistake or looking for "correct" answers every time. He tended to focus on students having a successful reading experience and understanding the meaning of the passage. When he did correct the students, it was usually through modeling. He gave praise and support to his students in verbal and physical ways: a "Well done!" or "You all can read so well" after a passage is read, or maybe a supportive touch on the shoulder or head.

Examining Situational Literacy Practice through Discourse

Pedro's enrichment reading group has also been socialized to use and understand literacy in very specific ways. For these students and their teacher, being socialized to read and write means being socialized to understand the context of the story you are reading and how the words and ideas that make it up form, create, and support that story. In Pedro's classroom, the reading process is often characterized by students' oral reading in turn. But, instead of reading from the board or from charts, they read from books. In the reading event transcribed below (discourse sample #2), students are reading aloud from a story about a girl who goes out to play in the rain. They read this story in turn, two pages of text at a time, with the teacher's guidance and prompting. Words are drawn from the text and written on the board and discussed when students have trouble decoding with them. Between the reading turns, the story is discussed, with examples and connections being drawn from the students' lives and experiences. Jacobo and Gloria are present but do not participate directly in reading the two pages that comprise this turn. Hilda and Sylvestre, also members of Susana's "low" reading group, are also present and do participate.

Discourse Sample #2: *"La niña y la lluvia"*

1	Student:	((A student has just finished reading))
2	Pedro:	**perfecto muy bien todos lo hicieron bien**
3		*perfect very good everyone did it well*
4		**porqué se está bañando la niña**
5		*why is the girl bathing*
6	Student:	((unintelligible))
7	Pedro:	**porqué se baño**
8		*why did she bathe*
9	Hilda:	**por que tiene jabón en los ojos**
10		*because she has soap in her eyes*
11	Pedro:	**no qué pasó con ella primero**
12		*no what happened with her first*
13	Hilda:	[((…))
14	Student:	[se ensució [con la agua
15		*{she got dirty {with water*
16	Hilda:	[no
17	Pedro:	**con la qué**
18		*with what*
19	Student:	**con la agua de la lluvia**
20		*with the rainwater*
21	Pedro:	**y ahorrita que está pasando allá**
22		*and at this moment what is happening out there*
23		((Points to the classroom window))
24	All:	**lloviendo está lloviendo**
25		*raining it's raining*
26	Pedro:	**lloviendo y ustedes cómo entraron**
27		*raining and you how did you enter ((the classroom))*
28	All:	((unintelligible))
29		**con agua**
30		*with water*
31	Pedro:	**con agua ustedes entraron mojados**
32		*with water you entered wet*
33	Sylvestre:	**moja:aos moja:aos**
34		*we:et we:et*
35		((He laughs at the double entendre he is making with the word mojados))
36	Pedro:	**ella ((la niña en el cuento)) se mojó la:as:s**

37		*she ((the girl in the story)) wet he:er:r*
38		((He lightly slaps his own cheeks))
39	Student:	**um::m**
40	Student:	**mejillas**
41		*cheeks*
42	Pedro:	y también la::a
43		*and also he:er:r*
44		((He grabs his chin))
45	All:	**barbilla**
46		*chin*
47	Pedro:	**también e:el:l**
48		*and he:er:r*
49		((He touches his hair))
50	All:	**cabello**
51		*hair*
52	Pedro:	**y qué le gusta beber la niña**
53		*and what does the girl like to drink*
54	All:	**agua**
55		*water*
56	Pedro:	**y porqué. dónde llega l'agua**
57		*and why. where does the water come from*
58	Student:	((unintelligible))
59	All:	**por su boca**
60		*through her mouth*
61	Pedro:	**por su boca muy bien. y qué van a hacer ustedes**
62		*through her mouth very good. and what are you going to do*
63		**entonces ustedes se van a ahogar verdad**
64		*therefore you are going to drown right*
65	Student:	**no:o**
66	All:	**Si::i!**
67		*ye::es:s!*
68		((Laughing))

In line 1, a student has just finished reading two pages of text, and Pedro initiates a review and discussion of the text by asking, in lines 4–5 and 7–8, "Why is the girl [in the story] bathing? Why did she bathe?" Throughout this discourse sample, as well as throughout the general reading discourse patterns in the classroom, Pedro assists his students' literacy learning in several ways.

First, he praises his students: at the beginning (lines 2–3) with, "Perfect. Very good. Everyone did it well" and toward the end (lines 61–62) with, "Through her mouth. Very good."

Second, he reviews and asks comprehension questions of his students: in lines 4–5 with, "Why is the girl bathing?"; 7–8 with, "Why did she bathe?"; 11–12 with, "No. What happened with her first?"; 17–18 with, "With what?"; 36–37 with, "She wet heeerrr...?"; 42–43 and 47–48 with, "And heeerrr...?"; 52–53 with, "And what does the girl like to drink?"; and in lines 56–57 with, "And why? Where does the water come from?"

Third, Pedro attempts to "connect" the events of the text to his students' experiences: in lines 21–22 with, "And at this moment, what is happening out there?"; 26–27 with "[It's] raining. And how did you enter [the classroom]?"; 31–32 with, "With water. You entered wet"; 56–57 with, "And why? Where does the water come from?"; and in lines 63–64 with, "Therefore you are going to drown, right?"

Fourth and finally, Pedro interjects "gesturally" to give clues to his students as to the meanings of the written texts: in line 23, ((Points to the classroom window)); 38, ((He lightly slaps his own cheeks)); 44, ((He grabs his chin)); and in line 49, ((He touches his hair)).

Through these praising, review and comprehension, connecting, and gestural prompts, Pedro assists students in co-constructing literacy abilities and textual understandings—students are invited and encouraged to create meaning with the teacher. Additionally, between his use of these discursive interjections, Pedro regularly laces in periods of more extended meaning-building through conversation, discussion, and dialogue with the students about the texts at hand.

Within this second setting, the data indicate that Pedro was apprenticing his students in behaviors that *would* ultimately empower and give them concrete successes in reading and writing. His students were learning to read for pleasure, instead of for the sake of progressing through formal stages of literacy development. They were learning to derive and give meaning to various texts of substantial length in their entirety versus trying to make sense of random sets of acontextualized consonants, vowels, syllables, and small words that had only their syllabic families in common. And, maybe most important, Pedro's students were learning to *become* successful readers by *practicing* being successful reader, as opposed to learning to be "remedial" and "low" readers by practicing being "remedial" and "low" readers. These bilingual students gained competence in a set of skills that served to define and produce them as competent and capable.

One day I asked the three students of Pedro's who are also students of Susana's if they prefer reading from books, lists of words off the blackboard, or words off homework charts (the latter two are options in Susana's class). Sylvestre touched the book he held in his hand and said, "This. Yes. Because like this you can learn more words than Ms. Rivera gives us." Gloria shared that she prefers to read off the homework charts and from books. Hilda commented, "Yes, me too, from books."

Understanding the Culture of This Classroom: A Ripple in the Waters of Dominant Pedagogical Hegemony

Pedro's was not a highly critical and postformalist classroom. During formal interviews and many informal conversations, Pedro seemed rather atheoretical and aphilosophical about his pedagogy. Although he never labeled it as such, however, his classroom *practice* seemed guided by certain elements of postformalism.

There was a certain collectiveness about this classroom and its practices. It was not only physically arranged and appointed to look like a home, but the learning activities and ways of being within the space had a very familial feel to them. The literacy activities did not lend themselves to group, social class, gender, or race problem solving. Rather, they were about socially contextualizing texts and the reading process for individual students in this pull-out program—and not much else. The activities and practices in Pedro's classroom did not necessarily help students to develop widespread social solidarity and to call for cultural and political changes, but they did call for changes in the practices of their regular classrooms—and changes in how they saw themselves as potential readers.

Pedro and his students were beginning, perhaps, to unravel some of the edges of hegemonic formalism. Students were encouraged to interpret texts for themselves and to focus on the relationships between humans (themselves and their classmates) and objects (stories and books) versus only between grammatical objects (consonants, vowels, and the syllables and words they formed). Yet these youngsters were not apprenticed in how to more fully deconstruct socially encoded texts and to read the larger world in all its different ways.

However, as Kincheloe (1993) notes, "Post-formal thinking and post-formal teaching become whatever an individual, a student, or a teacher can produce in the realm of new understandings and knowledge" (p. 145). So yes, some form of postformalism appeared to be present in Pedro's thinking and classroom, however subtle. At least a few ripples in the waters of dominant pedagogical hegemony were made by Pedro and his students. I choose to call this a form of pre-postformalism. Behind the colorful mural and trim paint, they were working collectively toward some sense of "connected consciousness," even if it was just in their own solitary classroom and program. In this way, Pedro facilitated a learning environment where formalist structures were challenged as students were redefined as capable readers and writers.

CONCLUSION

In this chapter, the discursive classroom interactions of one group of Latina/o learners was presented, analyzed, and critiqued within the context of a "low" Spanish reading group in a regular classroom and as "regular" students participating in a pull-out Spanish reading enrichment program. It was found that Susana Rivera tended to be guided by formalist notions of education and presided over a classroom where dominant hegemonic pedagogical structures maintained her learners as remedial. Pedro García, on the other hand, tended to be guided by pre-postformalist" notions of education and facilitated a learning environment where these structures were challenged as students were redefined as capable.

Gutierrez (1994) notes:

> As children participate in events, they help to shape activity, and in turn, are shaped by the activity of others in these socially constituted activities. Through this process of shaping and being shaped by activity...children acquire both linguistic and sociocultural knowledge for what it means to be a member of a community and to act in socially appropriate ways....[By] participating in the events of classroom life, students have particular opportunities to acquire situated understandings of what counts as literacy in particular classrooms. (pp. 3–4)

If we redefine what "social appropriateness" means in learning contexts from a position of postformalism and critical postmodernism— whose goals include furthering social justice and human solidarity, and creating environments for success for all learners in ways they will find meaningful in their everyday lives—then we, like Pedro, might turn what we do between the four walls of our classrooms day in and day out into opportunities that truly count.

NOTES

1. I do not for a moment wish to leave the impression that the data presented in this chapter in any way constitute that most honored and worshiped demigod of modernist social science research, the "truth." On the contrary, the data presented below, and the fleeting and very partial slice of "reality" of the classrooms studied, are quite contingent and interpretive. I heartily invite other colleagues to deconstruct and reinterpret this work. I do believe, however, that attempting to unpack and more fully understand our larger philosophical and historical educational concepts through the lens of classroom practice is a healthy and potentially creative intellectual process.

2. Throughout this text, and at the risk of being repetitive, I will consistently use quotation marks when referring to the reading group observed in Susan Rivera's classroom, for I hold that "low" or "high" reading ability is socially constructed and not the result of innate "intelligence" or "ability"— which are also themselves social constructs, in my estimation.

3. K-12, adult, and teacher education students alike, but especially the latter.

4. These "stages" could also be understood as intelligence benchmarks.

5. This is still a commonly held belief—especially in traditional educational psychology circles and in teacher education programs—despite the fact that it has been shown that many adults "fail" Piagetian tests of formal-operational intelligence, while children *under* the age of twelve have been shown to pass them (Kincheloe, 1993).

6. That is, this well-accepted, "commonsense" and now "habituated" perspective.

7. See, for example, Hughes, 1995.

8. In keeping with the critical postformalism that informs this chapter, and for a very insightful and stirring fictional account of all the subtleties hegemony and the attendant social pressures can bring to bear, see LeGuin, 1974.

9. Kincheloe and Steinberg would refer to critical sociocultural and sociolinguistic ways of viewing classroom discourse, interaction, and pedagogy as "critical constructivism" (Kincheloe, 1993; Kincheloe & Steinberg, 1993).

10. Gee (1990) defines "Discourse" and "Discourses" (capital *D*) in a manner that goes beyond just how we read, write, speak, or gesture. He holds that "Discourses" are "ways of behaving, interacting, valuing, thinking, believing, speaking, and often [also] reading and writing, that are accepted as instantiations of particular roles by specific *groups of people....* You learn a Discourse by becoming a member of the group; you start as a beginner, watch what's done, go along with the group as if you know what you're

doing when you don't, and eventually you can do it on your own.... Each Discourse incorporates a usually taken-for-granted and tacit theory of what counts as a 'normal' person, and the 'right' ways to think, feel and behave" (pp. xv–xx).

11. To protect their anonymity, pseudonyms will be used for the school, the teachers, and the students who are the focus of their research.

12. Postformalism holds that we learn more about an institution (in this case, Susana's classroom and pedagogical practices) by focusing our analysis on those most negatively affected by that institution (Kincheloe, 1993). And based on much research demonstrating the deleterious effects of ability grouping, tracking, and curriculum differentiation, I hypothesized that Susana's "low" reading group might fall into this category. For more on this, see the work of Oakes (1985) and Page & Valli (1990).

13. Pedro was a teacher I also knew of professionally, and through our conversations over time about his and ideal classroom practices, I believed Pedro's pedagogy was informed by elements of postformal teachng.

14. An explanation of the transcription conventions used in the organization of the data examples is presented below. They have been adapted from Atkinson and Heritage (1984) and Larson (1995). (Please note that traditional punctuation norms, such as capital letters at the beginning of sentences or the use of punctuation marks like the comma or question mark, are not part of these conventions. The period is used, but not in the traditional way.) The original language in which the two discourse segments presented in this study was Spanish.

The original Spanish transcription has been bolded:

50   Susana: **él siempre se rasca la mano rasca**

The English translation and transcription has been italicized:

51   Susana: *he always scratches his hand scratch*

Colons indicate sound stretch:

42   Pedro: **y también la::a**
43   *and he:er:r*

A period indicates a short pause:

56   Pedro: **y porqué. dónde llega l'agua**
57   *and why. where does the water come from*

The contents of double parentheses are either description or gestural activity:

27 Susana: **hasta aquí van bien**
28 *until here you're doing well rass*
29 ((She underlines "ras" with her finger))

Brackets denote overlapping speech and or gestures:

21 Susana: **rra[ss**
22 Gloria: **[rrass**

Stress or emphasis in an utterance is underlined:

37 Susana: **qué letra es ésta**
38 *what letter is this*

15. Mrs. Córdova, the more skills-oriented teacher who formerly ran the Spanish reading "pull-out" program, called her program "remedial," while Pedro now calls his current incarnation of the same program "enrichment."
16. A higher-level Spanish basal reader than what they are currently using in her own class.

REFERENCES

Atkinson, G., & Heritage, J. (1984). *Structures of social action: Studies of conversation analysis*. Cambridge: Cambridge University Press.

Cole, M. (January, 1991). "On putting Humpty Dumpty together again: A discussion of the papers on the socialization of children's cognition and emotion." *Merrill-Palmer Quarterly, 37* (1), 199–208.

Cole. M. (1996). *Cultural psychology: A once and future discipline*. Cambridge: Belknap.

Cole, M., & Griffin, P. (1983). "A socio-historical approach to re-mediation." *Quarterly Newsletter of the Laboratory of Comparative Human Cognition, 5* (4), 69–74.

Fairclough, N. (1992). *Discourse and social change*. Cambridge: Polity.

Freire, P. (1970). *Pedagogy of the oppressed*. New York: Continuum.

Freire, P., & Macedo, D. (1987). *Literacy: Reading the word and the world*. Massachusetts: Bergin & Garvey.

Gee, J. P. (1990). *Social linguistics and literacies: Ideology and Discourses*. London: Falmer.

Gutierrez, K. (1992a). "A comparison of instructional contexts in writing process classrooms with Latino children." *Education and Urban Society, 24* (2), 244–262.

Gutierrez, K. (1992b). "The social contexts of literacy instruction for Latino children." Paper presented at the annual meeting of the American Educational Research Association, San Francisco, California.

Gutierrez, K. (1993a). "Scripts, counterscripts and multiple scripts." Paper presented at the annual meeting of the American Educational Research Association, Atlanta, Georgia.

Gutierrez, K. (1994). "How talk, context, and script shape contexts for learning: A cross-case comparison of journal sharing." *Linguistics and Education, 5* (3), 335–365.

Gutierrez, K., & Larson, J. (1994). "Language borders: Recitation as hegemonic discourse." *International Journal of Educational Reform, 3*(1), 22–36.

Gutierrez, K., Larson, J., & Kreuter, B. (1995). "Cultural tensions in the scripted classroom: The value of the subjugated perspective." *Urban Education, 29* (4), 410–442.

Gutierrez, K., Rymes, B., & Larson, J. (1995). "James Brown vs. Brown vs. Board of Education: Script, counterscript and underlife in the classroom. Original manuscript." *Harvard Educational Review, 65* (3), 445–471.

Hughes, L. (1995). *The collected poems of Langston Hughes.* Ed. A. Ramperstad and D. Roessel. New York: Knopf.

Kincheloe, J. (1993). *Toward a critical politics of teacher thinking: Mapping the postmodern.* Westport, CT: Bergin & Garvey.

Kincheloe, J. & Steinberg, S. (1993). "A tentative description of post-formal thinking: The critical confrontation with cognitive theory." *Harvard Educational Review, 63* (3), 296–320.

Larson, J. (1995). *Talk matters: Knowledge distribution among novice writers in kindergarten.* Unpublished dissertation, University of California, Los Angeles.

Lave, J. (1988). *Cognition in practice: Mind, mathematics, and culture in everyday life.* Cambridge: Cambridge University Press.

Lave, J., & Wenger, E. (1991). *Situated learning: Legitimate peripheral participation.* Cambridge: Cambridge University Press.

LeGuin, U. (1974). *The dispossessed.* New York: Avon.

McLaren, P. (1989). *Life in schools: An introduction to critical pedagogy in the foundations of education.* New York: Longman.

Miles, M., & Huberman, M. (1984). *Qualitative data analysis.* London: Sage.

Oakes, J. (1985). *Keeping track: How schools structure inequality.* New Haven: Yale University Press.

Oakes, J., Gamoran, A., & Page, R. (1992). "Curriculum differentiation: Opportunities, outcomes, and meaning." In P. Jackson, (Ed.), *Handbook of research on curriculum.* New York: Macmillan.

Ochs, E. (1988). *Culture and language development.* Cambridge: Cambridge University Press.

Ochs, E., & Schieffelin, B. B. (1984). "Language acquisition and socialization: Three developmental stories and their implications." In R. Shweder & R. LeVine (Eds.), *Cultural theory: Essays on mind, self, and emotion* (pp. 276–320). Cambridge: Cambridge University Press.

Page, R., & Valli, L. (1990). "Curriculum differentiation: An introduction." In R. Page & L. Valli (Eds.), *Curriculum differentiation: Interpretive studies in U.S. secondary schools*. Albany: State University of New York Press.

Piaget, J. (1928). *The language and thought of the child*. New York: Harcourt, Brace.

Piaget, J. (1965). *The moral judgment of the child*. New York: Free Press.

Piaget, J. (1970). "Piaget's theory." In P. H. Mussen (Ed.), *Carmichael's manual of child psychology* (3rd ed.). (Vol. 1). New York: Wiley.

Pruyn, M. (1994). "Becoming subjects through critical practice: How an elementary classroom critically read and wrote their world." *International Journal of Educational Reform, 3* (1), 37–50.

Pruyn, M. (1996). *The social construction of critical student agency in one adult literacy classroom*. Unpublished dissertation, University of California, Los Angeles.

Pruyn, M., & Fischman, G. (1994). "'De nosotros sale nada': The social construction of literacy in a critically informed adult Spanish literacy classroom." Paper presented at the annual meeting of the American Educational Research Association, New Orleans, Louisiana.

Rogoff, B. (1990). *Apprenticeship in thinking*. New York: Oxford University Press.

Rogoff, B. (1991). "Social interaction as apprenticeship in thinking: Guided participation in spatial planning." In L. Resnick, J. M. Levine, & S. D. Teasley (Eds.), *Perspectives on socially shared cognition*. Washington, DC: American Psychological Association.

Scarr, S., Weinberg, R., & Levine, A. (1986). *Understanding development*. San Diego: Harcourt, Brace & Jovanovich.

Vygotsky, L. S. (1962). *Thought and language*. Cambridge: Cambridge University Press.

Vygotsky, L. S. (1978). *Mind in society: The development of higher psychological processes*. Cambridge, MA: Harvard University Press.

Walcott, H. (1988). "Ethnographic research in education." In R. Jaeger (Ed.), *Complimentary methods for research in education*. Washington, DC: American Educational Research Association.

Wenger, E. (1997). "Practice, learning, meaning, identity." *Training, 34* (2), 38–39.

Chapter 11

Informally Speaking: A Continuing Dialogue on Postformal Thinking

Ronald C. McClendon

and John A. Weaver

As witnesses to the emergence of a postmodern society, educators are faced with the task of developing a classroom and educational system that begins to address the issues and concerns postmodernity invents and highlights. Educators, however, are often philosophically, politically, culturally, or pedagogically estranged from the epistemological assumptions helpful in engaging the postmodern worlds we live in. Instead, educators resist, ignore, or underestimate the powerful forces, such as information technology, identity politics, popular cultures, and antiessentialist and foundational notions of identity and knowledge underlining postmodernity. As a result, educators respond to the shifts in education schizophrenically. At times they cling to old guideposts that permit them to continue the luxury of living the fantasy that school curricula can be predetermined and preordained, students' learning can be measured in a so-called quantified and objective manner, teachers can be evaluated by an assumed universal notion of excellence, administrators can be expected to act as the one true voice of the school, and educational scholars housed in teachers colleges can be relied upon to discover the universal laws of science that govern all school systems. At other times the fantasy is broken as teachers, students, administrators, and academics deconstruct the assumptions behind modernism and wander out into the uncertain, chaotic, complex, and nonlinear world of schooling where curriculum plans emerge, students become active learners, teachers are accepted as practitioners and not tellers at a bank for knowledge, administrators speak and act as one voice among many, and academics rely more on alternative forms of knowledge while never completely abandoning more traditional ways of knowing.

Yet during those times when educators wander into the wilderness of postmodernity, it is often done with what Joe Kincheloe and Shirley Steinberg (1993) refer to as a theoretical hesitation or stutter. Educators exhibit an uncomfortable feeling when they stumble into postmodern worlds, a feeling that they do not belong or that they are strangers in another country. This hesitation or stutter takes more substantive shape as well in the classroom. Educators are often intrigued or enticed by the bravado of postmodern thinking, but they often try to tame the untameable spirit of postmodernity by forcing it into old epistemological models. For instance, educators will adopt pedagogical strategies that promote student voices and self-organizing classrooms, but only within the confines of the traditionally structured classroom, where the teacher is the center of all learning. It is not that teachers are unaware that postmodern teaching requires a complete epistemological shift in how we educate. To the contrary, they are aware, perhaps too aware, that postmodernity requires educators to relinquish control of the classroom, and it is the uncertainty of such dramatic shifts that causes their hesitation.

This hesitation or stutter is not found only in the primary and secondary schools. In fact, it might be more prevalent in the university setting, where Cartesian-Newtonian teaching has been perfected, deductive thinking glorified, artificial hierarchies of knowledge erected, and fantasies of replication, correspondence, unity, and objectivity lived. What follows in this chapter is part of an ongoing dialogue we are having at the University of Akron in regard to developing a postformal institution and postformal classrooms where student voices are valued, alternative modes of evaluation are constructed, ways of knowing are deconstructed, accepted notions of scholarship are questioned, and pedagogy is nurtured.

We present two routes to developing postformal thinking within the university and classroom that reflect our personal notions of knowledge and learning as well as our insights into the politics and culture of the postmodern university as it influences our teaching. The two of us come from different cultures both ascriptively and academically, and we try to utilize these differences to shape our visions of a postformal classroom. Our dialogue represents one way we utilize alternative forms of knowing. That is, our dialogue is not only an attempt to construct a vision of postformal thinking but also a way to subvert traditional forms of knowing and, to some extent, writing in academic scholarship that exiles the subjective, sanctifies the objective, disguises the power of scientism, and perpetuates the myth of the culture of no culture (Haraway, 1997). In this chapter we will not adopt the traditional "scholar" persona. We will not adopt the third-person voice or suggest that research studies "speak." We do not believe multiple personas are inherently dysfunctional—to the contrary, multiple personas are needed to navigate through the worlds of postmodernity. However, the "scholar" persona constructs the subject in a way that denies it meaning and substance. We would prefer not to hide our visions of schooling behind the third-person voice or act like a failed ventriloquist trying to make research studies "speak." Rather, we prefer our visions to serve as a statement of who we are as educators and as a mark of our substance.

Ron is an African-American educational psychologist who sees the current approaches to constructivism as one paradigm within academic scholarship that already espouses some of the premises of postformal thinking. Ron's constructivist views put the major emphasis on the social construction of knowledge and to some extent reject the individualistic orientation of Piagetian theory (Airasian & Walsh, 1997). For Ron, it is less a matter of dramatically transforming the epistemological assumptions that undergird much of the teaching and learning approaches that mark contemporary classrooms than tapping into the work of cognitive psychologists in order to restructure classrooms and rethink tenets about learning. Therefore, Ron strives to accept a postformal university with multidisciplinary classrooms in which teachers and students cross and reconfigure academic borders, merging constructivism with pedagogy, affective dimensions with rationalities, and science with art.

John is a European-American educational foundationalist who is a postmodernist and sees the creation of a postformal university and postformal classrooms as contingent on the reconfiguring, if not the outright abandonment, of traditional forms of knowledge. In place of positivist, behaviorist, and Eurocentric approaches that co-opt the powerful labels of "objective," "neutral," "natural," and "truth" should be pedagogical approaches that expose power not only in regard to ascriptive forms of discrimination such as racism, sexism, and homophobia but also in relationship to academic knowledge. If academic knowledge is seen as a form of violence and repression then we can begin to see the power of alternative forms of knowledge such as science fiction, rap, storytelling, and autobiography without romanticizing these alternatives. For John, postformal thinking is the reconfiguring of knowledge as well as the restructuring of the curriculum in a manner that promotes boundless exploring, unencumbered by whimsical notions of what is scholarship, good teaching, and measurable learning.

John: Let me start with this premise. A postformal university has to be, I think, an abandonment of a Western tradition of academic work that devalues the affective dimension of teaching, scholarship, and life. We have constructed notions of reality that accept the so-called rational side of humans as superior. If affective dimensions are invited into the university dialogue, they often come in on the terms and standards founded in Western traditions that devalue these alternative forms of knowing from the start. Howard Gardner (1991, pp. 6–7), for instance, develops the idea of three characters, the intuitive learner, the traditional student, and the disciplinary expert, which represent types of learning. He warns that these characters do not develop in the human mind like preordained stages with smooth transitions. Instead, they coexist throughout a person's life and emerge at different times in an individual's developmental process. However, he creates these characters within a hierarchy in which the disciplinary expert is superior, or at least preferable, while the intuitive learner represents a childish phase in life that is to be dismissed as immaturity if it is predominant in adults. If the intuitive learner clashes with either the disciplinary expert or the traditional student, the intuitive is seen as expendable, obstructive, and less important. Yet it is in the intuitive learner that affective dimensions thrive, and Gardner limits the power of the intuitive in learning by placing it at the bottom of a hierarchy disguised as a natural dimension of the mind. Ironically, though, Gardner's work would not have the impact it has without his reliance on affective dimensions of learning. His work is thick with metaphorical images that serve as epistemological foundations on which to construct his theory of learning and intelligences.

Gardner's line of thinking is prevalent in universities and is one reason why students feel disconnected from the schooling process, whether it is primary, secondary, or postsecondary schooling. The message is clear that their cultures of MTV, body piercing, rap, science fiction, films, and so on are not welcome unless they can be probed and analyzed in the name of scholarship, while academic work is not subject to the same scrutiny. Academic work is held up as the unquestioned norm, as neutral and objective. Look at the curriculum, for instance—there is little room for students to connect their experiences with the official knowledge of schools. Schools with standardized tests, fixed curricula, and now statewide testing are still working from the premise that students are empty vessels and the job of teachers is simply to fill their minds with "facts" that someone else has determined to be important. In the university, attention is given to those forms of knowledge that can provide students with skills that will make them marketable, commodifying their minds as products to be sold to the highest bidder.

Ron: For me the issue is less about devaluing affective dimensions of thinking, because I think cognitive psychology addresses these dimensions, than it is about creating a synthesis between the rational and the affective. We do have an academic culture that facilitates the development of the former without developing and valuing the latter. I think that in Western society we do teach people to value the rational and to be as objective as possible. And in terms of Vygotsky (1978), Wertsch and Tulviste (1992), and other sociohistorical types of thinkers, a society uses certain tools, and in Western society the abstract, rational-man model is a main tool. But psychology is aware of this. Subjective experience has usually attached emotions to the way one sees the world. Take, for instance, the attraction to the idea of learning styles. What people refer to as learning styles are not cognitive ways of perceiving or thinking but those that relate to preferences. This is a focus on affective dimensions of learning. Take another example, situated cognition and anchored instruction. They need to be implemented more in schools because they are forms of postformal thinking and have been a part of educational psychology models since the early 1980s. However, paradigms are slow to change. It takes at least twenty-five years for theories to reach the field of practice of education.

John: Paradigms are slow to change not only in primary and secondary schooling but also in universities as well. We still live the myth of the culture of no culture, in which we believe our work is disconnected from politics and any other incumbrance of a complex world. I think Donna Haraway (1997, p. 24) summarizes this mentality, or what she calls a virtue, best when she writes:

> This is the virtue that guarantees that the modest witness is the legitimate and authorized ventriloquist for the object world, adding nothing from his mere opinion, from his biasing embodiment. And so he is endowed with the remarkable power to establish the facts. He bears witness; he is objective; he guarantees the clarity and purity of objects. His subjectivity is his objectivity.

Yet we know discoveries and learning are not done in these formal ways. We do not discuss the power behind these formal ways because formal ways of knowing get us grants, state tax dollars, and Department of Defense contracts that legitimate our power to evoke upon our students the vestiges of knowledge without exposing the informal ways in which we learn. For instance, if it were not for intuition, hunches, dreams, hallucinations, and imagination, Galileo would not have proposed the idea that the earth is not the center of the universe (see Feyerabend, 1988), Darwin would not have conceived of evolution (see Mazlish, 1993, p. 88), Babbage would not have invented the difference engine (see Morrison & Morrison, 1961, p. 33), and Szolard would not have come up with the idea of harnessing atomic power (see Rhodes, 1986). As Paul Feyerabend put it, if we relied upon the scientific method or formal ways of knowing to expand the frontiers of knowledge, we would still be in the Stone Age.

This is not to suggest that the scientific method is a complete myth. There is no doubt that the scientific method is an important way to be rigorous and disciplined in what we are trying to know. However, as Andrew Ross (1996, p. 3) proclaims, "Science does not have a monopoly upon rationality." Discovering or learning about anything is messy, fuzzy, and gray, but the scientific method has become such a mythical epic that we have convinced ourselves that good scholarship is precise, objective, dispassionate, and correspondent to a transcending reality. As Stanley Fish (1989, p. 376) has noted, we have successfully eliminated any "traces of fumbling, groping" that it takes to learn or understand something, and then we dress "up [our theories] in the vocabulary" of science and present it "in terms as formal and mathematical as possible." I think in a post-formal university we need to be permitted to fumble and grope and work in the messy and gray. We need to be permitted to go on journeys of passionate knowing and learning even though we may not know where we are headed. Students have to permit themselves these opportunities, too. We have to move away from what Gary Rhodes and Sheila Slaughter (1997, p. 25) call "supply-side higher education" and move toward "curiosity-driven research."

Ron: I think cognitive psychology attempts to describe the way we think and to devise methods to place what we know into a systemic order. We cannot know and evaluate things that are intuitive. Galileo had a perception of what was real and worked from there. Constructivists have attempted to deal with the notion that perception is reality, so therefore it is accepted that multiple realities exist at any give time. I think we have to begin talk about a postformal university with a conversation on perception. How do we perceive, and how do our students perceive? For instance, Piaget is often said to be a modernist who interpreted the scientific or rational as a symbol of advanced thinking. Yet at other times he is seen as a precursor for postmodernism. Perceptions of who Piaget was and what he wrote shape how we interpret him, but much of what is attributed to him is not something he advocated. He merely becomes a conduit of our perceptions and interpretations of what we think Piaget thought. Constructivists are aware of the importance of these acts of creating meaning (Airasian & Walsh, 1997). Approaches such as using the zone of proximal development facilitate appropriate constructions, socially shared cognitions, and the social transmission of knowledge (Brown, 1997; Wertsch & Tulviste, 1992). The process facilitates the construction of knowledge of the less experienced individual, in the same way as the parent nurtures the child or the teacher guides the student. This process of "scaffolding" was remarked upon by Bruner in the 1960s. Now we have advanced to people like Wittrock (1974, 1992), whose theories of generative learning view the brain as a model builder that controls the processes of generating meaning and plans of action that makes sense of experience and perceived realities. This clearly incorporates the whole idea of construction. I think that in the process of trying to move away from behaviorist notions of learning, educational psychologists have gotten on a better track.

John: Another issue that is important for creating a postformal university is attempting to rethink the scholarship and writing processes. Currently these processes are antiquated and are probably the best reflections of how tightly positivism and scientism still grip our notions of knowledge. I mean, look at the majority of journals—they are still run on the notion that knowledge can be segmented into parts and reduced to its simplest form. Many journals still require that we present our "findings" or "data" in a problem-method-results-discussion-and-implications format. Such an approach to writing is based on the notion that "facts" can be separated from "opinion" and the individual can be separated from the piece s/he is creating. Yet literary critics such as Michael Bèrubè (1995) and Bruce Robbins (1993), cultural critics such as John Fiske (1994) and bell hooks (1994), and rhetorians such as Donald McClosky (1994) and Herbert Simons (1990) clearly demonstrate in their work how "facts" cannot be separated from interpretation. For years the *American Educational Research Journal (AERJ)* would publish nothing but quantitative studies or a few qualitative pieces that clearly knew their place in the hierarchy of knowledge. This was challenged by Margaret Marshall and Loren Barritt's (1990) piece "Choices Made, Worlds Created: The Rhetoric of *AERJ*." They understood the implications of the dominance of quantitative work in education when they wrote: "Research journals have a lot to do with establishing what is considered important enough to talk about... as well as influencing how education gets talked about by professional educators" (p. 590). They knew that if one did not present ones views and ideas in a formal, disconnected way, one risks being shunned, discouraged, or at the very least pushed aside to the margins of journals, conferences, and education departments.

This is changing, of course. *AERJ* now does present some pieces that are grounded in qualitative approaches, although they still have published nothing on postmodernism or other epistemologically radical approaches. More diverse or funky journals are appearing that invite nontraditional approaches to the understanding of education. However, I don't think the transformation of education journals is as important as our coming to grips with the idea that academic writing is a process grounded in the blurring of fact and fiction. If we accept the blurring of these imaginary lines, we will see the power of science fiction, music, films, and other previously delegitimated forms of knowledge. We will realize that fiction often tells us more about the educational process than any quantitative piece that tries to isolate its "subjects," replicate the natural sciences, and separate its different forms of knowledge. A postformal university needs to encourage the development of nontraditional forms of writing. For tenure, we should be able to submit a fiction piece, have an art exhibit, create a documentary, write and perform a play we wrote dealing with education, or put on an interpretive dance recital as evidence of scholarship. Ph.D. or Ed.D. students should be encouraged to do the same. This would encourage the crossing of academic boundaries as we learn the crafts of writers, filmmakers, artists, and futurists in order to enhance our own teaching.

John: Let's move on to the issue of postformal classrooms. I think it is clear that postformal classrooms have existed for decades, so their existence is in no way contingent upon the creation of a postformal institution. Institutionally, one issue is how do we begin to reward a teacher who embarks with her/his students in creating a postformal classroom when the institution bases its evaluations for tenure and promotion on formal criteria that can be quantified? How do we foster a postformal classroom when the Foucauldian pressure of self-disciplining is so intense in universities and public schools?

Ron: A postformal classroom for me emphasizes instructional activities rooted in high standards and intellectual quality and in authentic, significant, and meaningful assessments of achievement (Sternberg, 1992). There also must be an understanding of the history of educational psychology and how we have developed in our thinking. You have a first stage that was response acquisition, and this is primarily behavior that says that learning is an accumulation of responses to certain stimuli. The way this plays out in the classroom is the teacher is supposed to stand there and elicit responses from the students and reinforce right answers, which of course facilitates repetition and the accumulation of knowledge. From the perspective of educational psychology, this is no longer an acceptable model, even though it still is a predominant model of teaching in many schools. Educational psychologists have made two subsequent moves in developing learning models. In the 1950s and 1960s, we moved from behavioral to information-processing models (Shuell, 1986). The human mind was no longer seen as built on Cartesian-Newtonian laws but was seen as a computer. We have come a long way since this shift as well. We recognize that the human being continues to be unique and different from animals and machines in terms of processing information. Situated cognitivists and advocates of anchored instruction recognize that the student is not a blank slate or a machine that records everything the teacher deems important (Cognition and Technology Group at Vanderbilt, 1990). The student is a constructor of knowledge. S/he changes, ignores information, and the affective dimension also plays an important role. The individual's unique background or cultural experiences play a key role in the processing of knowledge that affects what is constructed (Newmann, Marks, & Gamoran, 1995; Wittrock, 1979). This means that educational psychology is looking at relevant learner characteristics important in shaping knowledge, such as ethnicity, race, gender, and religion. They have looked at, for instance, what whiteness and blackness mean in terms of knowledge processing. The problem is that any good theory takes twenty-five years to reach the classroom.

There are some issues that still need to be addressed, however. For instance, teachers who do adhere to a constructionist model face the reality that the school curriculum and the statewide testing movement in states such as Ohio are founded in a behaviorist model of knowledge acquisition. So teachers are often forced to teach in a manner that fits these realities rather than the way they know students learn. Here this is a political issue. Teachers need to address these concerns with politicians who are still working from the notion that schooling is merely about the acquisition of knowledge. For example, a minority child having to compete for a limited number of positions at a university or college based upon certain types of tests, such as the ACT or SAT, will really be tested according to this child's ability to correlate his or her experiences with the assumptions and experiences of the test creators. Now, middle- and upper-class parents have recognized for years the importance of having their children in schools where the emphasis will be on gaining the types of information and skills that are valued on those tests; we call those "high-stakes" types of tests, because these tests influence the rest of your life (Sternberg, 1992). So I think these teachers are doing the right thing in teaching according to the test. I also think that where you will most likely find innovative attempts to change the learning model to fit the way educational psychologists think we learn is in the urban, minority school districts (Brown, 1997). In terms of learning, this may be correct, but in terms of accumulating the necessary cultural capital to do well on tests, it will not be to the advantage of these students. In this sense a postformal or any other innovative classroom can become a barrier to a child's success. It becomes a way to reinforce the privileging of whiteness as urban schools become the proving grounds for innovations based upon the assumptions of white academics and progressive teachers. I think if postformal schools are going to thrive, there will have to be a comprehensive change in the thinking of how students learn—from the politicians to the test makers, from the school boards to the parents, and from the teachers to the students. Postformal schools have to overcome the set of beliefs that often exists in conservative and progressive reforms and which subverts the education of the children. We must overcome those models that see the child of color as inferior, indifferent, or "at-risk." We have to create a classroom where we begin to see that students in urban centers and rural areas, especially, are aware of the fact that they are not getting the same education as students in suburban havens. In this type of setting the urban or rural child devalues education because she or he does not see it as having any bearing on future outcomes.

John: This is similar to the argument raised by Lisa Delpit (1995). According to Delpit, literacy programs invented to liberate and reconnect students with schooling can end up hindering people of color. I am certainly aware of these possibilities you raise, but a postformal classroom is about reconnecting the students and teachers with the schooling process. In my mind, there are numerous ways to make this reconnection. I like to use something that is generally not seen as academic knowledge to make this reconnection, such as rap or science fiction. I think it sends the message that knowledge is everywhere, and as students, they have the ability to create knowledge. Besides, I think rap and science fiction are postformal ways of knowing. Rap artists such as Leaders of the New School and feminist science fiction writers such as Octavia Butler, for instance, deconstruct current social structures and offer a vision for creating alternative worlds (Roberts, 1993). They connect the logical with the emotional, and self-knowledge becomes an imperative to knowing and learning. Leaders of the New School, for instance, talk about the nonsense peddled as knowledge in schools, but they also stress the importance of teaching yourself. They encourage their readers and listeners to seek out their own meaning and interpret what they see, read, and experience.

In my attempts to create a postformal classroom, this past spring I decided I was going to have my graduate and undergraduate students write their own rap songs portraying (1) how they, as future or current teachers, interpreted the schooling process, and (2) how they thought students saw the schooling process. I got mixed reviews. Whereas my graduate students wrote some wonderful pieces, my undergraduates did not want to write their own songs. My graduate students were surprised by how disconnected they felt, how obvious the problems that caused this disconnection were, and how clearly they saw students, for the most part, rejecting schooling. One group named themselves Naughty Teachers by Nature and wrote this:

> I teach to connect
>
> Where's the respect
> You sit there sleepin',
> While others are thinkin'
>
> *Chorus*
> Down with OPT [Ohio Proficiency Test]
> Yeah, you know me
> I make my own recipe
>
> Talkin' head
> Might as well be dead

Test scores, lecture bores
How can I learn when I don't get a turn

Chorus

Teachers bitch
Students bitch
That's why I'm absent from your shit

Chorus

Talkin' trash about your class
Stop whining and get off your ass
Make 'em feel what you teach is real

Chorus

Easier said then done
It won't always be fun
Get the kids involved
Give 'em a voice
Give 'em a choice!

Chorus

Houston Baker (1991, p. 204) asked his University of Pennsylvania graduate students what the poetry of the nineties was, and "to a man or woman [his] students responded 'rap' or 'MTV.'" So I posed the same question to my graduate students, and they too said rap. As you can see, these teachers knew what was causing the disconnection (tests) and what was needed to reconnect with their students (make it real and get them involved). They also began to envision a curriculum that demanded students claim their voice and get involved. Their vision is much like the visions William Doll (1993) and Patrick Slattery (1995) share with us. As my students were creating visions of their classrooms, they were also constructing a university classroom that was postformal as they claimed their voices and got involved.

I posed Baker's question to my undergraduates. They replied, "Oh, God, is it rap?" and some did not respond at all. When I told them I wanted them to write their own rap songs, they objected. I gave them a short history lesson on rap, stressing all the time that gangsta rap is only one form of rap. I played them songs they would know, such as Coolio's "Gangsta Paradise," and songs they didn't know, such as Leaders of the New School's "Teacher's Don't Teach Us Nonsense." There was no killing of cops, no violence, and no swearing. But they didn't want to hear it. They responded with their own experiences, saying that they would not use rap in the classroom because when they listened to rap or punk rock, they did it only to piss their parents off or to be part of the in crowd. They saw rap only through their own experiences as white middle-class rebels who had moved past that stage in life, so they thought their future students should do the same. They made a mistake, I think, that many people who privilege whiteness make. Since they co-opted rap music in order to resist their parents' culture, they believed that this is why rap artists created their poetry in the first place. They saw rap as a form of resistance in a dichotomous world of dominance and subordination. However, Jonathan Scott (1995, p. 170) reminds us that with rap "something interesting and complicated is going on, and one will find very few answers by looking to categories like 'oppositional' and 'counter-hegemonic.' Hiphop is hegemonic and refuses to be treated as a minority culture—as disadvantaged and excluded." These students in their formal classrooms will see their students, just as they see rap, as oppositional, disadvantaged, and excluded by choice. Their remedy will be to enforce more control and dispense more knowledge into the empty vessels called students. On the other hand, I think a postformal classroom will create a classroom that is similar to rap. It will have a nonsynchronous rhythm that plays to the beat of the classroom cultures, a sound that is noise to some but learning to the attentive ear, a message that is transformative for those willing to overcome media images and stereotypes, a mix that is eclectic and artistic and a pedagogy that is a hybrid—mixing and molding experiences and school knowledge to create a student who is never innocent, pure, or complete, but emerging and critical.

Ron: I am also concerned with the obstacles we will experience in our attempts to create postformal classrooms. For instance, how many complaints from students and parents will it take before we abandon what we know in regard to how students learn and go back to a modernist approach where we throw out facts and expect the students to regurgitate them back to us on a test? I want to move beyond the modernist approach, but students ask, "How am I being graded?" and "Are we being graded on this?" There is a great amount of research done on teacher, student, and parental expectations and the impact this has on student outcomes. If the expectations are different between the groups, there will be conflict. If you go into that conflict situation, the expectations of the parents (which are probably based on the modernist way many of them were educated) will probably give you a combination for a complaint. But the opportunity is there for the university to educate and inform the parents as to what the goals of the university are—to create thinkers and not vocational clones. The university has failed in this sense. Part of the problem is that many university officials are not interested in creating thinkers who can enter into a complex and nonlinear world and create their own solutions to unique problems they face. They want the clones who give back as alumni or who are valued by industrial leaders and other rational men perceived as driving the economy.

John: The challenge of a postformal classroom is to work within the constraints that modernist assumptions place upon us as natural and unquestioned givens. That students are clones whose end goal is to seek the employment opportunity they desire is one of those modernist assumptions. There are others that I mentioned before, such as a predetermined curriculum and the notion of knowledge as a fixed object. After thirteen to twenty years in a formal, modernist classroom, students and professors just accept—no matter how degrading, boring, and offensive it is—that these constraints are the way people learn. If someone attempts to take an alternative approach to learning and teaching, they have to overcome the myth that the modernist way is the true way. As postformal thinkers, we need to demonstrate to the students that there are alternatives that achieve more through self-reflection, student participation, and self-organization. In this sense, I find the work of bell hooks (1994) quite helpful. She reminds us that in postformal classrooms there will be a need to discuss in more depth epistemological assumptions undergirding the classroom because, unlike in an established pedagogical tradition, there is a need to justify one's approach and, literally, existence. Once the epistemological assumptions are understood, I think, we can begin to introduce alternative forms of knowledge on their own terms and standards. The latter point is important to stress. Oftentimes in classrooms we introduce alternative forms of knowing in order to dismiss them. There is still a common belief, for instance, in universities that qualitative approaches can be used under the same principles as quantitative approaches. The assumption is that qualitative approaches cannot be trusted unless they are controlled by "scientific" standards. It is like going through social studies in high school, where you discussed Marxism only to dismiss it. If we are going to embrace alternative forms of knowing, then we have to recognize that formal standards are not valid. We have to invent or create new standards.

I think this issue is most important in dealing with creating alternative forms of evaluation in a postformal classroom. Formal testing, as in standardized and statewide testing, is invalid in a postformal classroom. This means that we have to rethink dramatically how we adults come to know what children and young adults know. One response is to say we can never know. I think modernists, with their grade scales, bell curves, and objective tests, know this but are unwilling to break this illusion because they are scared of what is created after they admit that they really don't know what our students know. I am not suggesting that this fear of what comes after the abandonment of modernist notions of knowing and tests should not be taken seriously. Like any dynamic system in a postmodern world, a school system is capable of self-destruction at any time. We already have schools that have self-destructed from narcissism (societal ambivalence to social issues such as drug usage and AIDS), rugged individualism (vouchers), and—the most frequent form—modernism (the factory model). I think teachers and administrators feel that if we are honest with students, parents, and ourselves and admit that tests do nothing more than reveal our abilities to take tests, then they will add another form of self-destruction of public schools—the loss of legitimacy and authority to define what is worthy of knowing. However, I am an optimist and believe that dynamic systems are also capable of unlimited growth. To highlight this possibility, I like the examples of quantum physics. It took Heisenberg's (1958) uncertainty principle to demonstrate that when we look at an assumed objective world we really are looking at it through the method we use and the questions we ask. In other words, we cannot know the "real" world. This is also true of school knowledge: We cannot know what students actually know except through our methods and questions.

A second response, one I am more inclined to adopt, is to create alternative forms of evaluation. I think that students learn better by applying what they know and learn to something they experience every day. For instance, I teach an honors class and for their final project the students have to demonstrate through any medium how they interpret the ideas we discussed. One student demonstrated how chaos theory applied to interpretive dance. While she was showing the dance moves, she was explaining how chaos theory worked in her field. Another student wrote and sang her own song dealing with the issue of whose knowledge should we teach. Other students wrote science fiction short stories to chart their vision of the future (they were all dystopic stories). All of these students demonstrated to me that they understood the issues we discussed throughout the semester. While they were dancing, singing, and writing I was evaluating them. My approach to evaluating stems from Doll's (1993, pp. 172–173) idea that we should stop evaluating based on a notion of deficit and begin to work from the students' strengths. The medium these students chose represented their strengths, and by explaining their projects to the class, they were building on these strengths and making connections to ideas and theories that extended their strengths.

THE FUTURES OF POSTFORMAL PSYCHOLOGY

We want to end this chapter with a discussion on possible research agendas postformal psychology can nurture in order to develop postformal universities and classrooms. First, we think that a continued relationship between information technology and cognitive psychology is in order. The works of Paul Churchland (1996), Howard Gardner (1991), and Norbert Weiner (1954) are just a few examples of how fruitful these ventures are. As Churchland points out, creating a neural-network computer that is patterned after the brain is already a reality. This work so far is rudimentary, but how far off is a self-generating computer that acts like a brain and eventually becomes a brain? Gardner has demonstrated that present and future teachers need to be immersed in, not drowned by, information technology, because it is one of the best ways to nurture the development of the multiple potentials of all children. Weiner's vision is still applicable to information technology and cognitive psychology. In the infancy of information technology, it was Weiner who was grappling with the issue of access and the inequalities lack of access would cause, not just developmentally in students but also economically in society as a whole.

We think postformal psychology needs to steer from, but never lose sight of, these research projects. We feel postformal psychology can make its mark where formal psychology refuses to go because of its epistemological assumptions about learning and knowledge. Postformal psychology can continue the theme of learning and information technology established by cognitive psychologists and neurophysiologists by explaining, for example, the ways in which computer hackers learn. Most hackers do not have formal training, and most of the time they are the ones teaching computer-security programmers in multinational corporations and government agencies about breaking codes and gathering information. How do they learn, what are their cultures like, and who teaches them? More important, what is it about learning that hackers can teach us, and how can we incorporate these insights into school curricula? Also, postformal psychology can move into the realm of Saturday morning cyborg cartoons, science fiction novels, and video games and how children learn from these sources of knowledge. There have been some attempts to do this, such as Eugene Provenzo's (1991) and Peter Appelbaum's (forthcoming) work, but the overarching epistemological assumptions about learning construct a research paradigm that leads formal psychologists to ignore these realms of knowledge construction. That is, their elitism prevents them from seeing animation, science fiction, and video games as a form of learning and thinking.

Finally, we think postformal psychology needs to again take a cue from cognitive psychology and information technology. Part of the brilliance of people such as Bruner, Churchland, Gardner, and Weiner is their ability to construct a multidisciplinary team that looks at similar problems from different angles. Postformal psychology should take these efforts further. Instead of inviting just academics from traditional fields of study, such as anthropology, artificial intelligence, computer science, and philosophy, postformal psychologists have to invite cultural and literary theorists, sociologists of science, feminists, multiculturalists, Afrocentrists, and other scholars into the discussion on schooling and postformal thinking. Moreover, postformal psychology needs to invite computer hackers, skateboarders, video game players, cartoon creators, science fiction writers, and romance novel writers into the conversation. Although these are only two intitial steps, they are necessary in order to construct an infrastructure within the academy and to legitimate postformal thinking as a field.

REFERENCES

Airasian, P. W., & Walsh, M. E. (1997, February). "Constructivist cautions." *Phi Delta Kappan,* Feb., 444–449.

Appelbaum, P. (Forthcoming). "Cyborg selves: Saturday morning magic and magical morality." In J. Weaver & T. Vickory (Eds.), *Popular culture, critical pedagogy: Reading, constructing, connecting.* New York: Garland.

Baker, H. (1991). "Hybridity, the rap race, and pedagogy for the 1990s." In C. Penley & A. Ross (Eds.), *Technoculture* (pp. 197–209). Minneapolis: University of Minnesota Press.

Bèrubè, M. (1994). *Public access: Literary theory and American cultural studies.* London: Verso.

Brown, A. L. (1997). "Transforming schools into communities of thinking and learning about serious matters." *American Psychologist, 52* (4), 399–413.

Churchland, P. (1996). *The engine of reason, the seat of the soul: A philosophical journey into the brain.* Cambridge: MIT Press.

Cognition and Technology Group at Vanderbilt. (1990, August-September). "Anchored instruction and its relationship to situated cognition." *Educational Researcher,* 2–9.

Delpit, L. (1995). *Other People's children: Cultural conflict in the classroom.* New York: The New Press.

Doll. W. (1993). *A post-modern perspective on curriculum.* New York: Teachers' College Press.

Feyerabend, P. (1988). *Against method.* London: Verso.

Fish, S. (1989). *Doing what comes naturally.* Durham, NC: Duke University Press.

Fiske, J. (1993). *Power plays power works.* London: Verso.

Gardner, H.(1991). *The unschooled mind: How children think and how schools should teach.* New York: Basic Books.

Haraway, D. (1997). *Modest_witness@second_millennium. FemaleMan_Meets_OncoMouse.* New York: Routledge.

Heisenberg, P. (1958). *Physics and philosophy.* New York: Harper.

hooks, b. (1994). *Teaching to transgress: Education as the practice of freedom.* New York: Routledge.

Kincheloe, J., & Steinberg, S. (1993). "A tentative description of post-formal thinking: The critical confrontation with cognitive theory." *Harvard Educational Review, 63* (3), 296–320.

Marshall, M., & Barritt, L.(1990). "Choices made, worlds created: The rhetoric of *AERJ.*" *American Educational Research Journal, 27* (4), 589–609.

Mazlish, B. (1993). *The fourth discontinuity: The co-evolution of humans and machines.* New Haven: Yale University Press.

McClosky, D. (1994). *Knowledge and persuasion in economics.* New York: Cambridge University Press.

Morrison, P., & Morrison, E. (Eds.). (1961). *Charles Babbage and his calculating engines.* New York: Dover.

Newmann, F. M., Marks, H. M., & Gamoran, A. (1995). "Authentic pedagogy: Standards that boost student performance." Issue Report No. 8, Center on Organization and Restructuring of Schools. Wisconsin Center for Educational Research. University of Wisconsin, Madison.

Provenzo, E. (1991). *Video kids: Making sense of Nintendo.* Cambridge: Harvard University Press.

Rhoades, G., & Slaughter, S. (1997). "Academic capitalism, managed professionals, and supply-side higher education." *Social Text, 15* (2), 9–38.

Rhodes, R. (1986). *The making of the atomic bomb.* New York: Touchstone.

Robbins, B. (1993). *Secular vocations: Intellectuals, professionalism, culture.* London: Verso.

Roberts, R. (1993). *A new species: Gender and science in science fiction.* Urbana: University of Illinois Press.

Ross, A. (Ed.). (1996). *Science wars.* Durham, NC: Duke University Press.

Shuell, T. J. (1986). "Cognitive conceptions of learning." *Review of Educational Research, 56* (4), 411–436.

Scott, J. (1995). "Critical aesthetics on the down low." *The Minnesota Review, 43–44,* 164–171.

Simons, H. (1990). *The Rhetorical Turn.* Chicago: Chicago.

Slattery, P. (1995). *Curriculum development in the postmodern era.* New York: Garland.

Sternberg, R. J. (1992). "Ability tests, measurements and markets." *Journal of Educational Psychology, 84* (2), 134–140.

Vygotsky, L. (1978). *Mind in society: The development of higher psychological processes.* Ed., Trans. M. Cole, V. John-Steiner, S. Scribner, & E. Souberman. Cambridge: Harvard University Press.

Weiner, N. (1954). *The human use of human beings: Cybernetics and society.* New York: Doubleday.

Wertsch, J. V., & Tulviste, P. (1992). "L. S. Vygotsky and contemporary developmental psychology." *Developmental Psychology, 28* (4), 548–557.

Wittrock, M. C. (1974). Learning as a generative process. *Educational Psychologist, 11,* 87–95.

Wittrock, M. C. (1979, February) "The cognitive movement in instruction." *Educational Researcher,* 5–11.

Wittrock, M. C. (1992). "Generative learning processes of the brain." *Educational Psychologist, 27* (4), 531–541.

Chapter 12

Politics, Intelligence, and the Classroom: Postformal Teaching

Joe L. Kincheloe

and Shirley R. Steinberg

The power of psychology is sobering. Mainstream educational psychology has played a major role in shaping educational practice since the early twentieth century. The discourse of modernist educational psychology provides the portrait of reality on which teaching is based. Postformalists trace the effects of this picture as they expose the technical rationality behind the engineering of teaching. Such a rationality concerns itself with locating the best method of teaching based on statistical analysis of standardized test scores. The "common sense" about teaching that emerges from this form of rationality distorts educational practice, as it fails to question what exactly the statistical analyses are measuring and their relevance to the goals of education in a democratic society. As John Weaver and Ronald McClendon maintain in their chapter, teachers experience great pressure to teach in line with the psychological assumptions of state-mandated tests, regardless of their own professional understanding of educational purpose and the learning process. Assuming that school is primarily concerned with the acquisition of data, mainstream educational psychology and the testing bureaucracy attempt to strongarm teachers into specific deskilled roles.

The deskilled teacher emerging in this context according to Ann Watts Pailliotet and Thomas Callister in their chapter, is an identifier of technical problems relating to time, managerial, and learning efficiency. In such a mode, teachers measure students' ability to memorize one-dimensional verbal associations devoid of connections to the lived world. The classrooms created in this context are like the one Mark Pruyn observed in his research: boring places marked by drudgery and repetition where isolated students work on joyless and meaningless lessons painfully tied to their developmental level. These are the psychologically produced formal classrooms that demand the myopic formal thinking so unsuited for a progressive democracy. As Pruyn notes, students from marginalized backgrounds in these formal classrooms quickly come to see themselves as incompetent scholars, thus blaming their low cognitive abilities for their failure. The ideological work of educational psychology maintains the undemocratic status quo by validating the privileged and invalidating the knowledge and talents of the subjugated. Such students come to accept and embody mainstream psychology's sorting of them into different ability and vocational tracks.

In this context Gaile Cannella's assertion that modernist educational psychology helps position teaching and teacher education as technologies of regulation becomes visible to many onlookers. As it produces "truths" about children and their universal process of development, mainstream educational psychology constructs a "natural" form of thinking by which all other forms of thinking are evaluated. Teachers thus strive to suppress modes of reasoning that might interfere with natural reasoning. Forms of student (and teacher) thinking that fall outside the boundaries of natural development are judged harshly in this one-truth psychology and the teaching it mandates. Though it may be wrapped in a humanistic language of child-centeredness, this regulatory education assumes a defect whenever children hold values and manifest behavior contrary to a white middle-class norm. The culturally different (aka, nonwhite, non-middle-class) home is not respected as a proper place of learning. In this psychological context, an individualistic ethic is promoted that blinds teachers to the cultural assumptions directing their teaching.

Thus, postformalism seeks to understand both the nature of the cultural and theoretical assumptions of mainstream educational psychology and the various ways the discourse affects the political domain and teaching practice. As it comes to understand psychology's liberal tendency to abstract students from their communities, postformalism learns that the discipline's assessment of students' intelligence is shaped by their attachments to specific types of communities. Indeed, students do not simply bring certain traits from their communities to the school—they bring their identities. Pepi Leistyna emphasizes this point in his chapter, contending that critical educators need to stress the social nature of the mind. The ways we think and feel cannot be separated from our experiences in our social groups. When mainstream educational psychology falls into this trap, Leistyna concludes, it creates a personality vacuum.

Postformalists understand that the way around this involves a historically situated, hermeneutics-based psychology that studies students and their performance from a variety of perspectives (Usher & Edwards, 1994; Postman, 1995; Dewey, 1933; Tomlinson, 1988: Walkerdine, 1988; Burman, 1994; Ingleby, 1995; Sampson, 1995; Cushman, 1995).

In this psychologized, abstracted, and decontextualized state, schools do little to improve or democratize intelligence. Delivering fragmented data to students whose backgrounds are not understood accomplishes little. This is not to say that postformalists are opposed to providing students with information; too often critical concern with the delivery of fragmented bits of data to students is misread as an argument against content. Postformalists understand that teaching sophisticated thinking is impossible outside of a body of information to think about. The relationship between information and thinking is complex and must be explored by teachers and psychologists with great care. While content knowledge is necessary to higher orders of thinking, it does not necessarily follow that individuals who possess massive amounts of information in a particular domain think better than those who do not. As Dewey (1933) argued decades ago, information becomes knowledge only as it is comprehended—meaning that the various pieces of the information are understood in the ways they relate to one another.

Postformalists would add that in the process of reflection on the *internal* relations of the information, attention to its *external* relations would also take place. Such external relations would involve the information's connection to the life of the learner, the good of the community, and the understanding of other bodies of knowledge. Mainstream educational psychology often fails to appreciate the difference between the acquisition of information and the achievement of understanding. Postformal teaching engages students in reflective understanding at the same time they obtain information. The postformal thinker performs a form of cognitive triage when confronted with data, as he or she prioritizes, filters, connects, discards, and schematizes. Understanding this process, postformal teachers gain new insights into methods for dealing with subject matters of many varieties (Horton & Freire, 1990; Perkins, 1995).

TEACHING GROUNDED ON A RECONCEPTUALIZED NOTION OF INTELLIGENCE

Nothing is simple about teaching people to think critically; no set of easy steps can be delineated in some workshop conducted by an expert in educational psychology charging twelve thousand dollars per day. Ann Watts

Pailliotet and Thomas Callister emphasize this reality in their exploration of the problems educators encounter in this context, including student discomfort, conceptual difficulty, the power dynamics involved in the process, and the fear many parties express relating to the unprecedented expectations such an effort demands. Indeed, too much of the literature on critical thinking advocates the development of higher-order cognition without sufficient understanding of the difficulty of the teaching process required for success. The postformal definition of higher-order thinking is inseparable from what might be labeled wisdom—cognitive abilities that lead to a higher quality of life and to a more just and equitable world. No matter what discipline one is teaching, these politico-cognitive dynamics can be addressed and consciously cultivated.

Postformal teachers, thus, possess a meta-awareness of the psychological dynamics delineated throughout this book. Such an awareness allows them to constantly monitor the cognitive, cultural, affective, discursive, and political dynamics operating in their classroom and how they are affecting students at any particular time. Teachers ask themselves if students are involved in postformal processes in their learning activities. Is the distinction between those who are and are not so involved patterned around cultural lines? Are students' facilities or lack of such with the skills being taught based on cognitive or dispositional (affective) dynamics? How might students' familiarity with the discourse of the school culture shape their responses to classroom activities? What are the political (ideological) implications of the material being investigated? Do student performances reflect power relations in the existing society? How can the classroom and its activities be rearranged to disrupt the reproduction of those extant power relations in democratic and just ways? Such a postformal meta-awareness and the questions that emerge from it change the ways teachers approach their classrooms. Teachers who have studied such politico-cognitive analyses can never again simply pass along a body of unexamined information for memorization by a group of students whose cultural and class backgrounds are irrelevant.

CONNECTING STUDENTS TO THE REALITY OF THEIR EXISTENCE

As students become active postformal learners, critical teachers lead students beyond the school's attempt to adjust them to existing social schematas and conventional approaches to vocational life. Instead, teachers help students explore bodies of knowledge and develop thinking skills that put them in contact with the reality of their existence. "What will I make of the life I possess?" "What are the realities I must face as a result of my 'being'?" "What is the nature of this existence?" are questions postformal students confront in the context of various subjects and disciplinary discourses. Both Aostre Johnson and Paul Stein extend these ontological questions in their explorations of the narrow definitions of human possibility found in the discourse of mainstream educational psychology. Challenging this narrowness of ontological possibility offered by the culture at large and by the disciplinary imagination of educational psychology, as Pailliotet and Callister point out, does not necessarily make a teacher popular with students. Such a process involves teachers confronting students with the ways they have been socially constructed—a realization that limits self-determination and agency. Few enjoy hearing about the ways they are shaped by invisible forces outside of individual control. Thus, conflict is inevitable.

Teaching a postformal curriculum concerning the ways our consciousness is constructed and the possibility that emerges from such an understanding is a delicate educational task. As students explore the forces that have shaped their identities and belief systems, the process of rethinking their identities may be at times rocky, emotional, and contentious. Teachers must be willing to explore their own consciousness construction, opening themselves to the same personal vulnerability they ask of their students. As Pailliotet and Callister caution us, this can be accomplished only when a teacher has created a safe and supportive classroom environment. As students explore the genesis of their worldviews and self-concepts, they come to learn (in the words of Suzanne Gallagher) that they are more "inscribed" by the discipline of psychology than merely "described." Such students, Gallagher posits, come to realize that their own "misbehavior" in school as well as that of the schoolchildren they may encounter in the future can be read as a political search for self-direction and agency.

Indeed, postformalists such as Lana Krievis and Karen Anijar argue that such critical analysis of consciousness construction—in particular mainstream educational psychology's role in the process—may uncover the ways students have been victimized by the discipline's reductionistic classification system. In this context, healthy and intelligent individuals find themselves labeled deficient and even deviant. Should we be surprised when students act out their frustrations and resentments concerning such a demeaning classification procedure? As postformal teachers act on their appreciation of the sociopolitical and psychological dynamics at work in this process, they both bring comfort to students and engage them in meaningful learning experiences. This pedagogical process takes place at all education levels—from elementary school to college. Judging from Pepi Leistyna's description of his graduate educational psychology classes, this analysis of the etymology of consciousness and belief systems may be no less important at the graduate school level.

Operating on their understanding of the critique of mainstream educational psychology and the understanding of postformalism and the traditions on which it draws, critical teachers help students explore their relationship to their social, cultural, political, economic, and educational environment. Such an undertaking is not merely an attempt to, in the words of conservative critics, "make students feel good at the expense of becoming educated." On the contrary, it is a content-based, discursively savvy, complex analytical educational process that requires a deep understanding of a wide variety of knowledge systems, the skills to critique them, and the cognitive facility to develop new insights to replace inadequate academic constructs. If the development of such cognitive processes is not a manifestation of a rigorous education, then we are confused about the nature of rigor. In such a postformal learning situation, students analyze the way their memories and their amnesias are socially constructed and the relation of such psychological dynamics to structures of power and authority. In this context, postformal teachers connect the domain of the psychological to the political, in the process exposing issues of privilege around structures of race (whiteness), class (elitism), and gender (patriarchy). In these ways students gain profound insights not only into the nature of their existence but also into how they might want to rethink their existence and their goals as human beings (Farber, 1989; Martin-Baro, 1994; Shotter, 1993).

BEYOND FORMAL THINKING: CONNECTING SCHOOLING TO THE UNCERTAINTY OF EVERYDAY EXPERIENCE

The usefulness, be it political or otherwise, of schooling grounded on a mainstream educational psychology is undermined by its disconnection with the everyday life of the student. Schooling thus becomes technocratic and rationalistic to the extent that it is removed from the material and everyday world and the experience of students. When a student, for example, is confronted with a test-driven pedagogy that focuses on the learning of the formal organization of government in the United States, he or she may commit to memory that the three branches of government include the legislature, the judiciary, and the executive. How these branches operate in the complexity of everyday life is never broached, thus undermining any civic use of such information in the student's political life. How knowledge learned in this manner might be valuable to the student is not apparent to postformalists. The information is inert, devoid of connections to the lived political world. John Weaver and Ronald McClendon are aware of this dynamic when they describe the journey into the wilderness of uncertainty that the embrace of the complexity of everyday life entails. In this new and ambiguous terrain, no longer can teachers access the authority of certainty and infallibility granted to them by modernist psychology and the pedagogy of facticity it supports.

A postformal educational psychology encourages teachers to take the risk, to make the emancipatory leap. It induces teachers to deliver information or engage students in the production of information in connection to its use. This relationship between knowledge and use helps us understand why individuals with an extensive formal education are often unable to think outside of a particular frame or solve problems that confront them. Such individuals have not gained access to bodies of knowledge in relation to everyday life in general or their lives in particular; their knowledge has been accumulated in conceptual isolation. Here is where we can so clearly see the need for teaching that is unafraid of engaging the subject matter of academic disciplines in a contextualized and critical manner. Such teaching is critical in the sense that addresses the power dynamics of subject matter production and the democratic aspects of its use. From the time of John Dewey to the present, those who have challenged the shibboleths of the prevailing cognitive and educational psychological wisdom have been charged with a disregard for subject matter. Both Dewey (1933) and Paulo Freire (1998) were very clear that progressive teachers needed "to know something" and to confront their students with knowledge. Postformal teachers are comfortable with the notion that students should leave their classes with a multidimensional and adaptable grasp of various bodies of knowledge that can be deployed for personal and social benefit when needed. Freire remarked to us before his death that those "Freireans" who were not concerned with obtaining and imparting knowledge were missing the point of his educational philosophy. Of course, the possession of such knowledge without an exploration of just what purposes it might be used to accomplish is also a betrayal of the spirit of Freireanism (and Deweyanism as well). As post-formalists study subject matter, focusing on its production and its use, they contend that the analysis and teaching of information outside such a focus can be misleading as well as socially superfluous.

Without the epistemological questioning that accompanies what postformalists would label "the study of knowledge production," teachers and students fall victim to a naive empiricism. Such a cognitive naiveté has minimal ability to make sense of raw subject matter. Little attention is given to the process by which we interpret the meaning of the information or what inferences we might derive from its presence in our lives. Such are the limitations of a Cartesian-Newtonian view of knowledge and the cognitive processes that emerge within this modernist epistemological recipe. Such cognitive processes often confuse correlation and cause—the belief that just because one event follows another, it is caused by the previous occurrence. In this context a postformal psychology claims status as a critical hermeneutical psychology that focuses on the intricacies of the interpretive process whenever it engages with subject matter or the production and dissemination of knowledge. Democratic citizens who work successfully for social justice must be capable of making this cognitive leap into postformalism and the insights it grants into the politics of knowledge.

REFERENCES

Burman, E. (1994). *Deconstructing developmental psychology*. New York: Routledge.

Cushman, P. (1995). "Ideology obscured: Political uses of the self in Daniel Stern's infant." In N. Goldberger & J. Veroff (Eds.), *The culture and psychology reader*. New York: New York University Press.

Dewey, J. (1933). *How we think*. Lexington, MA: Heath.

Farber, K. (1989). *The use of psychological foundations to inform teaching for critical reflectivity*. Paper presented to the American Educational Research Association, Chicago.

Freire, P. (1998). *Teachers as cultural workers: Letters to those who dare to teach*. Boulder, CO: Westview.

Horton, J., & Freire, P. (1990). *We make the road by walking: Conversations on education and social change*. Ed. B. Bell, J. Gaventa, & J. Peters. Philadelphia: Temple University Press.

Ingleby, D. (1995). "Problems in the study of the interplay between science and culture." In N. Goldberger & J. Veroff (Eds.), *The culture and psychology reader*. New York: New York University Press.

Martin-Baro, I. (1994). *Writings for a liberation psychology*. Ed. A. Aron & S.

Corne. Cambridge, MA: Harvard University Press.

Perkins, D. (1995). *Outsmarting IQ: The emerging science of learnable intelligence.* New York: Free Press.

Postman, N. (1995). *The end of education: Redefining the value of school.* New York: Alfred A. Knopf.

Sampson, E. (1995). "The challenge of social change for psychology: Globalization and psychology's theory of the person." In N. Goldberger & J. Veroff (Eds.), *The culture and psychology reader.* New York: New York University Press.

Shotter, J. (1993). *Cultural politics of everyday life.* Toronto: University of Toronto Press.

Tomlinson, S. (1988). "Why Johnny can't read: Critical theory and special education." *European Journal of Special Needs Education, 3* (1), 45–58.

Usher, R., & Edwards, R. (1994). *Postmodernism and education.* New York: Routledge.

Walkerdine, V. (1988). *The mastery of reason: Cognitive development and the production of rationality.* New York: Routledge.

Chapter 13

Postformal Research:
A Dialogue on Intelligence

Leila E. Villaverde
and William F. Pinar

Joe Kincheloe has maintained that his work on rethinking intelligence has always owed a debt to Bill Pinar's curriculum theory. In this context I (Leila Villaverde) entered into a conversation with Pinar, asking him to respond to particular themes of this book: democratizing intelligence, politicizing cognition, and postformalism. The connections between Pinar's *currere* and Kincheloe and Steinberg's postformal thinking and the consequent redefinition of intelligence and experience are central themes for students of critical forms of cognition. The following are two of the questions I posed to Pinar about these dynamics:

> How would you see postformalism challenging or pushing the necessity of voice in *currere* as it deals with past, present, and future; race, class, and gender; place and power?

> What happens in the space for reflection on, knowing of, and experiencing the meta-awareness that *currere* affords and that our challenge of educational one only psychology demands?

Currere is "regressive-progressive-analytical-synthetical. It is therefore temporal and conceptual in nature, and it aims for the cultivation of a developmental point of view that hints at the transtemporal and transconceptual" (Pinar, 1994, p. 19). Kincheloe (1998) explains:

> In his attempt to analyze educational experience, Pinar connected his under-
> standing of phenomenology to psychoanalysis and aesthetics to produce a
> unique analytical form. *Currere,* the Latin root of the word, "curriculum,"
> concerns the investigation of the nature of the individual experience of the
> public. (p. 129)

Currere is an alternative to linear, traditional modes of research. It fully
engages memory construction and the effects of time, place, and psychological attachment on memory, creating a meta-awareness and analysis of
self. This method interlaces past, present, and future in order to develop
with more clarity the biographical details that have constructed and continue to construct one's consciousness, subjectivity, and identity. *Currere*
is crucial as we examine the ways and circumstances in which our knowledge was produced and validated.

I see *currere* as actuality, meaning it truly goes beyond reflection,
given a postformal perspective. It grounds us in a theorizing existence
where we continually contextualize our perceptions, internalizations,
imaginations, and synthesizing moments, understanding knowledge production with a critical system of meaning. *Currere* is central to the construction of knowledge as we begin to understand how schooling from a
teacher's or student's perspective intersects with their experience of it.
Currere necessitates the paradigm shift proposed by postformalism
(Kincheloe, 1993; Kincheloe & Steinberg, 1993) in order to change,
expand, democratize, and rethink intelligence.

Students need more experience in understanding and struggling with
modes of being and acting in the world, exploring other ways of knowing where "a cognitive revolution initiated by postformality reshapes the
school in a way in which life and its multidimensional connectedness
resides at the center of the curriculum" (Kincheloe & Steinberg, 1993, p.
310). Teachers need to accept the process of being changed and changing,
of being analyzed and analyzing, of being constructed and constructing,
of learning and teaching, of disembedding and connecting (Kincheloe,
1998, p. 134). In this book we have provided new forms of analysis,
research, knowledge production, and consciousness construction where
notions of validated knowledges and paradigms are expanded and redefined, therefore democratizing intelligence and offering different, new
ways of learning, teaching, struggling, and relating.

Pinar addressed my questions and comments beyond my expectations. He explained how *currere* and postformal thinking combine to create an autobiographical democratization of intelligence through his latest

work. The following is his response; I will conclude this chapter with a further attempt to unravel and connect explicitly the themes of this book with his ambitious project.

NOTES ON DEMOCRATIZING INTELLIGENCE...WITHIN

Gender and race conflate in a crisis. (Oates, 1996, p. 84)

The speaking subject is also the subject about which it speaks. (Foucault, 1987, p. 10)

An autobiographical democratization of intelligence does not occur solely within institutions such as the school or within disciplines such as education and psychology. It occurs within the human subject. There is a politics of reason within the self in which sites of identification and disidentification, modes of experience, and forms of understanding and misunderstanding must be reflexively grasped. To understand curriculum as *currere,* the running of the course takes us toward cultural studies, to provoke remembrance of things past and brutalities present. How? I offer a brief description of my current project as an example.

As a feminist man, it is clear to me I must confront my own manhood, understood of course not essentialistically, but historically, socially, racially, in terms of class and culture. The main issue of the twentieth century may have been—may remain—the color line, but this line does not stay within itself, by itself, dividing what would otherwise be a monolith: humanity. The color line traverses other planes, inhabits other problems, especially educational ones. Race and gender intersect and, as Gates (1996) observed, conflate. The racial crisis is gendered, and the crisis of gender is racialized. Within these intersections of race and homosexuality I want to work autobiographically to perceive the lives of four men and the historical moments they inhabited. In particular, I want to outline the shadows they cast over me and us, European-American men. In so doing, I sleep with bodies of knowledge that might help reconfigure the lived practices of male self-constitution, in so doing reformulating self and other: an autobiographics of alterity. Curriculum understood as *currere* is a form of social psychoanalysis, a complicated conversation with myself and others, the point of which is movement: autobiographic, political, cultural. I employ the method of *currere* in searching for a passage out of the impasse that is fin-de-siècle America, the impasse in this individual life which shares with others the dilemma of being an American, an American man, an American white man—in my case, an American white man who is queer.

It is clear that autobiography is not just about oneself but also about the other. It is, in Leigh Gilmore's phrase, a technology of self-production. It is as well a technology of the production of others. How can we understand this production of the "self" as a gendered and racialized production? How might the European-American male begin to grasp how his masculinity is racialized and how his "race" is gendered? To answer these questions I have undertaken a study of four men whose lives and times span the twentieth century and traverse the Western world. How might such work enable one to reexperience the present in fin-de-siècle America? How might an indirect autobigraphy or, to borrow from Gilmore (1994), an autobiographics of alterity, help us to move through the racial and gender sediments that contribute to the stasis that is the present moment? To begin we must return to a time past, still in the present.

The plan of the series is this: after two introductory volumes I move to the first man, the first historical moment. He is Robert Musil, the Austrian novelist, essayist, and journalist. Musil's novel of a Prussian military school—entitled *Young Törless* (1955), originally published at the dawn of the twentieth century—will help me to discuss the crisis of European culture, which was also a crisis of European masculinity. I am not a historian; I will not be making claims about history. Rather, I want to unearth—as in a kind of social psychoanalysis—those elements of the cultural and political crisis that signaled the beginning of the end of the age of European hegemony. These issues—among them mind and body, Christian and Jew—have largely disappeared from the European-American male screen of preoccupation. Disappeared, perhaps, but not gone: remembering fin-de-siècle Vienna may shed new light on our own time. Several of these elements are very familiar—anti-Semitism, fascism—but their relation to homosexual desire and repression are perhaps less known. To underline how this work points to us, I will make the Musil volume also a "tale of two cities." Juxtoposed to Vienna in first years of the twentienth century will be Atlanta, Georiga, where an American version of anti-Semitism and fascism occurred. The occasion was the lynching of Leo Frank (Dinnerstein, 1968). The meaning of these events—the cities, the men, the novel—for us represents a kind of cultural psychoanalysis, located in the "universal singular," an autobiographics of alterity.

From a depiction of this internal crisis of European culture I move in volume four to its last imperialist, colonialist gasp—not unrelated to its earlier internal crisis, of course. The location and time of this episode was North Africa in the 1950s and 1960s. From German-speaking Europe—Musil was Austrian and spent much of his life in Germany and Switzerland—we move to the Caribbean, to France (briefly), and finally to North Africa and the Algerian revolution. The man is—you have no doubt guessed by now—Frantz Fanon. Native to Martinique—what has been termed the the center of African culture in the "new world"—Fanon received his postsecondary education in France. His astonishing but short life of political activism and intellectual accomplishment was lived out in North Africa, dedicated to the emergence not only of an independent Algeria but of an Africa freed from colonial subjugation. Fanon knew—if in heterosexist terms—about the sexual dynamics of race, writing about them in his *Black Skin, White Masks* (1967), first published in 1952. His portrait of the "wretched of the earth"(1968)—first published in 1961—inspired many who would participate in the failed American revolution of the 1960s.

The third moment/man does not follow chronologically the Algerian war for independence. Having studied first the crisis and then the collapse of European empire, I want to back up a bit, to focus on the moment just after World War II, a moment of political opportunity in which socialists and communists, as well as various sectors of the center and right, fought hard to sculpt the emergence of postwar Europe. This was for many an optimistic time, a moment defined in large part by the American/European economic expansion, including the trend toward the globalization of capitalism, foreshadowing, as we know now, its (momentary?) triumph worldwide. The cultural costs, the political struggles, a singular and magnificent effort at a European Renaissance—these point to the third moment and the third man. The one who embodies them is Pier Paolo Pasolini: filmmaker, novelist, poet, essayist, theoretician (Greene, 1990).

In the sixth volume of my proposed series, I move to the last historical moment in this regressive phase of *currere,* the 1960s, and I focus upon the United States. What has been a series of high-risk discursive moves becomes in this phase higher-risk, in no small part because the United States has not yet fully come to grips with this moment. It appears we have moved somewhat out of the country's knee-jerk repudiation of it, but just barely. I want to rescue that moment, to reexperience it, not for the sake of its idealization or sentimentalization, not even for what we think of it now, but for what it was like then. To attempt that I will focus on the struggle for civil rights, specifically the history of SNCC (the Student Nonviolent Coordinating Committee) and the Black Panthers. The man is Eldridge Cleaver (1968), who, perhaps more than any other single individual, evoked the potential, personified the excesses of a revolutionary movement, and was condemned to live out its mangled, gendered fate. Many will protest: Cleaver is hardly a "great man," as one might say about Musil, Fanon, and Pasolini. I tend to agree. With the exceptions of Martin Luther King Jr. and Malcolm X, there were no great men engaged in the fight for a new American nation in the 1960s. (And I need not remind the reader that those two men were murdered. Among the candidates for the status of great women are Angela Davis and Fannie Lou Hamer. Here I focus upon men.) The fight was carried on primarily by the young, and perhaps one reason it failed—there were numerous reasons—was the conspicuous absence of "greatness" in the leadership. I do think Cleaver had a hint of greatness about him—although few can remember that today, after his religious and political conversions, his crack habit—but my interest is not to establish that. Rather, I want to portray this complicated, contradictory, and gendered embodiment of this fourth historical moment, an American moment in which politics, culture, and economics became intertwined in a struggle for civil rights, for dignity, for—as Cleaver and others insisted—"manhood."

After completing this regressive phase of *currere,* I move to the progressive, an imaginary exposition of what the future might be. These seven volumes—two introducing the project, four regressive moments/men, and the one progressive moment—I have worked on somewhat concurrently. Initially these volumes were chapters in one book; they grew too large to be contained within two covers. In order to maintain their sense of sequence and interrelatedness, I have worked on all seven more or less simultaneously. The analytic volumes—there are three planned at this stage—will wait until these are finished, as they represent analyses of the regressive and progressive moments. The outlines of these three books are visible to me: One will focus on the (gendered, racialized) American national identity, another upon the psychological dynamics of self-divison (emphasizing Lacan), a third on issues of representation. The final volume in the series, the synthetic, will attempt a mobilization of the re-formed male self in light of the psychointellectual labor undertaken. It is in one sense a photographic blowup of "curriculum," of curriculum as "complicated conversation," on this occasion, a conversation about masculinity, race, politics, and sexuality. *Currere* understood as an autobiographics of alterity requires us to focus not only on the production of whiteness and masculinity and their intersections and conflations, but on their dissolution and re-formation. As Fanon said: "For Europe, for ourselves, and for humanity, we must turn over a new leaf, we must work out new concepts, and try to set afoot a new man" (quoted in Gendzier, 1973, p. 270). To do this requires to engage in a gendered democratization of intelligence...within.

VILLAVERDE'S CONCLUSION

In this statement Pinar carefully explains the trajectory of his method, consciousness, and being. It's important to realize how his project models a postformal research methodology conscious of race, gender, social justice, history, context, place, and power relations. This proves an example instructive on a variety of levels. Through his current work, Pinar exemplifies analytical synthesis, prepares to approach the contents of consciousness as they appear through educational contexts and explores and loosens our identification with the contents of consciousness. He does this so that we can gain some distance from them and may be able to see from new vantage points those psychic realms that are formed by conditioning and unconscious adherence to social convention, therefore starting to deconstruct, democratize, and expand intelligence (Kincheloe, 1998, p. 129).

There are two concepts,"complicated conversation" and "autobiographics of alterity," that I would like to explore further, given both the social and individual components of the construction and expansion of validated knowledge (i.e., intelligence). The concept of a "complicated conversation" brings many images and circumstances to mind. For instance, a conversation should be by nature quite complicated, since it is the space where two or more individuals interact and communicate. In an educational context, conversations must be complicated by necessity. They must be problematized to maximize the pedagogical experience and insight. This conversational space includes the individual's identity, subjectivity, consciousness, race, class, gender, culture, resistances, vulnerabilities, historicity, and psychosocial contextualization (to name a few). All of these things, actually the awareness of an individual bringing all of these parts of themselves to the conversation, creates a complex space of communication and interaction. Yet this space is quite often taken advantage of, given the power hierarchies established within the school and society at large. Any school personnel—teachers, students, administrators, counselors, coaches, assistants, academicians, parents, and so on—must have an understanding of this or an ability to engage and participate in a "complicated conversation" to truly change the condition of education in the United States. This process must happen simultaneously in the personal and social realms. Let me reiterate what Pinar stated at the very beginning of his statement: "There is a politics of reason within the self in which sites of identification and disidentification, modes of experience, and forms of understanding and misunderstanding must be reflexively grasped." In the reflection there must be a critical awareness of the construction and production of our experiences, of our being, of the "other," exposing contradictions, complexities, and multiplicities of our reality.

As Kincheloe states in the introduction to this book, we challenge "the decontextualized and antidemocratic practices of 'experts hiding behind the mantle of objective science.'... Such a critique emerges as a product of democratic cooperation, a manifestation of what happens when experience is questioned in the light of historical consciousness intercepting personal experience." We debunk the necessity of rote knowledge and endless memorization drills and expose the benefits of relating school knowledge to students' lives. We also propose that both teacher and student become active researchers of their experience in and out of the schools. We strive for perceiving, interpreting, and internalizing "new ways of being human" with this process of reconceptualizing educational psychology. This is a political struggle, we realize, but we cannot continue to espouse an apolitical stance or to pretend that a right-wing agenda is neutral at the expense of the student's educational experience. Kincheloe (1998) adds,

> Thinking about thinking in post-formalism induces students to deconstruct their personal constructions of the purpose of their schooling; it induces men to expose the ways the privileged position of masculinity has shaped their self-images; it induces heterosexuals to refigure their identities vis-à-vis confrontation with the dynamics of heterosexism and sexual preferences; it induces workers to reconsider the workplace and its social dynamics as profound influences on identity formation. (p. 132)

An analysis of the "autobiographics of alterity" is important at this point, since it addresses what we have just discussed. Our autobiographies are continually writing and rewriting themselves, yet we cannot fall under the impression that all they contain is our personal confessions. An "auto-biographics of alterity" is a reformulation of self, exploring, analyzing, and redefining the self and other, dealing with the other's consciousness, oth-erizing the self and selving the other (Foster, 1995). This reformulation of self must be an extension of the "complicated conversation" delving deep-er into the construction of an individual's identity and all other axes that come into play in the autobiographic, cultural, gendered, political, and socio-psychodynamic conversation. At the core of both a "complicated conversation" and an "autobiographics of alterity" is an active, constant research of the context and conditions in which one finds oneself, the sys-temic nature of the institutions one negotiates, the perception of self, cop-ing skills, and agency, as well as how others are perceiving and reacting to one's actions. The continual research of these personal and social phenom-ena allows an individual to explore and critically analyze the social and individual contributions to the production of self. Therefore Pinar presents an excellent (and ambitious) example of how to incorporate *currere* and postformal thinking methods into a complex weaving of his own biogra-phy through the lives and histories of the four men he chose to examine. In *Rethinking Intelligence* we have addressed the necessity "to construct a sociopolitical cognitive theory that understands the way our consciousness, our subjectivity, is shaped by the world around us" (from Chapter 1). We urge teachers, students, and all school personnel, at least those committed to the improvement of educational spaces and to social justice, to engage in processes similar to the ones discussed throughout this book in the effort to expand and develop human growth, insight, and progress toward a radically democratic pedagogical space and society. The synergy pro-duced by the interaction of Pinar's *currere* with postformal thinking offers hope in the effort to rethink intelligence and the educational practices inevitably attached to definitions of intelligence.

REFERENCES

Cleaver, E. (1968). *Soul on ice.* New York: Dell.

Dinnerstein, L. (1968). *The Leo Frank case.* New York: Columbia University Press.

Fanon, F. (1967). *Black skin, white masks.* Trans. Charles Lam Markmann. New York: Grove Weidenfeld.

Fanon, F. (1968). *The wretched of the earth.* Trans. Constance Farrington. New York: Grove.

Foster, H. (1995). "The artist as ethnographer?" In G.E. Marcus & F. R. Myers (Eds.), *The traffic in culture: Refiguring art and anthropology.* Berkeley: University of California Press.

Foucault, M. (1987). "Maurice Blanchot: The thought from outside." In M. Foucault & M. Blanchot (Eds.). Trans. Brian Massumi. New York: Zone.

Gates Jr., H. L. (1996). *Colored people: A memoir.* New York: Alfred A. Knopf.

Gendzier, I. L. (1973). *Frantz Fanon: A critical study.* New York: Pantheon.

Gilmore, L. (1994). *Autobiographics: A feminist theory of women's self-representation.* Ithaca, NY: Cornell University Press.

Greene, N. (1990). *Pier Paolo Pasolini: Cinema as heresy.* Princeton: Princeton University Press.

Kincheloe, J. L. (1998). "Pinar's *currere* and identity in hyperreality: Grounding the post-formal notion of intrapersonal intelligence." In W. Pinar (Ed.), *Curriculum: Toward new identities* (pp. 129–142). New York: Garland.

Kincheloe, J. L. (1993). *Towards a critical politics of teacher thinking: Mapping the postmodern.* Westport, CT: Bergin & Garvey.

Kincheloe, J. L., & Steinberg, S. R. (1993). "A tentative description of post-formal thinking: The critical confrontation with cognitive theory." *Harvard Educational Review, 63* (3), 296–320.

Musil, R. (1955). *Young Torless.* New York: Pantheon.

Musil, R. (1990). *Precision and soul: Essays and addresses.* Ed. and Trans. B. Pike & D. S. Luft. Chicago: University of Chicago Press.

Pinar, W. F. (1994). *Autobiography, politics and sexuality: Essays in curriculum theory, 1972–1992.* New York: Peter Lang.

Contributors

Karen Anijar is assistant professor of curriculum and instruction at Arizona State University. She is the author of many journal articles and a forthcoming book: *Teaching towards the 24th Century: The Social Curriculum of Star Trek.* Her areas of research include consumerism, commodification, science fiction, and youth and popular cultural studies.

Gaile Cannella is an associate professor of early childhood and multicultural education at Texas A & M University. She received her Ed.D. in early childhood education from the University of Georgia. In addition to numerous research articles in professional journals concerned with the education of young children, she has written on social justice and teacher education. Her latest book is *Deconstructing Early Childhood Education: Social Justice and Revolution.*

Suzanne Gallagher teaches at Gwyneed-Mercy College in Gwynedd Valley, Pennsylvania. Her research interests deal with critical literacy and the discipline of educational psychology along with ethical and moral imperatives.

Aimee Howley is professor of Educational Studies at Ohio University. Teaching primarily in the Educational Administration Program, her research examines critically the theory and rhetoric that informs educational practice in the U.S. She is particularly concerned with the ways power relationships are shaped in rural schools and communities.

Craig Howley is an educational writer and researcher who works from his small farm near Albany, Ohio, where he milks the cows daily and raises a few hogs and a large garden. Formerly he directed the ERIC Clearinghouse on Rural Education and Small Schools. He has written about school size and inequality, the political economy of rural life, and the contradictory ends and means of schooling in the U.S.

Aostre N. Johnson is currently the director of Graduate Education Programs and an assistant professor at Saint Michael's College in Colchester, Vermont. She teaches courses in curriculum and human development and is particularly interested in re-visioning curriculum and educational practice in light of aesthetic and spiritual dimensions of being.

Joe L. Kincheloe is the Belle Zeller Chair of Public Policy and Administration at CUNY Brooklyn College and a professor of Cultural Studies and Education at The Pennsylvania State University. He is the author of many books and articles, including *Teachers as Researchers: Qualitative Paths to Empowerment; Toil and Trouble: Good Work, Smart Workers and the Integration of Academic and Vocational Education; How Do We Tell the Workers?;* and *Changing Multiculturalism: New Times, New Curriculum* with Shirley Steinberg.

Lana Krievis teaches in the Covina Valley School District, Covina, California. Her interests are in pedagogy and deaf education.

Pepi Leistyna is an assistant professor at the University of Massachusetts, Boston, in the Department of English as a Second Language / Bilingual Studies. Leistyna's research has centered around issues of language and experience, democracy and education, and the implementation of critical multicultural curricula in public schools. Leistyna conceptualized and co-edited the book *Breaking Free: The Transformative Power of Critical Pedagogy,* and most recently authored *Presence of Mind: Education and the Politics of Deception.*

Ronald C. McClendon has a PhD. in Counseling Psychology. His career has included a number of years in private industry and human resource consulting. Currently, Ron teaches developmental psychology and educational psychology in the Teacher Education Program at the University of Akron, Ohio.

Wiliam F. Pinar is St. Bernard Parish Alumni Endowed Professor at Louisiana State University. He is the author of many books and articles in curriculum theory and autobiography and is the founding editor of *The Journal of Curriculum Theorizing.* His latest books are *Curriculum: Toward New Identities, Queer Theory and Education* and the second and revised edition of *Contemporary Curriculum Discourses.*

Marc Pruyn is an assistant professor of social education in the Department of Curriculum and Instruction at New Mexico State University. His first book, *Discourse Wars in Gotham-West,* has just been published by Westview Press. Marc lives in Las Cruces, New Mexico, with his partner and daughter.

Linda Spatig is a professor at Marshall University in Huntington, West Virginia, where she teaches courses in social foundations of education and qualitative research methods. Her recent publications concern the experiences of teachers and low-income mothers involved in a Head Start to Public School Transition Demonstration Project. Her research addresses schooling and social inequities.

Paul Stein is a doctoral candidate at the Margaret Warner Graduate School of Education at the University of Rochester. His research and publications deal with spirituality, psychology, and curriculum theory.

Shirley R. Steinberg teaches at Adelphi University in Garden City, New York, and at the Adelphi Urban Campus in lower Manhattan. She is an educational consultant and a drama director. Among the numerous books she has written and edited with Joe L. Kincheloe are *Measured Lies: The Bell Curve Examined; White Reign: Deploying Whiteness in America; Kinderculture: The Corporate Constructions of Childhood;* and *Unauthorized Methods: Critical Strategies for Teaching.* She is the senior editor of *Taboo: The Journal of Culture and Education.*

Ann Watts Pailliotet is assistant professor of education at Whitman College in Walla Walla, Washington, where she teaches preservice literacy methods, critical reading of children's literature, and media literacy. She is a past winner of the National Reading Conference Student Outstanding Research Award and College Composition and Communication Citation for outstanding classroom practice. She is the co-editor of *Intermediality: The Teachers' Handbook of Critical Media Literacy.*

Leila E. Villaverde is a lecturer/instructor in the College of Education at The Pennsylvania State University. She is the editor, with Nelson Rodriguez, of the forthcoming *Dismantling White Privilege: Pedagogy, Politics, and Whiteness.* She has also published on art, politics, research, and education. She teaches and supervises preservice teachers across the curriculum.

John A. Weaver teaches at the University of Akron, Ohio, and his research interests are popular culture, information technology, and curriculum theory. His recent books include work on cyborg culture and science fiction and popular culture. He also greatly fears the dissolution of critical pedagogy vis à vis *South Park* ideology.

Philip Wexler is the Michael Scandling Professor of Education and Sociology and Dean of the Warner School at the University of Rochester. He is the former editor of the American Sociological Association Journal, *Sociology of Education*. Among his publications are: *Sociology of Education; Beyond Equality; Social Analysis of Education;* and *Becoming Somebody*. He is the co-editor, with Richard Smith, of *After Postmodernism: Education, Politics and Identity*.

Index